The Germanic People

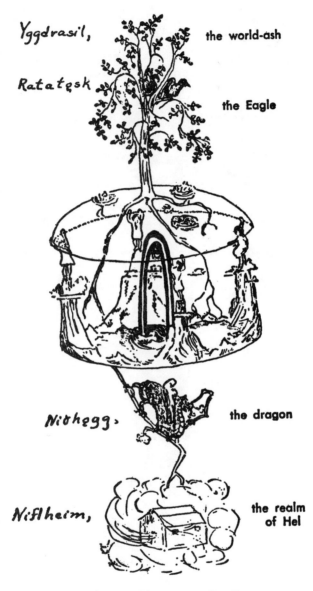

Yggdrasil, the world-ash

Ratatøsk

the Eagle

Niðhegg, the dragon

Niflheim, the realm of Hel

The World Tree Iggdrasil

The Germanic People

THEIR ORIGIN, EXPANSION AND CULTURE

By

Francis Owen

Professor Emeritus, University of Alberta

BARNES
&NOBLE
BOOKS
NEW YORK

This edition published by Barnes & Noble, Inc.,
by arrangement with Doris Owen.

1993 Barnes & Noble Books

ISBN 0-88029-579-1

Printed and bound in the United States of America

M 9

Foreword

The problem of the origin and expansion of the Germanic people is intimately connected with the problem of the origin and expansion of the Indo-European speaking peoples, since it is universally admitted that Germanic is a group of the Indo-European language stock. An attempt has been made in this book to establish a synthesis and perhaps find an acceptable solution, by making use of available material in the fields of linguistics, archaeology, anthropology and history.

It is quite impossible for any one individual to master completely all the material in these four fields of study, and the author has had to a great extent to depend on the investigations of others. It is to be hoped that a representative selection has been made and that no important expression of opinion has been neglected.

In addition to the works cited in the Bibliography, a long list of books on the subject which were read during the years of preparation of the material for this book has been made but has been omitted in the interest of economy of space.

I am greatly indebted to several of my senior and graduate students who during the last twenty-five years have assisted in the collection of material, especially Mrs. E. Newton, R. Zuar, E. Müller (later Professor at the University), I. Johnson, E. Milbradt, L. Wilcox, J. E. Oyler (at present Professor at the University of New Brunswick), A. Malycky, and D. Owen, my wife, who collected data on the origin and distribution of northern amber and also made many of the line drawings and maps.

Very valuable help has also been rendered by Dr. W. D. Asmus, Director of the Provincial Museum at Hanover, Germany, with whom I have discussed many of the problems of the book and who has provided reference material and illustrations.

I also wish to express appreciation of the assistance given by (Fräulein) Dr. G. Asmus, Hanover, for very useful criticisms of the sections on anthropology.

Acknowledgement is also hereby made of the courtesy extended by the following in granting permission to use quotations from published works:

The sons of F. B. Gummere; *The Oldest English Epic.*

Penguin Books, Ltd.; S. A. Handford: *The Conquest of Gaul.*

Clarendon Press, W. H. Fyfe: trans. of Tacitus' *Agricola* and *Germania.*

American-Scandinavian Foundation; H. A. Bellows: trans. of *The Poetic Edda.*

Dent and Co., R. K. Gordon: *Anglo-Saxon Poetry.*

Dassent, G. W.: trans. of *The Story of Burnt Nyal.*

Harvard University Press, Cook and Tinker: *Select Translations from Old English Poetry.*

Acknowledgement is also hereby made to the following museums for permission to use reproductions of exhibits:

Provinzial-Museum, Hanover.

National Museum, Copenhagen.

Translations of poetic selections not otherwise acknowledged were made by the author.

I am very greatly indebted to Professor E. Reinhold of the Modern Language Department of the University of Alberta for assistance in obtaining financial aid and in the placing of the manuscript with a publisher.

For financial help in the collection of material I am indebted to the University of Alberta and to the Humanities Research Council of Canada as well as for generous subsidies in aid of publication from money furnished by the Canada Council.

FRANCIS OWEN. 1959

TABLE OF CONTENTS

LIST OF MAPS AND ILLUSTRATIONS

The Palaeolithic and Mesolithic Background

Germanic is a group of the Indo-European Language stock. The original speakers of Indo-European belonged to the Caucasian or White race. From the skeletal evidence there is fairly good reason to believe that representatives of this race were present at Swanscombe, Galley Hill and elsewhere in Europe as early as the Second Interglacial, but it was not until Upper Palaeolithic times during the Fourth Glacial that members of the Caucasian race appeared and remained in Europe in appreciable numbers.

The Quaternary Ice Age which may have begun about 600,000 years ago has been divided into glacial and interglacial periods of varying length. In Europe these have been named after four Swiss rivers: Günz, Mindel, Riss and Würm. According to some calculations the Würm or Fourth Glacial began about 120,000 years ago.[1] But it is no longer regarded as having been a time of continual cold; there were periods of temporary climatic amelioration. These are called Interstadials. The Fourth Glacial has been divided into three cold and two relatively mild periods: Würm 1, Interstadial 1, Würm 2, Interstadial 2 and Würm 3. At the end of Würm 3, the third cold period of the Fourth Glacial, Europe entered either a Third Interstadial or a Fourth Interglacial. The future will determine which it was. This was approximately 11,000 years ago.[2]

Europe must have been very different during glacial times from what it is today. Extreme cold, however, will not of itself produce glaciation. Conditions must be such as to cause huge accumulations of snow in elevated areas. An average annual lowering of the temperature of about six degrees Fahrenheit, if other conditions are favorable, may be sufficient to cause an advance of the ice. Pressure causes the ice formed from the masses of snow to flow.[3]

In Europe there were two main centres from which the ice slowly spread, grinding and leveling up everything before it. One of these centres was in the Alpine area, the other and the major centre was in the Scandinavian North. Between the two advancing ice-fields there was a narrow corridor in Central Europe which was not glaciated. Conditions in the corridor must have been somewhat similar to those prevailing in the Barren Lands of Northern Canada or in the Siberian region along the Arctic. The winters would be very cold but the short summers would be reasonably warm, certainly warm enough for wandering bands of hunters to follow the herds of reindeer and other cold-loving animals. Only in the mountainous areas were France and Spain glaciated during the fourth advance of the ice, a fact which is of considerable importance in the cultural history of Western Europe. Great Britain was outside the scope of the Fourth Glacial.

It is obvious that the moisture which provided the material for the huge masses of snow and ice, in some areas two miles deep, must have come from the surrounding waters. This caused a lowering of the water level and an extension of the continental shelf, thus producing land-bridges at such places as Gibraltar and Tunis-Sicily-Italy. Between England and France there was low-lying land bisected by a Channel River, and meandering rivers where the North Sea now is. In time the lowering of the water level would be to some extent offset by the depression of the land under the weight of the accumulated ice. When the ice melted, the melt-water was returned to the adjacent seas and some measure of equilibrium would be again restored.

Whatever may have been the original place of origin of the Caucasian race there can be little doubt that the Southern Mediterranean area from west to east prior to the Fourth Glacial was inhabited by people of this primary race of mankind. There is also evidence of the presence in some regions of Palestine and North Africa of Neanderthal Man. Some mixture may have taken place.

The culture of Caucasian Man in the Mediterranean has been named Capsian, a latinized form of Gafsa, in North Africa. From the Mediterranean was derived the early Upper Palaeolithic culture found in Europe, called Aurignacian from a French place-name. The immigrants brought this culture into Europe across the Straits of Gibraltar in the west, from Tunis to Italy in the centre and in the east around the Caspian Sea. It is highly probable that their appearance in Europe was during the First Interstadial of the Fourth Glacial. That would be about 80,000 years ago.

Of the four main Upper Palaeolithic cultures the Aurignacian then belongs to the First Interstadial, the Solutrean and Gravettian to the Second Interstadial and the Magdalenian to Würm 3, the last major phase of the advance of the ice.

With the possible exception of Grimaldi which may be Negroid, all of the types of *homo sapiens* who replaced Neanderthal Man and whose skeletal remains have been found associated with various aspects of Upper Palaeolithic cultures, can with considerable certainty be classified as Caucasian, but there are naturally many cranial and skeletal differences. To be sure, this differentiation into secondary racial types is based upon a relatively small number of fossils. These types have been named after the places where characteristic specimens have been found: Cro Magnon, Combe Capelle, Brünn, Predmost, Chancelade and Oberkassel.

Some authorities group all of these types rather loosely as Aurignacian Man; some as Cro Magnon Man. Since Aurignacian is a cultural term it is not advisable to use it in an anthropological sense. The term Cro Magnon should be restricted to a particular type. For present purposes it is sufficient to differentiate two main types: The Cro Magnon and the Combe Capelle.

The Cro Magnon people were as a rule tall, with moderately broad heads, with narrow noses, broad faces, pronounced chins, presenting in general rather a rugged aspect. Several complete skeletons have been found. It has been suggested that the tall stature of Cro Magnon Man (some over six feet) is the result of so-called "hybrid vigor," a mixture of the typical Caucasian with some variety of Neanderthal Man, but this explanation is of a speculative nature, even though mixture may have taken place.

The Combe Capelle type is shorter in stature, more gracile, with a long, narrow skull, a broader nose than the Cro Magnon, presenting in general a more primitive appearance.

Other Upper Palaeolithic types may be regarded as variants of these two. But taking into consideration all of the types associated with Upper Palaeolithic cultures it might be said that there was no greater range of variation than can be seen in the present population of Europe.

The Caucasoids differed from other primary races such as the Negroid and the Mongoloid as the result of certain mutations which produced facial and skeletal changes and a decided tendency to depigmentation. The cause of mutations is not definitely known; they appear to be present in all living forms. If the mutation has survival value it may became a fixed characteristic, and a new type comes into existence.

There are several sub-divisions of the Primary Caucasian, but three of them are of major importance: these are the Mediterranean, the Alpine and the Nordic.[4] The others, such as Dinaric, Armenoid, East Baltic, may be considered as having resulted from a mixture of two or more of the three basic types.

There are no living typical representatives of racial varieties. There are only approximations to the types set up by the anthropologists for purposes of classification. Changes, whether the result of further mutations or race mixture, have in many cases altered the basic forms.

The modern Mediterranean is, generally speaking, perhaps the closest to the original Caucasian type. The stature is short, the head dolichocephalic (long and narrow), the face long and narrow, the nose also narrow, the eyes brown to black. Approximations to this general type can be found in many areas of the Mediterranean, but especially in Southern Spain, Sicily and among the Berbers in North Africa, as well as in Eastern Mediterranean regions.

There are many problems connected with the origin of the Alpine secondary race which have not yet been solved. In hair and eye color the Alpine is like the Mediterranean. He is moderately tall; very sturdily built. The head is brachycephalic, that is, with a tendency to roundness, the nose broad and with a low bridge, the face broad, the skin somewhat lighter than in the case of the Mediterranean. Approximations to this type can be seen all across Central Europe from France to Russia.

The Nordic secondary race shows the most pronounced deviations from the Primary Caucasian. The Nordic shows a much greater degree of depigmentation than the Alpine or the Mediterranean. Not only has the skin been affected, but also the color of the hair and the color of the eyes. It may have been an adaptation to specific conditions of an Ice Age environment, if it is true that depigmentation has a definite survival value under environmental conditions which provide only a minimum of sunshine. In any case, the Nordic is blond, with fair to straw-colored hair, with blue to grey eyes. The Nordic is tall; taller than the Alpine and much taller than the Mediterranean. In head measurement he is dolichocephalic verging on mesocephalic. He has a long, narrow, prominent nose and a long, narrow face, except where the Cro Magnon element is dominant. In general he presents a much more rugged appearance than the Mediterranean. The area of greatest density of the Nordic type at the present time is in Northern Europe and in areas which have been colonized from there.

The secondary types of the Primary Caucasian can be found all over Europe, but nevertheless it is true and a matter of common observation that, as one travels from the north of Europe to the south, one can see that the three types, Nordic, Alpine and Mediterranean, with their variants, are dominant in the north, centre and south respectively, with, of course, many areas of transition.

The people of Upper Palaeolithic times were hunters and food gatherers. This does not mean they were all nomadic. In many districts such, for example, as the Garonne and Vezère river valleys in France nomadic life was not necessary. There was an abundance of game, and the climate, even during Würm 2 and Würm 3 must have been reasonably favorable, since these areas were far removed from the worst effects of the glacial conditions. During the Interstadials the people lived to a great extent in the open, but during the colder phases, in the caves and rock shelters.

It was in these caves and shelters that Upper Palaeolithic hunters left a record of many of their interests in the drawings and paintings on the walls of the caves, on pieces of bone, ivory, slate and reindeer horn. Bears, mammoths, bison, deer, wolves, reindeer, many smaller animals and winged fowl are found pictured in great profusion, and in many cases with realism and technique surprising at such an early stage. As far as is known, this is the first appearance of the pictorial art in the history of human culture. Many of the drawings were colored. There was also some clay modelling and statuary.

The presence of certain signs, impressions of mutilated fingers, representations of medicine men, would seem to indicate that the original and primary purpose of the cave art was connected with fertility practices designed to maintain a constant supply of the game necessary for food. Perhaps totemic cults were already in existence. Nevertheless, there can be little doubt that the artistic impulse was present in a marked degree. The artists may have had a very practical purpose, yet they were greatly concerned with form and symmetry, with accurate description and color contrasts.

The chief artifacts were the stone knife, the spear and arrowhead, the bow and the engraving tool. These, with the bones of animals that were eaten, are found in cultural layers in the caves and in open encampments, making it possible to some extent to reconstruct the manner of life of these early settlers in Europe, some of whom are the direct ancestors of the modern Europeans.

Ceremonial burials, often in the floors of the caves, with the inclusion of food and weapons, would indicate a vague concept of a continued existence after death. In many cases the bodies of the dead were painted with red ochre to simulate the life-sustaining blood. The dead were buried in shallow earth graves.

It is reasonable to assume a widespread language stock, divided into many separate languages and dialects all along the Southern Mediterranean coast. This language stock was associated with the Capsian and derived or related cultures. For lack of a better term this stock will be referred to as the Mediterranean language stock. Some form or forms of this language must have been introduced into Europe both in the east and in the west by the immigrants from Capsian culture-areas, that is, by the originators of the Aurignacian culture north of the Mediterranean.

It is true that this is a hypothetical language stock, but

there are compelling reasons for such an hypothesis. The Semitic-speaking peoples are basically Caucasian, as are also the speakers of Hamitic languages, although no doubt there has been considerable miscegenation with Negroid peoples. A common origin of Semitic and Hamitic has been suggested. There are languages in the Mediterranean area which might be described as linguistic fossils. Examples are: Basque, Berber, perhaps Etruscan, ancient Ligurian, ancient Egyptian, extinct languages of Asia Minor and Greece, many of the non-Indo-European languages of the Caucasus. Some of these languages at least are related and presumably formed units in a much larger linguistic complex. Knowledge of this widespread stock is not much further advanced at the present time than was the knowledge of Indo-European about a century and a half ago.

With the climatic amelioration and the gradual melting of the ice at the end of the Upper Palaeolithic cultural period the cold-loving animals moved slowly toward Northern Europe. Many of the hunters followed, and indications of their presence can be found in the North European Plain from Berlin to Hamburg. These hunters penetrated into Schleswig-Holstein and were the first permanent settlers of that region.

Another area of settlement of Upper Palaeolithic hunters was in Upper Saxony and Thuringia. This was before the invasion of the forest and it must have been an excellent country for game.

With the advent of the Mesolithic cultural period, or the Middle Stone Age, following upon the Upper Palaeolithic, there was a new invasion of Europe by people from the Southern Mediterranean. These were the bearers of a microlithic culture, a late development of the Capsian. The practice was to shape minute flint points for arrowheads, fish-hooks and for a variety of composite implements and weapons made by inserting the microlithic flints into bone or wooden handles.

The cultures of the Mesolithic period in Europe can now be fairly definitely defined. In Spain and in an area north of the Black Sea there are indications of a Late Capsian microlithic culture. In Northern Spain, France, Western Germany and Great Britain is found the Azilian-Tardenoisian, a microlithic culture imposed upon a Late Magdalenian or Azilian. This microlithic culture is also found in Central and East Germany and in Poland where it is known as the Swiderian-Tardenoisian. It also extended into the Danube area. In Italy there was a Late Magdalenian, called the Epi-Grimaldian (see Map I).

The bearers of these cultures were still in the food-gathering stage. They could not have been very numerous, and consequently in such an area as Central Germany where there were descendants of the Upper Palaeolithic hunters the impression made upon the physical type would not have been very significant. Whatever mixture took place would be a mixture of Proto-Nordic and Basic Mediterranean where the cranial characteristics at least exhibit a considerable degree of similarity.

Around the shores of the Baltic, in Denmark, Southern Sweden and Southern Norway a Late Magdalenian culture had survived down to about 8300 B. C. This is called the Göti-glacial era. The Baltic was an ice-dammed lake. The climate was Arctic to sub-Arctic. The flora was mainly dwarf birch and willow, and the fauna consisted of tundra and steppe forms. Lemmings and reindeer were plentiful. Typical culture stations have been discovered at Meiendorf near Hamburg, Stallmoor and Ahrendsburg.

It has proved possible to establish an absolute chronology for the Scandinavian North on the basis of varve-counting. Since this area is undoubtedly the home of the Germanic people it is of interest to have a general understanding of the physical background. Varves are sediment-layers which have been deposited in the lakes and shallow waters since the beginning of the recession of the ice-sheets. Every year two layers were

deposited, a thicker and coarser one in summer and a thinner
and finer one in winter, since the finer grains would be held
longer in solution. Two varves indicate a year, and by comparing results in hundreds of places it has proved possible to
establish an accurate time-sequence with but a small margin of
error.[5]

The results of pollen analysis which indicate the nature
of the flora and hence the climate have also contributed
materially to the information about the Scandinavian North
since the recession of the ice.

The Mesolithic has been divided into three cultural periods:
Period 1 corresponds to the Finiglacial of the geologists, from
about 8300 to 6800 B. C. The early part was the Yoldia Sea
phase of the Baltic,[6] which was then a salt-water body.
Sweden and Norway formed a huge island, the rapidly melting
ice raising the level of the surrounding waters to such an
extent that the water of the Arctic ocean, the North Atlantic
and the Baltic, mixed. The temperature was gradually rising.
The forest (birch, pine and willow) was encroaching on the
tundra and steppe. The climate is called the pre-boreal. The
lemming had disappeared. Peatbogs (moorlog) were being
formed and it is by the analysis of the pollen preserved in
these bogs that the nature of the flora has been determined.

The second part of this period was the Ancylus Lake phase,[7]
but this extends also into period 2. It lasted for about a
thousand years from 7800 to 6800 B. C. The land, relieved
of the tremendous weight of ice, rose and shut off communication with both the Arctic and the North Sea. The Baltic
became a fresh-water body. In the North Sea there was
increasing transgression by the water on the low-lying lands
between Jutland and England, especially in the neighborhood
of the Frisian Islands and the Dogger Bank. The temperature
was boreal-continental, that is, warm and dry. The forests
were of birch, pine, elder, hazel, oak, elm and lime, the
last three constituting what is called the oak-mixed forest. The

earliest instance of the domesticated dog in Northern Europe has been recorded. The average July temperature has been estimated at 55 degrees Fahrenheit at the end of period 1, rising to 60 to 65 degrees at the end of period 2.

Typical culture stations of period 1 are Ahrendsburg, Remouchamps and Lyngby, of period 2, Maglemose. Some influence of the microlithic culture has been noted. Lyngby shows the ax or adze of reindeer antler which consists of a flint ax inserted into the hollow sleeve of a piece of antler. These axes show the beginning of adaptation to forest conditions.

The Maglemose culture of period 2 had developed out of the Late Magdalenian, the Tardenoisian (microlithic) and the Lyngby cultures. It was a fishing culture supplemented by the hunting of small game animals and birds. The people had also learned the art of making dug-out canoes, since wooden paddles for such craft have been excavated from the peat-bogs. This is the earliest instance of the initial stages of water travel in Northern Europe. The making of these canoes must have been closely associated with the development of the ax. A throwing-stick has also been found. There was a wide variety of fishing implements.

Nor were the esthetic arts neglected. Perforated animal teeth and pieces of amber were used for personal decoration. Artifacts of many sorts were adorned with geometric motives and net-patterns.

The Maglemose people established their habitations by the banks of rivers, by the shores of the lakes and on small islands, but many of their camp sites show signs of seasonal migration, indicating that they were occupied during the summer and autumn months only. The size of the communities must have been relatively small, as is usually the case in a hunting, fishing and food-gathering economy.

In the third period of the Mesolithic in the North, the Litorina Sea phase of the Baltic,[8] the water transgressed over the land between Southern Sweden and Denmark, and there was once again a connection with the North Sea, so that the Baltic was no longer a fresh-water lake, although not so salty as during the Yoldia phase. Period 3 lasted from 5000 to 3000 B. C. The climate was Atlantic, that is, warm and moist. This is the beginning of the climatic optimum of the Scandinavian North, much warmer than it is at the present time. The mixed-oak forest was dominant. The distribution of the hazel, determined by pollen analysis, is a certain indication of the milder climate. There was continued transgression of the North Sea bed by the water, and Southern Sweden ceased to be joined to Denmark.

This was the period of the kitchenmiddens (Danish: *kjökken-möddingar;* German: *Muschelhaufen*), also designated as the Ertebölle culture after a place-name in Denmark. Many of the settlement-sites are now below the surface of the water, while elsewhere, settlements which were formerly on the shore are now some distance inland. Kitchenmiddens are heaps of kitchen refuse. These refuse heaps are composed of the shells of oysters, snails, the remains of many kinds of fish; the bones of birds such as duck, goose, swan, gull; game animals such as deer and wild boar; also otter, marten, fox, bear and beaver.

Some signs of huts have been discovered, so it is possible that the actual dwelling-places were nearby in more sheltered localities. Hearths have been found in these shell-mounds, which indicates that the food was cooked on the spot, probably often on low rafts, the refuse being thrown over the sides.

The characteristic artifacts were arrowheads, flint ax-blades for insertion into horn-sleeves, hafted stone axes, and something entirely new in the history of European culture: pottery. The pots were of cylindrical shape with a pointed bottom and totally lacking decoration except the impression of the thumbnails around the brim. They were handmade and then baked. Prior to this time the containers had doubtless been of wood, leather and perhaps also of woven reeds. The women of the shell-mound culture apparently carried on some form of weaving. The bone combs which have been found are scarcely suitable for any other use except combing wool.

It is important to note that these people no longer lived a nomadic or semi-nomadic life; they were fairly closely bound to certain localities by the presence there of their means of subsistence. The depths of the shell-mounds and their extent, often a hundred yards in length and from three to five feet in depth, indicate continued use over a long period of time. Such a pile of refuse could not have been accumulated in one generation.

The inhabitants of Northern Europe during the Mesolithic were in part the ancestors of the Germanic people. The conditions described form part of the Germanic background. The language spoken had developed out of a language-form of the Upper Palaeolithic, and this in turn must have had its origin in the Southern Mediterranean area. This was not an Indo-European language.

Unfortunately the fossil evidence from the Mesolithic period is much less satisfactory than from the preceding Upper Palaeolithic or the following Neolithic. The stratigraphic evidence in many cases is far from convincing. For present purposes, however, it makes little difference whether the fossil remains found in the North belong to period 1 or period 3, provided they are either Mesolithic or early Neolithic. There is no indication of any significant migration into the North during this period of time, apart from those already described. That means that the Mesolithic inhabitants were basically of the same physical nature as the Upper Palaeolithic hunters, and these were to a very great extent of the two dominant types: Combe Capelle and Cro Magnon.

While, however, the two main types from Upper Palaeolithic times were dolichocranial, a new type had arisen towards the end of the Upper Palaeolithic or early in the Mesolithic. This was the Alpine type or sub-race of the Primary Caucasian. This was the beginning of what has been called the "Alpine

wedge." The first definite indications come from a cave called
Ofnet in Bavaria. Two nests of skulls were found there,
one of them containing twenty-seven skulls, the other six.
The heads had evidently been severed from the body before
burial. There has been no satisfactory explanation of this
practice. The find is important, however, for other reasons.
Some of the skulls are dolichocranial, some mesocranial and
some brachycranial. It is generally considered that we have here
an indication of two distinct sub-races and a mixture of the
two. Whether this new Alpine type is a development of
certain tendencies already existing in the Cro Magnons or
is an intrusion from the east is still a matter of dispute.

Other brachycranial skulls have been found at Furfooz in
Belgium and at Grenelle near Paris, but the stratigraphic evidence is not such as to permit of very accurate dating. What
evidence there is points to the Mesolithic period.[9]

In various districts in France, in Late Mesolithic or Early
Neolithic times, skulls and skeletons have been found which
are representative of the Mediterranean sub-race of the Primary
Caucasian. They are short in stature, slenderly built, dolichocranial, with narrow faces and noses. The average cranial
index is 71-72.[10] Remembering the expansion of the Late
Capsian-Microlithic culture into Europe, this appearance of the
Mediterranean type might be expected. The microlithic cultural
influence extended into Northern Europe, but it was not apparently accompanied by any significant migration of people.

Two skulls have been found in Mark Brandenburg (Pritzerber
See) which, it is claimed, were associated with artifacts of
the Lyngby culture, both belonging to the Combe Capelle
type.[11] A Swedish find at Stangenäs, described by Arnborg,[12]
shows characteristics of both Combe Capelle and Cro Magnon.
A skull from Grosz Tinz, Silesia, with mainly Combe Capelle
and some Cro Magnon characteristics, may be either Mesolithic
or Neolithic.[13] Two skulls from Grube, Oldenburg, are claimed
to be of Mesolithic age.[14] They are on the lower brachycranial

margin. Two incomplete skulls were found in Kiel Harbor during dredging operations which may belong to the close of the Mesolithic. They show Cro Magnon characteristics.[15] Still another comes from Ellerbek near Kiel which may also be Mesolithic. It is essentially Cro Magnon.[16] A skull has been found at Borreby, Denmark, associated with the Lyngby culture which appears to be of the Alpine brachycranial type.[17] If this is correct it would indicate an intrusion from further south.

As far as the evidence goes, it is only possible to say that the Cro Magnon and the Combe Capelle types predominate. If the Mesolithic inhabitants of Northern Europe were in the main descendants of the Upper Palaeolithic hunters, if there was no significant intrusion of any other type during the Mesolithic, and if the early Neolithic types in the North still show the same characteristics, the conclusion must be that the Mesolithic inhabitants of Northern Europe were definitely part of the physical make-up of the Germanic people. It also follows that they were Proto-Nordic.[18]

This chapter began with the assertion that Germanic is a language group of the Indo-European language stock. We must now attempt to isolate the Indo-Europeans and show how it happened that this language stock was introduced into the North of Europe.

The Neolithic

Background

From a purely technical point of view the term "Neolithic" refers to a new kind of technique in the manufacture of stone implements and weapons. This is the technique of polishing. It was new, however, only in the sense of general application to flint and other kinds of stone. The technique of polishing had already been used in the Mesolithic period in the making of bone and horn implements. But Neolithic in addition to meaning "New Stone Age" can also be used to describe a way of life. This new way has been called the Neolithic Revolution.[1]

From the earliest time down to the beginning of the Neolithic period man was a hunter or fisher and a food-gatherer. His only attempt at increasing his food supply was by the use of magic and ritual. The change from food-gathering to food-producing was perhaps the most important milestone in the history of human culture. It has completely changed the course of history.

The domestication of food plants and animals placed a much greater emphasis upon sedentary community life. It brought about the establishment of agricultural villages, a possibility of a store of surplus food, a greater division of labor and the formation of classes. The possibility of food storage against a future lack involved individual and social responsibilities which had not previously been so pronounced. It also brought a radical change in diet; the consumption of cereal foods reduced the amount of meat which was required.

There was a rapid development in the art of pottery making, in part because of the necessity of storage facilities, and in part because of the needs of a sedentary life.

Food surpluses led to trade to exchange food commodities for other goods from outside or raw material. This trade required transportation either by using domesticated animals as beasts of burden or by the development of water transport in addition to human carriers. Surplus commodities and trade usually involve some system of records. Although this may not have been the reason for the invention of written symbols, it was certainly an important factor in their development for practical use.

With a plentiful food supply there was a rapid increase in population. In many areas this meant expansion to virgin soil, a migration of agricultural populations, sometimes of a peaceful nature, sometimes warlike. Race and language mixture also took place.

Food-production is so intimately associated with the soil that fertility cults, such as that of the Earth Mother, were a natural by-product. Priests, temples and rituals soon followed. The ability to make astronomical calculations to determine the proper season for the cult-rituals and the favorable period for agricultural operations increased the power of the keepers of the temples and kept the agriculturists dependent upon them. Out of the worship of the Earth Mother and the Sky God there developed a great variety of local burial customs, great stone monuments, places of sacrifice and worship and a widespread cult of the dead.

Eventually, with more advanced weapons and techniques came the formation of city, states and empires. Man had then reached the stage of organized war. Prior to this time wars had been of a tribal nature, motivated by personal quarrels, disputes over hunting grounds and women.

It should be kept in mind that most of these revolutionary changes had become an integral part of the lives of the people in Egypt and the Near East before Europe had emerged from the mists of the Mesolithic. The beginnings of food-production in the river valley of the Nile and in the valleys of the Fertile Crescent can be placed at about 6000 B. C. That is three thousand years earlier than the beginning of the Neolithic period in Northern Europe. The first accurate calendar was established in Egypt in 4236 or 4241 B. C., and there were agricultural communities long before that. By that time imperialism was already flourishing.

It is generally accepted that the first knowledge of agriculture was either in Mesopotamia or Egypt, or in both. Hoe or garden methods were undoubtedly the earliest. As there was no knowledge of fertilizers and little understanding of soil conservation there would be expansion with the exhaustion of the soil and the increase in population. Apart from such regions as the Nile and the Fertile Crescent, where there is either natural irrigation or where artificial irrigation is technically a fairly simple matter, there must have been a steady movement of agriculturists seeking new land. Any migration from the Near East into Eastern Europe would be associated with the westward advance of a Mediterranean type of man, with some Alpine mixture. This conclusion corresponds to the available anthropological data. These agriculturists mixed with and absorbed the food-gathering peoples among whom they came and taught them the art of cereal food-production and the domestication of animals.

In Southeastern Europe the direction of the new cultural movement was around the Caspian Sea and westward north of the Black Sea to the Danube and then up the river following the distribution of the loess deposits which make favorable agricultural soil. The new economy finally reached the Rhine and the North German Plain. It seems clear, however, that Western and part of Northern Europe also received a knowledge of agriculture from the southwest as the result of cultural dissemination and also some migration along the Atlantic littoral in association with the northward expansion of the Mediterranean type of man in Spain, France and Great Britain. It is reasonably certain that most of the cultures of Neolithic Europe had an agricultural basis by 2500 B. C., perhaps by 3000 B. C. in Southeastern Europe. The emphasis upon grain cultivation or stockraising would vary in accordance with the conditions of terrain and climate.

The Indo-Europeans are to be found associated with one of the Neolithic cultures of Europe. The important cultures may be listed as follows:

  a) The Painted Pottery culture of Southeastern Europe.
  b) The Banded Pottery culture of the Danubian area.
  c) The Western European culture (Iberian Peninsula, France and Britain).
  d) The Swiss Lake Dwelling culture.
  e) The Northern European Megalithic culture.
  f) The Single Grave-Corded Ware-Battle Ax culture of Upper Saxony and Thuringia.
  g) The Bell and Zoned Beaker cultures.

The main area of the Painted Pottery culture was north and west of the Black Sea, an area of very fertile agricultural land. The bearers of this culture had an implement called after its shape, the "shoe-last." It was used as a hoe. They made clay figurines of animals and women, which would indicate that their religion was based upon some form of the fertility cult. They used spiral and meander decorations on their pottery which was hand-made and sun-dried. But before drying, this pottery was elaborately painted, several colors being used. It is a highly advanced ceramic art, probably as advanced as any before the discovery of the potter's wheel.

Painted Pottery appears to be of Asiatic origin. It is found in Turkestan, on the Asiatic steppes and as far east as China. Important stations in the Near East are Susa and Anau. It is probable that this form of pottery developed in close association with agricultural settlements in East Mesopotamia and then spread in various directions. An attempt to derive the Painted Pottery from the Banded Pottery of the Danube has not proved successful.[2]

The settlements of the Banded Pottery culture are found in the loess areas of the Danube valley. These settlements have yielded evidence of the remains of oxen, goats, sheep, and pigs, also proof that wheat, barley, millet and flax were cultivated. The typical, polished, stone implement is here also the shoe-last celt. The pottery is unpainted, but has banded and spiral ornamentation. Fertility statuettes are quite common. The people do not seem to have been very warlike, since the only thing resembling a weapon is a disc-shaped mace-head.

There can be little doubt that the clay fertility statuettes of both the Banded and the Painted Pottery cultures are in origin connected with the fertility traditions of Western Asia. In all probability the bearers of the Banded Pottery culture were an early wave of agriculturists whose migration began before the introduction of the painting technique. There are some significant resemblances between the Painted and Banded Pottery cultures but there are also significant differences. Neither one can be derived from the other.

The Western European culture covered a wide area and included a number of local cultures. The type of pottery is represented by the Michelsberg ware, a simple unornamented type, showing very little artistic originality. Characteristic of the Western European cultures are the megalithic structures of Spain, France and the British Isles with their chambered graves, menhirs, stone circles, alignments and the Long Barrows of Britain. Uniformity in such a complex of structures did not, of course, exist. It is merely a matter of convenience to classify them all as Western European.

One thing seems to be certain: there was a spread of the Mediterranean racial type all along the way from Spain by the Atlantic littoral to the British Isles. This contact between Southwestern Europe, Northern France and the British Isles can be demonstrated by the presence of Mediterranean skulls in the graves and Long Barrows.

The agriculturists of the Banded Pottery culture exhibited definite expansive tendencies. They expanded to the west, influencing the culture of the Swiss Lake Dwellings and producing a number of mixed cultures as the result of contact with the Northern Megalithic culture which had expanded into Central Germany.

The culture of the Swiss Lake Dwellers shows possibly the greatest degree of variation of all the Neolithic cultures. It was a continuation and elaboration of the same idea which was responsible for the raft-dwelling sites of the Maglemose and kitchenmidden people of the North. Over two hundred of the Lake Dwellings have been found in Switzerland. Mainly for purposes of protection, these dwellings were built on platforms resting on piles driven into the bottom of the lakes in the shallow waters near the shore. Most of the pile-dwellings have been discovered during periods of low water and reconstructions have been made from the ruins found. That these people were fishermen, is proved by the finding of fishhooks, harpoons and nets. They also knew the art of weaving. Flint axes in stag-horn sockets have been found in large numbers. They were also acquainted with agriculture and had domestic animals. Sickles have been discovered, dried grains, dried apples, stones used for the crushing of grain. The bones of many domestic animals have been identified.

There was a brachycranial element among the Swiss Lake Dwellers, and this seems to have been the dominant type until strongly influenced by invasions from the North. In all probability these people became acquainted with agriculture as the result of cultural influence from the Danubian area.

The typology of the megalithic graves in Northern Europe is quite clear, especially in Jutland, the Danish Islands, in Schleswig-Holstein and in the peripheral regions, Southern Sweden and Northwest Germany. They are classified according to three types: (a) the dolmen, from a Celtic word meaning "round table"; (b) the passage or corridor grave; and (c) the stone cist. This is not only the typological but also the chronological order.

The dolmen is a small chamber designed to contain several burials, erected on the surface of the ground by means of large stones set upright. These are the so-called "erratic blocks" left by the waning ice-sheets. Four or five of these blocks form the walls, and over these large cover-stones were laid. The interstices in the walls were filled in with smaller stones and the whole was then covered by a mound of earth, leaving only the top of the cover-stones exposed. In many cases a circle of smaller stones marks the circumference of the earth-mound (Fig. 1).

The next stage in the evolution was the erection of a short corridor made of two or more smaller stones. With the extension of this corridor over which covering stones were laid the dolmen became a passage grave (French *allée couverte;* German *Ganggrab*). This had a much larger chamber, often with smaller auxiliary rooms. Sometimes the passageway was also used for the disposition of the dead (Fig. 2).

A variation of the dolmen, and sometimes a combination of the dolmen and the passage grave was the long grave (German *Langgrab*), where in a roughly rectangular enclosure often two hundred feet or more in length two or three dolmens were placed, with or without a corridor entrance.

The stone cists were made of thin stone plates, giving the effect of a long stone coffin. This is the corridor of the passage grave without the chamber into which the corridor provided a covered entrance. Probably a shortage of erratic blocks may have had something to do with the change in the method of construction.

The sphere of influence of the Northern Megalithic culture extended beyond the areas where the characteristic graves have been found. This is indicated by the finds of pottery, implements and weapons, articles of amber and art motifs over a much greater territorial area than the comparatively restricted one in Northern Europe.

The Northern Megalithic pottery shows considerable variety of form and adornment. The ornamentation is of the geometrical type, the pattern being incised into the clay before firing, and as a rule designed to separate the lower and upper parts of the vessel. This is in strong contrast to the method employed in the Painted and Banded Pottery cultures where the whole surface is ornamented as a unit. Both the dolmens and the passage graves contain characteristic types of pottery (Fig. 3).

A typological and chronological series of flint axes can also be established. The first of the series is the ax with pointed butt, which is widely distributed in Western Europe. Then comes the thin-butted ax characteristic of the dolmens. In the passage graves the common types are the thin-bladed and the thick-butted ax. These axes were implements, not weapons. Some of them appear to have been designed for cult purposes; they are beautifully shaped and polished (Fig. 4).

For weapons mace-heads, chipped-stone daggers and double-headed axes were used (Fig. 5).

Amulets and necklaces of Baltic amber are quite common in the graves. Nothing is known about the clothing of those times, since the conditions were not favorable for the preservation of the materials, but weights used for looms have been found, an indication that the people must have been acquainted with weaving.

All the artifacts so far mentioned came from these community graves. The fact that the dolmens gave way to the passage graves and these in turn to the stone cists indicates a long-continued residence. Sometimes as many as a hundred skeletons have been found in some of the larger chambers. When the floor of the chamber had no more free space the bones of the dead were pushed aside to make way for others. It is consequently often quite impossible to reassemble the individual skeletons.

When the elaborate construction of the graves, the deposition of pottery with the burials, articles of adornment, work implements and weapons are taken into consideration, it is safe to assume that there must have been a very highly developed cult of the dead. And this cult was undoubtedly associated with the mysteries of the fertility cult. This dominance of the fertility cult had a very great importance later in the religious ideas of the Germanic people.

The graves were constructed of imperishable materials, but the houses, being of wood, have for the most part disappeared. In only a few cases has it been possible to reconstruct the dwellings from the discolored earth and charred remains. In wooded areas one would naturally expect to find the wooden and rectangular type of house, and this seems to have been characteristic of the North, as compared with the round houses or huts of Western Europe. The walls were made of wood and clay, and the roof was probably thatched. The hearth was usually inside (Fig. 6).

Even with the primitive agricultural methods which prevailed the food supply was greatly increased, as compared with the pre-agricultural days of food-gathering. This led to an increase in the population. The result was an expansion of the Northern Megalithic culture, the first great exodus from Northern Europe. In some cases this expansion was apparently a peaceful one; in others the evidence would indicate an occupation by force. Southern Sweden was overrun, also Northwest Germany and Holland. The expansion carried the culture into Middle Germany, where there were local cultures at Salzmünd, Walternieenburg and Bernburg. During the period of the stone cists the culture extended into Thuringia where the Rössen mixed culture arose. From there, there was another offshoot to the Middle Rhine. Another movement carried the culture to the region of the Swiss Lake Dwellings. This is shown by the presence of pottery of megalithic style and northern axes. The new-comers were doubtless in the minority and established a military and political supremacy in much the same way as the Normans did in England.

Another colonial expansion carried the Northern Megalithic culture to Bohemia and Moravia. The district between the Oder and the Vistula was also affected. This is the East German group. Still farther east there was a Kujavian settlement, where the characteristic grave was the long stone, an extension of the Middle German group. Between the middle and the head waters of the Volga there was yet another centre, which later became the Fatjanove culture. At Kuban, east of the Black Sea, there are some excellent examples of the stone cists (Map II).

This is a long way from the original home and testifies to the vigor and expansive strength of this northern culture. In the Kuban mounds are found indications of contact with the richer civilization of the South, the result of either trade or plunder, or of both. It looks as if some young leader with a select band of followers had heard of the treasures of the South and had gone to try his luck. He and his successors had graves built for themselves of the traditional type and probably made a very comfortable living by making occasional raids on the southern neighbors.

In the days before the invention of the wheel, pottery was made by hand and was the work of women. Pottery, being fragile, was not easily transported, at least under primitive conditions of transportation. As a rule, when a characteristic style of pottery is found in a district it can be concluded that there is evidence of migration, especially if the area is far removed from the centre of origin. Undoubtedly the same is true of grave-forms, because of their traditional and cult significance. Implements, weapons and ornaments are more ambiguous; their dissemination may have been the result of trade or barter. The one certain proof is of course, the finding of skeletons.

The term "Northern Megalithic" has been used in order to draw a sharp line of distinction between this culture and other megalithic cultures of Western Europe. These show characteristic structures which do not appear in Northern Europe, such as the tri-lithon technique of Stonehenge, the large stone-circles, the menhirs and the alignments.

There has been much speculation about the place of origin of the cult of the dead and the practice of erecting large stone monuments and graves. It may have spread from one centre such as Egypt; it is also possible that it may have originated independently in widely separated regions. The fact that the dominant type of man found in the Long Barrows of Britain is Mediterranean indicates contact with the South. But the people buried in the graves of the Northern Megalithic culture were not Mediterranean; they were Nordic.

The Northern Megalithic culture is, for our purpose, of supreme importance. That is also true of the Single Grave-Corded Ware-Battle-Ax culture of Upper Saxony and Thuringia. The characteristic type of pottery of this culture is a beaker or drinking-cup with cord ornamentation, made by winding twisted cords around the wet clay. The prototype may well have been the leather bottle of earlier times (Fig. 7).

It is also called the Single Grave culture because here are found single burials as compared with the community graves of the Northern· Megalithic culture. These graves are usually covered with a low mound of earth. The most typical consist of a shallow grave dug into the earth, paved with small stones on which the body was laid. The sides of the grave were often lined with planks, and there was also a wooden covering, often in the form of a triangular roof. In some of the mounds especially in the Scandinavian North, there are four graves, one above the other, each one a single burial. Such burials do not indicate a nomadic way of life (Fig. 8).

This Single Grave-Corded Ware culture is also distinguished by the term "Battle-Ax" because of a characteristic type of weapon which is usually associated with the burials. There were two types: a facetted hammer-ax common in Central Germany and a boat-shaped ax found in the North (Fig. 9).

As was the case with the Northern Megalithic culture, there were also various local varieties of the Corded Ware or Single Grave culture. In addition to the Upper Saxon-Thuringian group there was another between the Oder and the Vistula, a settlement on the Middle Rhine, an East Prussian group, one in Southern Sweden, another in Central Jutland and Schleswig-Holstein. The influence of the culture spread far and wide. In the South it affected the region of the Swiss Lake Dwellings. In a somewhat mixed form it made its appearance in Britain. There was also a very extensive field of influence in Eastern Europe: in Austria, Hungary, Roumania, the Southern Russian steppes, and in the area between the middle and head waters of the Volga (Map III).

One view is that Middle Germany, that is, Upper Saxony and Thuringia, was the original home of the culture and that it radiated from there in all directions as the result of emigration and cultural dispersion. According to this view, it had its basis in the Mesolithic culture of Middle Germany. That is the view adopted here. Jutland and Schleswig-Holstein have also been favored as the place of origin. Still another interpretation points to the Southern Russian steppes.

It has, however, been shown, that the Single Grave-Corded Ware culture was an intrusive culture in the North,[3] expanding directly down the Elbe into Northwest Germany and

thence into Schleswig-Holstein and Jutland, or from the area
of the Oder, where the East German group was, across the
Baltic into Southern Sweden on the one hand and on the
other westward along the Baltic coast into Schleswig- Holstein
from where it later spread into Northwest Germany, Central
Jutland and then into the rest of Denmark.

The theory that the people of this culture came from the
steppes of Southern Russia, assumes that they were a nomadic
or semi-nomadic horde.[4] The oldest culture in this region,
apart from that of the descendants of the Upper Palaeolithic
and Mesolithic hunters, was the Painted Pottery, as we have
seen. This Painted Pottery culture must have come from
the Southeast at a date prior to that of the appearance of any
of the Middle European, Western or Northern cultures. It
was an expansive agricultural culture, seeking new *Lebensraum.*
The bearers of this culture were basically Mediterranean or
Eurafrican, as they have been called. Further, the area of the
Painted Pottery culture was overrun first by the people from
the Northern Megalithic sphere and later by others of the
Single Grave-Corded Ware. It is difficult to see how the bearers
of this culture could have originated in Southern Russia. It
is true that the *kurgans* in that region were Single Graves and
contain examples of the Corded Ware pottery, but many of
them belong to the Bronze and even to the Iron Age. The
older graves would be the result of the expansion of the
Single Grave-Corded Ware people into Southern Russia from
the West as part of the general expansion described above.

The Central Asiatic steppes as the original home are simply
impossible. There is no evidence of the use of such a device
as the Corded Ware technique, nor is there any indication of
the presence of anything like the Single Grave, the facetted
battle-ax or the boat-ax. This explanation is a survival of
the traditional belief *ex oriente lux.*

A study of the geography of the Corded Ware settlements
in Middle and Northern Europe shows that the bearers of this

culture were inclined to inhabit areas which were not particularly well-suited to grain production. This was true of the Central part of Schleswig-Holstein and Jutland, part of Northwest Germany, the foothills of Upper Saxony and Thuringia and the sandy plains of East Germany (as they were at that time). These areas were much better suited to the raising of flocks and herds, and this seems to have been the main source of wealth of the early Single Grave-Corded Ware people. This does not mean that they had no knowledge of grain production but merely that the raising of cereals was secondary in their economy.

The fact that the people of this culture buried their dead in single graves strengthens the argument that they had a Mesolithic, and at a greater distance, an Upper Palaeolithic background. The flat, single grave was the usual procedure. The erection of a shallow mound over the grave could be attributed to the influence of the Northern Megalithic culture.

That the people of the Single Grave-Corded Ware culture in their original home in Upper Saxony and Thuringia were physically of the Nordic type can scarcely be disputed, and this is equally true of all the areas into which these colonizers carried this culture, either by peaceful expansion or military conquest.

According to the results obtained by Retzius[5] and Fürst[6] 51.4% of the crania of Neolithic Scandinavia were dolichocranial, 40% mesocranial and 8.6% brachycranial. For Denmark alone the proportion was, according to Nielsen[7]: 29.6% dolichocranial, 47.9% mesocranial and 22.5% brachycranial out of 142 skulls taken from 60 different burials. The evidence of the dolichocranial skulls and the mesocranial, with other indications as to stature found in the long bones, shows that the great majority of the people was of the Nordic variety.

There was still another culture which played a minor role in Neolithic Europe. This has been called the Bell Beaker culture after the characteristic shape of the drinking glass which is associated with the culture. It is first encountered in the Iberian Peninsula but it may not have originated there. It had a most remarkable and rapid expansion in various parts of Western Europe, in Middle Europe and at least as far east as Hungary. In the Rhine district this culture came into contact with the people of the Corded Ware. A mixture took place and from this centre there was an expansion northwards and at the end of the Neolithic period or early in the Bronze Age a colonial settlement was made in Britain. This hybrid culture is called Zoned Beaker. According· to Hubert[8] the bearers of this culture were the first to introduce an Indo-European language, an early form of Gaelic, into the British Isles, but this thesis has not been generally accepted.

The people of this culture were predominatly brachycranial, a physical characteristic supplied by the Bell Beaker element. In England they erected the Round Barrows, in sharp contrast to the prevailing type. They may also have been responsible for the introduction of bronze into the British Isles.

If it is granted that the original speakers of Indo-European were physically predominantly of the Nordic type, it should now be possible to eliminate some of the bearers of Neolithic cultures from consideration. The people of the Painted and Banded Pottery cultures can be excluded; they were basically of Mediterranean type. The Swiss Lake Dwellers before the instrusion of other elements from the North were mainly Alpine. The people of Western Europe and of the British Isles associated with the erection of megalithic graves were predominantly Mediterranean. The brachycranial people of the Bell Beaker culture can also be eliminated. This leaves two cultures for further consideration: those of Upper Saxony and Thuringia and Northern Europe, the home areas of the Corded Ware and Northern Megalithic cultures respectively. Attempts to identify the colonizing movements of the people of the Northern Megalithic culture with the expansion of the Indo-European language stock have not proved successful.[9] On the basis of the archaeological and anthropological evidence the conclusion must be that the people of the Single Grave-Corded Ware-Battle Ax culture were the original Indo-Europeans. Let us see if the linguistic evidence offers support for this point of view.

If a language map of Modern Europe is examined it will be seen that most of the languages spoken in Europe at the present time belong to the Indo-European language stock. The exceptions are: Basque, Hungarian, Finnish, Esthonian, some Finno-Ugrian languages in Northwestern Russia, Turkish in European Russia and several languages in the Caucasian area.

Indo-European languages are, however, not restricted to Europe, nor were they in early historical times. The problem has always been: Are the Indo-European languages of Asia the result of colonial expansion from Europe or has the movement been in the reverse direction?

Indo-European languages, the living and the known extinct, are classified as follows (Map IV):

1. Indo-Iranian or Aryan:
   a) Indic: the language of the *Rig Vedas,* Sanskrit, Prakrit, Pali, Modern Indic, of which the most important are: Sindhi, Bengali and Hindi.
   b) Iranian: Avestan, the language of the writings of Zoroaster, Afghan, Old Persian, the language of the cuneiform inscriptions, Modern Iranian, Kurdic, Ossetic (in the Causasus).
   c) Sacian (extinct).
   d) Scythian (extinct).
   e) Sarmatian (extinct).
2. Tocharic, in East Turkestan (extinct).
3. Thraco-Phrygian (extinct), Thracian in ancient Thrace in the Balkans, Phrygian in Asia Minor.
4. Armenian.
5. Hittite (extinct) in Asia Minor; at least some forms of the language.

6. Mitannic (extinct) in Asia Minor.

7. Hellenic: Ionic, Attic, Doric, West Greek, Macedonian.

8. Illyrian in Central Eastern Europe (extinct if possible survival in Albanian is excluded).

9. Albanian.

10. Balto-Slavic:

   a) Baltic: Old Prussian (extinct), Lithuanian, Lettic.

   b) Slavic: Bulgarian, Serbian, Croatian, Slovenian, Russian, Ukrainian, Polish, Czech, Slovakian.

11. Italic:

   a) Oscan-Umbrian (extinct).

   b) Latin, from which are descended the Romance languages: Italian, Spanish, Catalonian, Portuguese, Provençal, French, Rhaeto-Romanic, Roumanian.

12. Celtic: Continental Celtic (extinct), Cornish (extinct), Welsh or Cymric, Breton (a reintroduction into Northwestern France from Britain at the time of the Anglo-Saxon invasions), Gaelic in Scotland, Erse in Ireland, Manx on the Isle of Man (almost extinct).

13. Germanic:

   a) North Germanic: Icelandic, Norwegian, Danish, Swedish.

   b) West Germanic: English, German, Dutch, Flemish, Frisian.

   c) East Germanic: Gothic, Burgundian, Langobardic and many others (all extinct).

A general division of Indo-European into West and East Indo-European can be made on the basis of the development of the front palatals *k, g, kh, gh* which in Indo-Iranian, Balto-Slavic, Armenian and Albanian appear as voiceless or voiced sibilants under certain conditions, whereas in Hellenic, Italic, Celtic and Germanic they retain, or retained before later changes took place, the palatal *k* or *g* sound. The languages of the first division are called *satem* languages, those of the second *c* (k) *entum*. There would appear to be a fundamental division into the two great dialect fields, in spite of some discrepancies. One centre of dispersion would be Southeastern Europe, the other Northern and Central Europe.

Tocharic in East Turkestan is more closely related to the *centum* division than to the *satem*. This might be compared with the appearance of a Celtic language in Asia Minor, Galatian, which survived until the time of St. Paul. Both may be regarded as isolated expansion groups.

The dialect division into *centum* and *satem* languages indicates a cleavage in an original linguistic and cultural unity. This original unity appears in the interrelationships between such hyphenated groups as Thraco-Phrygian, Indo-Iranian, Balto-Slavic, Italo-Celtic, Germanic and Latin. These interrelationships can only mean an expansion of Indo-European speaking peoples from some area where linguistic and cultural unity were possible.

Archaeological investigations have shown conclusively that there was a highly-developed culture in Northern India before the introduction of an Indo-European language. India could not have been the *Urheimat*. Neither could Iran nor Asia Minor. Indo-European was introduced into these areas in early historical times. Greece can also be excluded. The Hellenic-speaking peoples were not native to the country, as survivals of place-names from native languages plainly indicate. Nor can there be any doubt that an Indo-European language was introduced into the Italian Peninsula, presumably by the Terramare and Villanova people from about 1500 B. C. on. Indo-European was introduced into Spain in the form of a Celtic language at the time of the Celtic expansion of the La Tène culture of the Iron Age. Gaul also was indo-europeanized by the Celts, as were the British Isles.

After this elimination we have left the mass of Central Europe from Southern Russia to the Rhine plus Northern Europe. It has been shown that the anthropological evidence excludes the people of the Painted and Banded Pottery cultures, of the Swiss Lake Dwellings, the Bell Beaker culture and the people of the Western European cultures. The bearers of these cultures were all either predominantly Mediterranean or Alpine. The original speakers of Indo-European must have been Nordic. The archaeological evidence will not support the thesis that the Indo-European language stock had its origin in Northern Europe, although the dominant physical type there can be identified with that of early speakers of Indo-European. This leaves only the Corded Ware culture of Upper Saxony and Thuringia to be associated with the original Indo-Europeans.

If the map of Europe showing the expansion of the Single Grave-Corded Ware-Battle-Ax culture is compared with a map showing the probable areas of the various Indo-European languages before the expansion into Asia Minor and Northern India (Map IV), it will be seen that there is a remarkable concordance between the two. The area of the Germanic language corresponds to that of the Northern Megalithic and the Corded Ware culture of Northwest Germany, Schleswig-Holstein, Jutland, the Danish Islands and Southern Sweden. The Banded Pottery and the Swiss Lake Dwelling cultures correspond to the areas of the Italic-Celtic, the Illyrian and the Hellenic. In Southeastern Europe where people of the Corded Ware culture came into contact with the Painted Pottery agriculturists are found the Thraco-Phrygians and the Indo-Iranians. The Balto-Slavic would be the result of the eastward expansion of the Corded Ware culture along the Baltic.

Undoubtedly many peoples and languages which arose out of this expansion-complex failed to maintain themselves as individual units. This has left many linguistic gaps. The Illyrians are one example within Europe, although their disappearance took place much later. But the movement from Southeast Europe into Asia Minor furnished many such cases: the Hittites, the Mitanni, Sacians, Tocharians, Lydians and the Lycians. The history of the Germanic people during the Age of Migration furnishes many parallel examples.

After the completion of the first stages of the Great Migration associated with the expansion of the people of the Northern Megalithic, Corded Ware, Painted and Banded Pottery and Bell Beaker cultures, there emerged three important centres from which further movements of peoples took place. These were the Danubian area of Central Europe, the Northern Balkans and Southern Russia, the latter including the territory now known as Roumania and Bulgaria. From these areas came the peoples who are known to history as Celts, Italians, Achaeans, Dorians, Hittites, Mitanni, Indo-Iranian, Scythians, Sarmatians and many others whose names have not survived. The amalgamation of the peoples and cultures of the Northern Megalithic and the Single Grave-Corded Ware-Battle Ax cultures which resulted in the formation of the Germanic people, was followed by a relatively long period of internal development before the first phase of Germanic expansion began.

Nothing is known of the Proto-Indo-European of the Neolithic period except what can be deduced from a comparison of words in Indo-European languages of a later date. And results obtained by this method are often ambiguous.[10]

Linguistic evidence indicates that the Indo-European people had the Sky God as their basic religious concept, but it is also quite clear they took over some of the *Magna Mater* fertility beliefs of those from whom they learned agriculture. This resulted in theological and mythological confusion, at least in the opinions of modern investigators.

Archaeological investigation supports the evidence of linguistic research that the Western Indo-Europeans at least lived in houses, not in tents so characteristic of a nomadic life. This is indicated by words for door, house, door-frame, and by such a German word as *winden,* referring to the construction of walls out of intertwined reeds or twigs (German *Wand*: wall).

Words for plough, furrow, bread, grain, pig, ox, sheep,

goat, steer, cow have also been deduced by the comparative philologists. These show a knowledge of cereal crops and stockraising. But there does not seem to be any common word for "horse."

There has been a great deal of controversy about the date of the introduction of the horse into Central and Western Europe. It appears to have become almost a dogma that the Indo-Europeans came from the steppes in a rapid invasion of Europe using the domesticated horse as a means of transportation. But this romantic picture of mounted Indo-Europeans galloping across Europe like the Huns of later times is not supported by the evidence. The migrations were rather with ox-drawn wagons, the adults trudging wearily alongside, as in the days of the Goths and Alaric.[11]

There is evidence that Indo-Europeans introduced the horse into Western Asia, not as an animal to be yoked to the plough, but for the drawing of war-chariots and then for riding. In Western Europe horses had survived in a wild state but most zoologists agree that the horse was first domesticated on the Asiatic steppes, presumably by nomadic people. This domesticated horse was lighter and swifter than the wild horse of Upper Palaeolithic times. The knowledge of the domesticated horse must have spread from the east by cultural diffusion. Apart from sporadic appearances the horse did not become general in Central, Southern and Northern Europe until the Bronze Age.

The concept of the Indo-Europeans as horse-mounted or chariot-driving warriors belongs to the Bronze Age. That is where Homer places the chariots and where the historical records of Egypt and the Near East place them. In Europe the Bronze Age belongs to the second millenium. And it is in the second millenium that the Indo-European avalanche descended upon the Near East with such devastating effect.

This does not mean that isolated advance parties in the third millennium did not try their fortune in the fabled lands of the South. Many adventurous chieftains may have led their followers southwards, and after having saved the tottering thrones of over-sophisticated petty princes, married the daughters and eventually established new dynastic lines. But these advance bands soon became merged with the native population, leaving as sole evidence of their existence their Indo-European names and some of their physical characteristics in the ruling class. There appear to be many instances of this kind in the background of Homer's story.

The presence of Indo-Europeans can often be deduced from the personal names composed of two root-elements. This practice was widespread, as is indicated by such compounds as Mene-laos, Dio-medes, Themisto-kles, Dubno-rix, Sigu-fried, Gisel-her, Kriem-hild, Deva-dattas, Beo-wulf and hundreds of others.

The fact that the Indo-European decimal system shows signs of having been influenced by the Babylonian duodecimal or sexigesimal has been used to indicate propinquity at an early stage and therefore to support a Central Asiatic origin of the Indo-Europeans. This Babylonian system has left traces even in the Germanic languages, the farthest removed from the Babylonian centre of influence, in such expressions as "twelve" which breaks the decimal system, "sixty" equal to five twelves, "one hundred and twenty," the English long ton, twelve inches, the division of the day into twenty-four hours, the hour into sixty minutes, the circle into three hundred and sixty degrees and the year into twelve months. Hirt,[12] however, attributes this to cultural influence, remarking that with the age of the Babylonian culture and with the wide radius of its influence there is no difficulty in accepting an extension of this influence to Europe. Possibly trade during the Bronze Age played an important role. Hirt points out, also, that if the two cultures had been contiguous in early times the impact of the Babylonian on the Indo-European would have been far more penetrating than a partial influence on the system of counting.

The beech-line has played an important role in the Indo-European problem.[13] This is a line drawn roughly from what was formerly called Königsberg to the Black Sea. It is claimed that the beech does not, or at least did not, flourish east of this line in earlier times. The word for beech occurs in quite a number of Indo-European languages, even though it does not always have the same meaning. In Greek the word was applied to the oak tree. That would hardly have happened if the beech had been native to Greece.

Conclusions based upon the presence or absence of such words as autumn, snow, salmon, *mare,* and others can rarely lead to definite results, since the possibility of borrowing must be taken into consideration, and since it is hazardous to fix an exact time for the presence of such words in a language before there is any manuscript evidence. There is little written material from the second millennium, unless the decipherment of some of the Cretan scripts proves to yield information. The *Rig Vedas* are early, some of them possibly as early as 1500 B. C., but there is no reason to assume they were committed to writing until much later, and that implies the possibility of additions and changes in spite of oral traditionalism.

From the time when manuscript or pictorial evidence was available, ancient geographers, historians and writers have provided us with some descriptions of considerable value.

The early Greek writers made no distinction in their physical description of the Celts and the Germanic peoples.[14] The Celts of the period of expansion are portrayed as tall, fair-skinned, blond warriors with grey or blue eyes. Livy, Diodorus and Polybius have left descriptions of the Celts which leave little doubt about the physical appearance of this people. Later, by the end of the period of Celtic expansion, mixture with native populations of other types, Alpine and Mediterranean, greatly modified the appearance of the Celts, although many of the leaders may have remained unmixed. Many plastic representations from Roman sources have survived and these show quite clearly that the dominant Celtic characteristics were of the Nordic kind, even when allowance is made for idealization on the part of the artist.

The original population of the Italian Peninsula was mainly of the Mediterranean type, but the dominant type among the *Italici* was Nordic. Both Sieglin and Günther have collected a vast amount of material from Roman sources, from literary and historical records, from Roman statuary and from personal names, showing clearly that the type of the ruling classes of the ancient Romans was Nordic. A great many well-known persons are described as blond. Blond hair was ascribed to the deities such as Amor, Apollo, Aurora, Bacchus, Ceres, Diana, Jupiter, Mars, Mercury, Minerva and Venus. Two hundred and fifty persons are known who bore the name of Flavius (blond) and there are many with names such as Rufus (red) and Rutilius (reddish).[15]

The intrusion of Indo-Europeans into the Aegean area, although on a relatively small scale, may have begun before 2000 B. C. The two main migration waves came later. There can be no doubt that those who introduced an Indo-European language were basically of the Nordic type.[16] Most of the gods and heroes of the *Iliad* and the *Odyssey* were blond; Athena was blue-eyed, Aphrodite was described as having golden hair, Helen had silken blond hair, light-colored eyes, a dazzling white skin. The Greek word *iris* meaning rainbow was used to describe the human eye. It would be very strange indeed if a dark-eyed people had made such a comparison.

To be sure, artists idealize, and it would be naive to believe that the Greeks even approximated the symmetrical beauty of the product of their artists, but the important point is that the Greek artists in the great majority of cases portrayed an idealized Nordic type of beauty, and they would certainly not have done that if this type had been strange to them.

The Nordic type in Greece ultimately suffered the same fate

as in Italy. It became submerged in other racial elements, mainly Mediterranean and Armenoid.

The South Russian Scythians of the Iron Age were mainly of Nordic type.[17] This is also true of the inhabitants of Southern and Central European Russia in the Bronze Age. From these areas came the Asiatic Indo-Europeans: the Iranians, the Sacians and the Indo-European-speaking invaders of Northern India. Two migration routes were open, one by way of the Caucasus and the other around the Caspian Sea. Both routes appear to have been used.

The native population of India was composed of racial elements of dark complexion such as Veddas, Australoids, Negritoes and also a southern expansion of a Mediterranean strain. The Indo-European invaders did not have numerical superiority, but they were physically superior and they were able to establish themselves securely. The caste system was introduced in order to maintain segregation. The Sanskrit word for caste, *varna,* means color. No doubt other factors in later times were of great importance in the development of the caste system, since it is today no longer based upon a difference in skin color.

Among the Brahmans, the highest Indian caste, fair skin and fair hair are still fairly frequent. Fair hair and blue eyes or grey are reported from Kashmir. Nordic traits are found in the Ganges district, in the Pamirs and Hindukusch. In the shape of face, stature and general physical build the Sikhs approximate the Nordic type. The Aryans in the Hittite inscriptions of Boghaz-koi are called *Hari,* which means "the blond people." Wall paintings in the temple of Ashanta indicate the difference between the native Indian type and the tall, blond Nordic. Passages in Sanskrit literature refer to the natives as being of dark color — *krishma varna* — and as *anas,* that is, noseless, whereas the newcomers refer to themselves as Indra's white friends. Indra himself, an Aryan god, is described as blond, red-bearded, and with some of the characteristics of the Germanic Thor. The fire god, Agni, and the sun god, Surja, have golden hair. Uschas, the goddess of the dawn, is delineated in much the same way as Eos among the Greeks and Aurora among the Romans. There can be little doubt that Nordic was the prevalent type among the invaders of India in the second millennium B. C.[18]

Skulls of Nordic type have been found in the burials of the royal families of the Hari and the Mitanni. Indo-European names of rulers are common. This is also true of the Hittites.[19]

The Sacians in West Turkestan, called Turkomen in modern times, also show traces of a former Nordic element. The Alans, who werè associated with the Goths, probably belonged to this group. The modern Ossetic people in the Caucasus may be a remnant of the Alans. They still speak an Indo-European language and Nordic traits, especially blondness with blue eyes, are still quite common among them.

The Medes and Persians belonged linguistically to the Iranian group of the Indo-Iranian branch. According to descriptions in classical literature, representations in the palace paintings and on Persian coins, the ruling element at least were of the Nordic type.[20]

Largely owing to the isolation of their mountain territory the modern Kurds, probably descendants of the ancient Medes, have preserved many of the traits of the Nordic type in stature, eye color, color of the hair and fairness of skin.

The conclusion that the Nordic type was the dominant type of the original Indo-Europeans in the East is supported by the investigations of Kappers and Parr, who find the long-headed Indo-European type in a great many localities throughout the Near East from the Caspian Sea to India.[21]

The purpose of this chapter has been to establish the fact that the original Indo-Europeans were of the Nordic racial type. The next task is to show the Indo-Europeanization of Northern Europe and the formation of the Germanic people.

The Germanic People in the Bronze Age

The settlement of Northern Europe from the recession of the ice of the Fourth Glaciation to the end of the Neolithic period has been briefly described. Many geological changes took place in the North during the approximately ten thousand years which elapsed between these two points of time: the stage of the Baltic Ice Lake, the *Yoldia* Sea, the *Ancylus* Lake and the change to conditions more or less like those of the present during the *Litorina* phase. The latter was a period of optimum climate for Northern Europe, a phase which lasted well into the Bronze Age but which began to deteriorate about 800 B. C.

We have seen how Northern Europe was first settled by bands of wandering hunters following the reindeer and game animals retreating northwards as the land became free of ice. We have also seen how the epi-Magdalenian culture mixed with microlithic elements was succeeded by the Maglemose and kitchenmidden cultures. Then came the participation of the North in the Neolithic Revolution with its tremendous impact upon the traditional way of life, the material increase in the food supply accompanied by a marked increase in the birth rate, the search for new land, migrations, the introduction of new customs and art-forms, introduction of new language-forms, physical and cultural mixtures.

Along with the Neolithic Revolution came a new religious

concept, the cult of the dead, resulting in the construction of innumerable large stone graves. In addition, there are in certain areas the single graves of the Corded Ware culture. Then too in some of the peripheral districts the flat graves of the Mesolithic bear witness to the fact that some of the people of Northern Europe had been relatively unaffected by the new and stirring events and had continued undisturbed the old traditional forms and burial customs.

The Northern Megalithic was in all probability an intrusive culture in the North; the Corded Ware culture of the Single Grave people was brought to the North by a wave of migration which has been identified with an Indo-European speaking people. It appeared in Northern Europe before the end of the Neolithic period, probably as early as the time of the passage graves. Between that time and about 1200 B. C. a cultural unification was completed in the older settled districts of the North, and the resulting culture can definitely be attributed to the Germanic people.[1]

The territorial extent of this unified Germanic culture at about 1200 B. C. was, however, not very great. Sprockhoff points out that the Northern Megalithic culture at the height of its development extended over a much greater area. Large parts of North Germany, especially Northwest Germany, which belonged to the territory of the Megalithic graves, were entirely outside of the Germanic cultural sphere at this later date.[2]

Sprockhoff maintains that with the coming of the Corded Ware people, many of the inhabitants of Schleswig-Holstein left (or were forced to leave) their homes and pushed across the Weser to the West and into Mecklenburg and Pomerania to the East. These were people who clung to the traditional forms and carried them along into exile. That this was not a voluntary exile may be indicated by the fact that the newer lands which they occupied were far from being as rich agricultural soil as that which they had left. Only an external force can explain such a change of home.[3]

In addition to this movement to the south, part of the population of Jutland under pressure of the same external force moved eastward into the Danish Isles. This force can only have been that of the Corded Ware or Single Grave people. Proof of this can be found in the fact that the pottery of the Single Grave people overlies that of the Northern Megalithic in many of the areas affected.[4]

According to Sprockhoff, and this corresponds fairly closely to the results obtained by Kersten, the Single Grave culture is oldest in the southern part of the Jutish Peninsula, and from there expanded in a northerly direction into Jutland proper, then into the Danish Islands, and perhaps into Sweden.[5] There is not, however, general agreement that the Single Grave culture of Southern Sweden is an extension of that from Jutland. It may have had its origin in the East German group.

In Holstein the Northern Megalithic culture was almost completely dominated by the invaders and many of the inhabitants were forced into exile. In Schleswig and Jutland the occupation was not so far-reaching. In the Islands the new culture overlies the older without any evidence of a forced displacement.

The assimilation of the two cultures and peoples into a Germanic cultural and linguistic unity did not take place at the same time in all parts of the North. The unifying factor was the culture of the Single Grave people.[6] Their grave forms crowd out the previously prevailing Megalithic community graves. The graves of the older Bronze Age are mound graves with single interments, with a gravel base, a coffin of stone plates, sometimes a structure resembling a low house, often a hollowed-out tree trunk, or simply a burial in a sand grave. The pottery also of the Older Bronze Age is mainly derived from the beaker pottery of the Corded Ware culture.

Kersten comes to the conclusion that the people of the invading culture established themselves as a ruling caste in Northern Europe, wherever they penetrated, influencing the cultural development of these regions, and being in turn influenced by the native culture. He shows that this cultural assimilation had as one of its most significant results the florescence of the Northern Bronze Age, and that it is very probable that this artistic development owed a great deal, perhaps a major part, to the older Megalithic population.[7]

There is no evidence of any subsequent invasion of Northern Europe after that of the Corded Ware people. It follows, then, that the Germanic culture, people and language were the results of these two factors: the Northern Megalithic and the Corded Ware-Single Grave cultures.

Montelius divided the Bronze Age of Northern Europe into five periods:

Period I: 1800-1600 B. C.
Period II: 1600-1400 B. C.
Period III: 1400-1200 B. C.
Period IV: 1200-1000 B. C.
Period V: 1000-800 B. C.

At first glance it looks like an arbitrary division, and modifications have been suggested, but on the whole it corresponds fairly closely to the sequence of the cultural development. Periods I and II may be classified as the Older Bronze Age, period III as the Middle and periods IV and V as the Younger.

The early artifacts still show the influence of imported wares, but many of them have already ceased to be copies. But it is only towards the end of the period that wares of purely local manufacture make their appearance. A specific Northern Bronze style does not occur before period II.

Jacob-Friesen claims that the influence of the Northern Bronze Age in periods II and III was sufficiently vigorous to justify the statement that large areas of Lower Saxony were Germanic territory.[8]

The typology of the Northern Bronze Age has been fairly well-established. Period I is characterized by flat and flanged axes, triangular daggers, short-shafted dagger-axes, lanceheads, armbands and neck-rings. The ornamentation is linear. In period II appear the stop-ridge axes, socketed axes, the beautifully ornamented hammer-axes, swords, daggers, razors, combs, arm-rings and the earliest form of the safety pin or brooch, as it became. The characteristic ornamentation is spiral. In period III are found the winged axes, brooches with a wide bow, kettle-wagons, half-moon-shaped neck-rings and razors with horse-head handles. In period IV there are winged and socketed axes, razors with a swan-head handle and spectacle brooches. The decoration is done with concentric circles. In period V there are spectacle brooches, socketed axes, needles with a head of concentric circles and pins with cupshaped heads, antenna swords, bronze vessels with suspension rings (Fig. 15).

Some authorities add a period VI to the Bronze Age. This period belongs partly to the Bronze and partly to the Iron Age. That is to be expected, since the Iron Age (Hallstatt phase) began in Central Europe long before it played any important role in the North. Period VI was a time of transition.

There were two methods of making bronze artifacts: the closed mould method and the *cire perdu*. When the closed mould was used two halves were prepared, either of metal or clay, each half representing a half of the artifact to be made. These were placed together and the molten metal was poured in through a small opening. When the metal hardened, the moulds were removed and the polishing began.

In the *cire perdu* method a wax model of the desired artifact was first prepared. This was then enclosed in a clay covering with a hole at one end for the pouring in of the molten metal and another to serve as an exit for the wax when it melted. The molten metal was poured in, and when it hardened, the clay covering was removed and the artifact was then polished, after which the process of ornamentation began.

The house urns and the face urns of the area between the Oder and the Vistula may give some idea of the type of store-

house and dwelling in use at that time, although they belong
to the transition from the Bronze to the Iron Age (Fig. 16).
These urns were really burial urns. The ashes of the deceased
were placed in one of these vessels. The spirit of the dead
was supposed to feel more at home when deposited in something similar to its home when living. Some of the vessels
suggest a structure on piles, evidently designed for storage
purposes in places where flooding might be expected. At
Buch, not far from Berlin, a village settlement has been
excavated. A street runs through the centre of the village,
the houses are rectangular, detached and in line, with thatched
roofs, and a large "community hall" is at one end of the
village.

The clothing worn by Bronze Age men and women of the
Germanic North has been reconstructed from the tree-trunk
burials. The dead were often buried in a large, hollowed-out
oak log, fully clothed and accompanied by many personal
possessions such as weapons, tools and articles of adornment.
The clothing was made of sheep's wool, both natural color
and bleached, with a mixture of deer or ox hair (Fig. 10).

The men wore a garment reaching from the shoulders to the
knees, fastened at the neck by a brooch, with a girdle at
the waist fastened by a buckle. The girdle was made of
leather or linen. Above this was worn a mantle or cloak,
also fastened at the neck or shoulder by a brooch. On the
head was a close-fitting, felt hat. The shoes were of a sandal-
like nature, and often something like the modern military
puttees were wound around the ankles and the lower part of
the leg. The upper parts of the legs and the arms were left
bare, evidence of a mild climate (Fig. 10).

The women wore a close-fitting jacket, high-necked and
covering the arms to the elbows, a long, broad skirt, long
enough to cover the ankles, bound at the waist with a long
girdle with tassels at the ends, and with a highly ornamented
girdle-plate at the waist. Examples of skirts of knee length

for young women have also been found. The hair was bound
in a net at the back of the head. A bronze collar was worn
around the neck. Arm-rings and arm-bands have been found
in the graves and various types of small bronze caskets
worn by the women for the keeping of small articles of
toilet use (Fig. 10).

To be sure, not everybody could afford the more expensive
kind of ornament, but on the other hand, the probability is
that among the freemen there was no class which could be
described as really poor, just as there was no class which was
inordinately rich. The simple economy of the Northern Bronze
Age did not produce the extremes of poverty and wealth. The
climate was beneficent and the harvests were plentiful. There
was enough for everyone.

At the end of the Older Bronze Age a change in the custom
of the burial of the dead took place. Up to this time inhumation had been the rule, although there were some instances of cremation even during the Neolithic period.

The *raison d'être* of cremation may have been the conviction
that in this way the return of the dead from the grave to
haunt the living would be more effectively prevented. But
cremation may also have arisen as a result of lighting fires
in the grave for the burning of a sacrifice and in the process
burning some part or all of the body of the deceased. Then
again, the change in burial practice may have been brought
about by a change in religious belief, a new emphasis on the
survival of the spirit rather than the survival of the body.
All three factors may have played a role.

In a grave-mound on the *Lüneburger Heide* the custom of
a tree-trunk burial was associated with an early stage of
cremation. The burned bones of the dead were found stretched
out at full length. The presence of the original tree-trunk
container could be determined by analysis of the decayed
remnants.

The usual procedure in cremation was to place the body on

a funeral pyre. The ashes and any unburned bones were then gathered and placed in a funerary urn. This urn was placed in a shallow grave over which a low mound was erected. Sometimes hundreds of these burial urns are found together, constituting a regular burial place.

At the end of the Bronze Age boat-graves are found in Gotland. They represent perhaps a primitive belief in the water barrier which the dead had to cross, as in Grecian mythology. The contemporary rock-carvings show that the sun-boat was a familiar idea, and it is also possible that there may have been a transference from sun-worship to burial practice. Or again, we may have here an indication of the fertility cult, if the hundreds of little bronze boats are to be explained as the feminine counterpart of the male phallic symbols. A purely materialistic explanation would be the desire of the individual to be buried in his favorite boat.

Although the description comes from the early eighth century of the present era in England, there can be little doubt that the description of Beowulf's burial is a survival from much earlier times. At the time of the composition of the *Beowulf* in the form in which it has come down to us, cremation had ceased to be the normal practice in England. But Christianity had not yet been accepted in the Scandinavian North, and many of the older burial customs were still practiced.

> Then fashioned for him the folk of Geats
> firm on the earth a funeral pile,
> and hung it with helmets and harness of war
> and breastplates bright, as the boon he asked;
> and they laid amid it the mighty chieftain,
> heroes mourning their master dear.
> Then on the hill that hugest of bale-fires
> the warriors wakened. Wood-smoke rose
> black over blaze, and blent was the roar
> of flame with weeping (the wind was still),

till the fire had broken the frame of bones,
hot at the heart. In heavy mood
Their misery mourned they, their master's death.

. . . .
. . . .
. . . .

. . . . The smoke by the sky was devoured.
The folk of the Weders fashioned there
on the headland a barrow broad and high,
by ocean-farers far descried:
In ten days' time their toil had raised it,
the battle-brave's beacon. Round brands of the pyre
a wall they built, the worthiest ever
that wit could prompt in their wisest men.

. . . .
. . . .
. . . .

Then about the barrow the battle-keen rode,
atheling born, a band of twelve,
lament to make, to mourn their king,
chant their dirge, and their chieftain honor.[9]

Although advanced methods of agriculture during the Neolithic period are more or less doubtful, it is quite certain that the people of the North were acquainted with the ox-drawn plough in the Bronze Age. There are many illustrations of ploughs on the rock-carvings of Southern Sweden (Fig. 11).

As far as is known, the ripened grain still had to be harvested with the old-fashioned sickle of Neolithic times. Nothing certain is known about the method of threshing, except by comparison with what is known of conditions elsewhere in early historical times. Presumably the grain was trampled out or beaten out by sticks or flails on the threshing floor, and the chaff winnowed out by the wind, methods described in many passages in the Hebraic writings preserved in the Bible. The grain, however, was made into flour by hand-mills. Such devices date back to Neolithic times.

Primitive water transportation by dug-out canoes had been greatly improved during the Neolithic period. There is a considerable amount of evidence for maritime communications between the Mediterranean and Western and Northern Europe during the Neolithic period. If the Corded Ware culture of Southern Sweden is to be derived from the Oder or from the East German group the people must have crossed the Baltic in boats. There must also have been communication between the many islands of the Baltic. The rock-carvings offer definite proof of the advance in the craft of boat-building (Fig. 12).

It is interesting to note that the type of Bronze Age boat appears later in Viking times, although it has undergone some modifications.

The bronze cult-wagons are evidence of the knowledge of the principle of the wheel. They also offer proof of the presence of the domesticated horse in Northern Europe during the Bronze Age.

We may regard the people of Northern Europe in the areas described as the Germanic people. Unfortunately the practice of cremation has left little physical evidence. G. Asmus lists in all only seven finds from Schleswig-Holstein and Mecklenburg, and these were not preserved in a very satisfactory condition.[10] Naturally the conclusions that can be drawn from such an inadequate sample cannot give a good picture of the racial conditions of the Bronze Age. Insofar, however, as conclusions can be reached, these fossil skulls come within the range of variation of the Nordic type.

Retzius examined twenty Bronze Age skulls from Sweden and Nielsen twelve from Denmark.[11] Both groups showed in general the same characteristics, and in both brachycrany occurs. In Sweden thirteen were dolichocranial to seven brachycranial; in Denmark four dolichocranial to five mesocranial and three brachycranial. It is evident that the physical characteristics are about the same as they were in the Neolithic period, if these skulls were representative. The arrival in the North of people of the Corded Ware-Single Grave culture made very little change in the physical characteristics of the inhabitants, since the bearers of this culture were Nordic, as were those of the Megalithic culture in the North. Chemical analysis of the preserved hair of the Bronze Age tree-trunk burials show depigmented, that is, blond hair.

To what extent does the Germanic language show signs of the cultural amalgamation of the Northern Megalithic and Corded Ware peoples in the Bronze Age?

Germanic differs materially from other Indo-European languages. This Common or Primitive Germanic has been reconstructed by comparing all the surviving languages of the group. It was the spoken language before the beginning of the Germanic dispersion. The most important differences between Indo-European and Germanic are:

(a) The systematic change of *p, t, k* and *ph, th, kh* into voiceless spirants: *f, th, x* (*ch*). Compare such words as Latin *pater*, English *father*; Latin *tenuis*, English *th*in; Latin *canis*, English *h*ound (Eng. *h* from an earlier *ch*).

(b) The change of Indo-European *b, d, g* into *p, t, k*, that is, the unvoicing of these voiced explosives. Compare such words as Lithuanian *dubus*, English *d*eep; Latin *decem*, English *t*en; Latin *gena*, English *ch*in (*ch* from an older *k* as in German *Kinn*).

(c) The change of the aspirated voiced explosives *bh, dh, gh* into the voiced spirants *v* as in English li*v*e, *th* as in brea*th*e, *g* as in German dialect sagen. Compare such words as Latin *frater* (*f* from an older *bh*), English *b*rother (where an older *bh* has become *b*); Sanskrit *dhadati*, English *d*o (where an older *dh* has become *d*); Sanskrit *dhoghos*, English *d*ay (where an older *g*: daeg has become *y*).

(d) The change of *p, t, k* to *b, d, g* instead of to *f, th, ch* as would be expected, when not under the accent. Compare the sound of English o*f* (unaccented) with the accented o*ff*. This is what is known as Werner's Law. The changes under (a), (b) and)c) are known as Grimm's Law or the Germanic consonant change.

(e) The fixation of the originally free accent on the strongly accented root syllable (as a general rule). This means the change from a musical to a stress accent.

(f) The disintegration of the Indo-European flexional categories, and as a result of this, the weakening of the final inflexional endings and the drift towards an analytical stage by the use of prepositions and word order to express what was formerly done by inflexional forms. English has traveled the furthest in this direction, with the Scandinavian languages next in order (Icelandic excepted).

Meillet attributes this differentiation between Germanic and Indo-European to the influence of the substratum.[12] Hirt believes that the change of accent plays a very important role in a language mixture, that is, when a people by force of circumstances is under the necessity of learning a foreign language and giving up their own. He also claims that language mixture is the cause of a great number of sound changes.[13] Braun expresses the same point of view and also Prokosch.[14]

In the case of migration and invasions three situations may arise: (a) Both languages may survive. Examples are: English and French in Canada; Swedish and Finnish in Finland; French, Italian and German in Switzerland. (b) The invaders may adopt the language of the country invaded. Examples are: Bulgaria and the Normans in Normandy. (c) The invaders may establish their own language in the territory invaded. Examples are: Magyar in Hungary, Latin in Gaul, Celtic in Spain, Latin in Spain.

If the Germanic is the result of the substratum, the same is probably also true of other Indo-European languages which were introduced into territories where other languages were spoken. Other languages of the stock do appear to have been affected, although the changes in the Germanic were carried through in a more systematic manner than can be shown for some of the others. Several of the Indo-European Caucasian languages and Armenian were subjected to changes somewhat similar to the Germanic consonant change. Restriction of the accent in Greek and Latin is not an Indo-European characteristic. The change in both Latin and Greek of the *mediae aspiratae bh, dh, gh* into *tenues aspiratae ph, th, kh* or modifications of these, belong to the same category as the changes which took place in Germanic. In Old Irish, Germanic and Early Latin is found the accentuation of the first, usually stressed, syllable. The phenomenon of *Umlaut,* the modification of a vowel by a following vowel, appears in both Irish and Germanic. There is a general tendency in the *centum* languages either to give up the inflexional system or to modify it greatly. Both Latin and Greek reduced the original number of cases (8) of the Indo-European, and the verbal system also is materially simplified, at least in comparison with that of Sanskrit. Lettish is a colonial language of the Lithuanian in territory where formerly Esthonian or some closely related language was spoken, and Lettish has adopted the peculiar "glide" pronunciation of the Esthonian (also found in Swedish). In Old Irish there are indications of a consonantal shift which in some respects can be compared with the Germanic. The Indo-European languages of Asia Minor and India differed radically from what is regarded as the reconstructed Indo-European.

It is an historical fact that Latin was introduced into Gaul, Spain and Roumania. It was in every case approximately the same kind of Latin, that is, the common spoken language of the soldiers, merchants and colonists. These languages, however, developed along quite different lines, and the changes were such that these languages have long been mutually unintelligible.

Differences between the Spanish of the New World and that of Spain have been explained as the continuation of certain phonetic tendencies in South and Central America which had already manifested themselves in the language in Spain, and there is consequently no evidence here of an Indian substratum.[15] But the conditions under which Central and South American Indians learned Spanish (or Portuguese) can scarcely be compared with those prevailing at the time of the expansion of the Roman Empire or the circumstances prevailing when the Indo-European languages were expanding over Europe and part of Asia.

We have a very modern example of a new language formed as the result of language mixture, the "pidgin" English of the South Pacific. This was the combination of a restricted English vocabulary and a language without formal grammar in the Western European sense. Similar combinations of a native language and French are also known. These become a *lingua franca,* and under circumstances different from those prevailing in the modern world such a *lingua franca* could become a standard language. This did actually happen in the case of the Greek *koine.*

It is quite easy to explain the change of *p* to *f* as the result of a purely phonetic change, the strong aspiration of the *p* resulting in *ph,* and when the lip tension becomes too strong the sound breaks down through *pf* to *f.* But this does not really solve the problem: Why the strong aspiration and at the same time the accentuation on the first or root syllable? There must be some underlying phonetic principle behind the phenomenon. This common principle is the imposition on a people whose speech habits are different, of a language formerly strange to that area. Many of the speech habits of the native language are then transferred to the new.

The Germanic world was much more restricted at the end

of the Older Bronze and in the Middle Bronze periods than it was during the Iron Age. It was a relatively closed area, extending over the Danish Islands, Jutland, Schleswig-Holstein, a considerable part of Lower Saxony, Mecklenburg, part of Pomerania as far as the Peene river and Rügen, Southern Sweden and a few localities in Southern Norway. In a restricted area such as this, a cultural fusion could be completed in a much shorter time than would be possible over a more extended area.

The enlargement of the Germanic territory began, according to some authorities, about 750 B. C., but almost certainly no later than 500 B. C. It is reasonable to conclude that the formation of the Germanic language was completed before the beginning of the dispersion of the Germanic people.

Attempts have been made to determine the time of linguistic changes by reference to certain loan words which were affected. *Kannabis* is an example. This is claimed as a Thracian-Phrygian word, meaning "hemp," taken into Greek and then introduced into Germanic. The change from *kannabis* to hemp, the change of *k* to *ch* (later *h*) and *b* to *p*, the deletion of the middle vowel *a,* show that the word has been thoroughly germanicized. But unless we know when hemp was first known to the Germanic people the sound changes do not give us a solution to this problem of time.

Furthermore, words may be borrowed from one language into another and follow the general pattern of the borrowing language, long after a specific series of sound changes may have taken place. What the English language has done to many borrowed words goes far beyond the bounds of words borrowed in a similar way by Germanic. This by no means invalidates the operation of Grimm's or Werner's Law. Such borrowings belong to a later stage.

Cultural influence often follows trade. Northern Europe during the Bronze Age was outside of the Southern and Central European cultural orbits, but there were nevertheless important contacts. There was some trade between the North and the South.

Neither tin nor copper are native to the Scandinavian North. Bronze is an alloy of these metals, the best results having been obtained by a mixture of 10% tin with 90% copper. Bronze was known and used much earlier in the Near East and in Egypt than in Europe. This must have been before 3000 B. C. At that time there were flourishing cities in India, Mesopotamia and Egypt, as well as in Greece and Crete. Europe at that time had just entered the Neolithic stage.

The earliest trade in bronze and bronze artifacts which developed in the North was with Italy. It is most likely that the required tin came from Cornwall and perhaps also from Spain. Some copper and tin appear to have reached the North from the Harz area, where both were mined. In exchange the North could offer skins and amber. The pelts of the cold-loving animals were greatly treasured in those days, just as they are today. There was an almost inexhaustible supply of amber in the North Sea and the Baltic. Amber ornaments appear early in Eastern Europe. On the basis of chemical analysis the amber beads found in Mycenean graves by Schliemann came from the North. Definite trade routes were established for this exchange of commodities. These routes were by way of the Vistula and Dniester to the Black Sea, much the same route as that taken later by the Viking traders, the Elbe-Moldau-Danube route, from the North Sea to the Mediterranean by way of the Rhine and Rhone rivers, the maritime route by way of the North Sea, the English Channel and the Straits of Gibraltar.

It is a curious fact that amber was no longer used so lavishly by the people of the North during the Bronze Age as during the Neolithic. The people had apparently discovered that amber was very much in demand by the traders from the South and elsewhere, and that they could get copper, tin, gold and silver for it in exchange.

The bronze industry developed quite early in Bohemia and Silesia, no doubt because of their strategic position on the Eastern trade routes. The spiral ornamentation which reached such a high state of perfection in the North was probably introduced from Central Europe.

After the initial period of importation and imitation the Northern artists equalled, if they did not surpass, those of the South. The artifacts show an excellence of form, a clarity of conception and a masterly execution which witness to the high attainments of the artists. From the point of view of artistic excellence this was a period of high tide in the North of Europe.

The Pre-Roman
Iron Age

Iron made its first appearance in Hittite Asia Minor in the fourteenth century before the present era, and from there a knowledge of the metal spread to Europe. Soon there arose in Austria and South Germany a new culture which has been given the name of Hallstatt after a settlement and cemetery of salt-miners in Upper Austria. This culture was strongly under the influence of Italy. From this general area the culture spread rapidly and became differentiated in various regions, but everywhere there are the same peculiarities, such as the same type of swords, safety pins and pottery styles. This beginning of the Iron Age in Europe is dated about 1000 B. C.

At the beginning, iron was used only for certain purposes and bronze still remained the important metal for most things. Iron has obviously a great advantage over bronze in the making of weapons of war, since it is a much harder metal, and the possession of iron swords must have given the owners a feeling of superiority.

The second phase of the Iron Age is called La Tène after a place name on Lake Neuchâtel in Switzerland. This was a Celtic culture and was carried into many parts of Western Europe as the result of cultural diffusion and the Celtic expansion.

In Northern Europe the Early Iron Age lasted for over a thousand years, from about 800 B. C. to A. D. 500. The first two hundred years, a transitional period from 800-600 B. C. is often called period VI of the Bronze Age. A further division can be made into a Pre-Roman and a Roman Iron Age. The North was relatively isolated during the first, but during the second was very greatly influenced directly and indirectly by the prestige of the power and culture of the Roman Empire.

The new metal made its way but slowly in the North. It was not introduced by an invading people using iron swords but by diffusion and trade. Such a warlike introduction of the new metal into the Germanic North has long been an accepted dogma for many historians, but there is neither archaeological, anthropological nor historical proof of any such movement. The theory has rested upon the conviction that the Germanic people were relatively late arrivals in Northern Europe and were part of a mass movement into Central and Western Europe from somewhere in the East.

Until the beginning of the present era any very considerable Germanic expansion in a southerly direction was blocked, to the east along the Baltic by the Illyrians and to the west and south by the Celts, with the Roman power in the background. It was necessary for the people of the North to obtain raw material through the mediacy of the Celtic traders. To a certain extent one might almost say there was a "Celtic Iron Curtain" which in many ways was quite effective in creating at least a partial isolation of the North of Europe. This is the explanation for the presence in the Germanic language of so many culture-words of Celtic origin. 'Iron' is an example.

But the North was ready for expansion. This had begun even before the end of the Bronze Age in those areas immediately adjacent to and south of the Schleswig-Holstein zone, and eastward along the Baltic. It seems as if during the Bronze Age in the North there had been a gradual accumulation of dynamic energy which was continually threatening to break out of the ethnic bounds of the culture, and this energy was finally unloosed in the Iron Age. For a time the struggle was against the Celtic power and then, after the collapse of the Celts, against the Roman. Finally the Germanic wave rolled with overwhelming force over the whole of Central and part of Western Europe, causing the collapse of the first really universal Empire. There must have been some reason for this migration-urge (Map V).

Several reasons can be given: the Germanic people of the North had beyond a doubt heard of the accumulated wealth in urban centres further south, and the lure of sudden riches and booty must certainly have played a prominent role, just as it did in later Germanic history when Germanic tribes were knocking so persistently at the doors of the Roman Empire. At this particular time it would be the wealth of Celtic foundations which stirred the blood of the more adventurous and excited their cupidity. Such motives have always played a part in war and colonial expansion.

But that was a minor motivation. It is insufficient as a satisfactory explanation of the gradually accumulating waves of people from the North. Even though these waves were often dashed to pieces against the opposition, still new waves were formed in the restless sea of people, and some of these were more successful.

We have seen that Northern Europe enjoyed an optimum climate during the latter part of the Mesolithic, the Neolithic and for the most of the Bronze Age. Even with the primitive agricultural methods employed during the Neolithic, there was an abundance of food and a consequent surplus of population. This was the cause of a movement of people during the Neolithic which laid the foundation of the Europe of today. Along with the beneficent climate of the Bronze Age, the relatively high cultural attainments of the people, the explosive energy of a vigorous people, there were many improvements in agricultural methods: better ploughs, better breeds of stock, better means of transportation and a wider outlook, culturally and materially. This resulted in a rapid increase in the population, an increase eventually of such a nature that the land could not provide sufficient food to maintain the standard of living.

There was still another reason why the food supply was rapidly becoming inadequate to feed the population. The climate was changing to a cold, damp one, to more unpleasant winters and to summers not nearly so favorable to the production of crops and the raising of flocks and herds, in spite of the improved methods.

Then, too, parts of the Southern Baltic land area were gradually being flooded. The water level was rising. This would cause a very serious disturbance of the settlers in the coastal areas affected. A process of impoverishment would begin. Eventually a proportion of the inhabitants would be forced to emigrate. The emigrants would be the more vigorous, the more adventurous, the more determined, and often the more needy and consequently the more desperate. These were the ones who were ready to challenge an unknown future and stake their all on a desperate move. It was the principle of the Roman *ver sacrum* applied by necessity and the urge to survival.

Methods of criticism change with the times. In the days of Rationalism it was the custom to regard all tales from ancient literature and sagas of floods and other stirring events as the product of pious fiction. With the change in methods of investigation, with the study of folklore, ethnology, archaeology and comparative linguistics, it was realized that there was some foundation for many of the so-called "old wives' tales." Long years after the event the descendants of the Goths at the time of Jordanes told about the floods which had caused their first movement away from the homeland. Roman historians learned from captured *Cimbri* and *Teutones* that they had been forced to emigrate by a terrible natural catastrophe which had caused large areas of the shoreland to be flooded and rendered unfit for habitation. And now the geologists substantiate the ancient story. Further, excavations in Northwest Germany have proved that many changes in the coastline have taken place.

These changes in the shore lines are explained as readjustments of land and water levels as the result of the melting of the glaciers and the consequent rise in the water level, but in many cases accompanied by a rise in the level of the land when relieved of the vast weight of the accumulated ice.

There is still another possible cause of the emigrations from the North. This was a change of climate. R. L. Carson describes the investigations of a Swedish scientist, Otto Petterson, in connection with changes which have taken place in the North.[1] Petterson links events in the deep, hidden places of the ocean with the cyclic changes of climate and their effect on human history. As the ocean water presses in towards the Baltic it dips down and lets the fresh water roll out above it. At the deep level where salt and fresh water come into contact there is a sharp level of discontinuity, like the surface film between water and air. Petterson established a connection between this phenomenon and the herring fishing which flourished in this area (Gulmarfjord) in the Middle Ages about 1300. Then the herring withdrew into the North Sea and the herring industry of the district collapsed.

According to Petterson there are alternating periods of mild and severe climate which correspond to the long-period cycles of the oceanic tides. The world's most recent period of maximum tides and most rigorous climate occurred about 1433, its effect being felt, however, for several centuries before and after that year.

There was not very much snow and ice on the European coasts, he claims, and very little ice in the seas around Iceland and Greenland during the latest period of more favorable climate. The Vikings were sailing over the North Atlantic in those days and there are records in Irish Tales of monks passing freely between Ireland and Iceland. Between Britain and the Scandinavian countries communication was frequent and easy. There is very little mention in the Icelandic sagas about the dangers of drifting ice on exploratory voyages to Greenland and Vinland. It is not until the thirteenth century that we hear of travel difficulties. It is known that by the end of the fourteenth century many of the old sailing routes had to be abandoned and new ones found that were considered safer. Some of the settlements in Greenland were located in places which would have been impossible in later days. Many of the old buildings appear to have been buried beneath the invading ice.

In early Scandinavian literature we hear of a great catastrophe which overtook the North. This was the *fimbul* winter when the frost giants ruled. This could be a recollection of the Ice Age, but it could also refer to later events. It will be recalled that when Pytheas described his journey to the North he spoke of a sluggish, congealed mass in the sea. This could only have been floating ice.

Petterson explains that the direction of the ocean currents was altered, including the Gulf Stream. The areas of low pressure were shifted. This materially affected the climate of Europe.

There appears to be an eighteen-hundred-year cycle. That means that these climatic changes were approaching a climax about a central point 500 B. C. We have here a very specific cause of the first major Germanic migration and for their continuance for several centuries. Once such tremendous movements are under way the pressures arise from all points and there is no cessation until the restless waves of people either find a permanent place in which to settle or are swallowed up by the tides.

The areas marked on the map indicate the extent of Germanic expansion at the end of the Bronze Age (Map V). Schulz claims that both the Vistula and the Oder are outside of the bounds of the area where the Germanic people were formed.[2] The lower Oder was an eastern boundary line. The Illyrian people occupied the area of the Middle Oder in the Older Bronze Age from where they had gradually expanded to the mouths of both the Oder and the Vistula. Germanic expansion eastward along the Baltic was at the expense of the Illyrians at first.

The tribes of the *Basternae* are the first whose names are known from the records of those days. They are reported as having reached the Black Sea by about 230 B. C., where they participated in the siege of Olbia in 220 B. C.[3] It has been suggested that the *Basternae* were descendants of the people who made the face-urns, but this culture has also been attributed to the Illyrians. The name has been interpreted as being a cognate of English 'bastard,' meaning that the *Basternae* were a mixed people. If the face-urn people were Illyrians, it could easily have happened that such a mixture took place when a Germanic tribe from Northwest Germany moved eastward along the Baltic at the end of the Bronze Age.

The *Basternae* were drawn into the political struggles around the lower Danube and the Black Sea, and different rivals. for power tried to make use of them as mercenary troops. In 29 B. C. and in the following year they suffered serious defeats by Roman armies. With the arrival of the Goths about A. D. 170 the fortunes of the *Basternae* suffered a permanent eclipse. As a result of Gothic pressure they appear to have raided the territories of the Eastern Empire in Asia Minor. In A. D. 280 they were permitted by the Emperor Probus to settle in Thrace. They must have survived in Thrace until the sixth century, for Justinian founded near Odessa a castle named *Basternae*.[4]

There is a great variety of opinion in respect to the original home of the Vandals.[5] North Jutland is the traditional place of origin, but the *Silingi* who were a Vandal tribe may have come from Seeland. In a slavicized form *Silingi* became the later *Schlesien*. If the Vandals or part of them came from

North Jutland they may have left that area at approximately the same time and for the same reason as the *Cimbri* and *Teutones*. The exact time is, however, uncertain.

The Vandals can be traced with considerable certainty in Southern Posen and Silesia, in Poland along the upper and middle Vistula and across the lower Vistula into the Masuren area and adjacent parts of Poland. It seems clear that with the arrival of the Goths at the mouth of the Vistula and their expansion, pressure was exerted on the Vandals as well as on other tribes such as Burgundians and Langobards who had preceded the Goths. Various tribes of the Vandals were. known to Tacitus, Ptolemy and Pliny, but the ultimate fate of some of them is not known. They were presumably either annihilated in tribal wars or were eventually absorbed by other tribes. Only two of the Vandal tribes made the long journey into Spain: the *Hasdingi* and the *Silingi*. This march began before 400. After many adventures in Central Europe they arrived at the Rhine and after a fierce battle with the Franks who were acting as *foederati* of the Western Roman Empire, they forced the passage of the river in 406-407. For three years the invaders looted in Gaul. In 409 they crossed the Pyrenees and poured into Spain where they finally settled down and accepted an official status as *foederati*.

But agreements and alliances at that time were often of short duration. In 416 the Visigoths under Wallia appeared in Spain with a commission from the Emperor to destroy the Vandals and their allies, the Alans and Swabians, contingents of whom had accompanied the Visigoths on their march west. Some of the Vandals and Alans suffered severely as a result of the Visigothic attacks. but before the Vandals could be completely annihilated, the Visigoths were recalled by the Emperor, perhaps because he feared that the prestige of the Visigoths might become too great and might endanger his own security, which was none too solidly based.

In a clash with the Romans in 421 or 422 the Vandals

won a decisive victory; afterwards they spread over the whole of Southern Spain and occupied the southern ports. The name of the Spanish Province Andalusia goes back to an original *Wandalusia.*

In 428 Gaiserich, one of the great figures of the Age of Migrations, became king of the Vandals. In 429 he led his people across the Straits of Gibraltar into Northern Africa. At this time the Vandals were about 80,000 strong. Resistance was easily brushed aside and the Vandals conquered the whole of Roman North Africa as far as Tripolis, and in 439 they captured the city of Carthage. They now had not only a powerful army but also a strong fleet. They controlled the trade routes of the Western Mediterranean and the grain supply of Italy from North Africa. After varying relations with the Western Empire they captured and sacked the city of Rome itself in the year 455.

In 477, the year of the death of Gaiserich, the Vandals were at the peak of their power. But a decline soon began after the death of the great king. In 533 the Vandal kingdom was destroyed by Belisarius, the brilliant general of Justinian of the Eastern Roman Empire[6] (Map VI).

The name of this particular tribe has left its impression on the modern world by the word 'vandalism' which was in those days used as a term of reproach in reference to the acts of the Vandals. Actually there is no reason to believe that the Vandals were any worse, or any better, than other peoples and armies on the move or engaged in warfare, whether of Germanic or Roman origin. Such armies usually expected to live off the country. In addition, recruits were often attracted into the service by the promise of booty in the capture and looting of cities. Neither the Roman nor the Germanic generals were noted for their humanitarianism, nor was the practice of warfare a gentle art for them. It is, however, too late to render justice to the Vandals; the name will continue to survive in this not entirely deserved connotation.

At the end of the eighth century Paulus Diaconus composed a histc../ of the Langobards on the basis of oral tales,
epic songs, accounts which have since been lost and other available information. Langobardic tradition supports the conclusion
that the Langobards were forced to migrate as the result of
serious climatic disturbances. Their original home has been
placed in Southern Sweden (Scania) and also on the island
of Gotland. Ptolemy locates them on the Elbe river and between
the Elbe and the Weser in the second century of the present era.
If they came from Gotland they probably crossed the Baltic
and landed somewhere in the neighborhood of Latvia, and after
coming into violent contact with the Vandals, moved along
the shores of the Baltic into Mecklenburg and then later into
the area indicated by Ptolemy.

About the end of the third century the Langobards were
in Lower Austria and Southern Moravia. But the former area
on the Elbe was not completely abandoned, since in the Lüne-
berg district and in Eastern Holstein there remained parts of
the tribe called the 'Bards.' As such they were known to the
poet of the *Beowulf*. It is likely that this remnant was finally
absorbed by the Saxons.

Somewhere in the region close to the northwestern Carpathian
Mountains, the Langobards at the beginning of the fifth century
fought with the Huns, called Bulgarians in the Langobard
saga. They appear to have remained for some time in this
area, to have been converted to the Arian form of Christianity
by Gothic missionaries. In 508 they defeated the *Heruli* in
a great battle. After a series of alliances and wars in Central
Europe the Langobards under their king Alboin invaded Italy
in 568. There followed a long period of almost continual
warfare between the Langobards and the imperial troops. In
the meantime they were induced to adopt the Athanasian creed,
which probably facilitated their settlement in the area now
called Lombardy. In the course of time they mixed with the
native population, and Germanic traits are still present there[7]
(Map VI).

There is much more agreement that the island of Bornholm was the original homeland of the Burgundians. The time of their emigration was between 150 and 100 B. C. The Burgundians are mentioned in history for the first time by Pliny who places them in Northeastern Germany between the Oder and the Vistula.[8]

To this new home across the Baltic (for the Burgundians must have used the water route), the emigrants brought their special burial customs: the *Brandgrubenbestattung*.[9] The body, and whatever artifacts and weapons were to be buried with the dead, were all placed upon a funeral pyre and burned. The remains were then collected and placed in a hollowed-out grave which was covered with earth and stones. In some cases a large urn was used for the bones and the rest was then sprinkled over the urn before the grave was covered. It is by these graves that the presence of the Burgundians can be demonstrated. Indications of Burgundian settlement have been found over a fairly wide area, but although a considerable number of Burgundians must have emigrated, Bornholm was by no means completely evacuated. A portion of the tribe remained on the island and only joined their relatives in about 300 while the latter were preparing to make another important move.

After having landed at the mouth of the Oder the Burgundians first conquered those West Germanic peoples who were east of the lower Oder, after which they gradually spread eastward to the Vistula and beyond. This brought them into conflict with the Vandals who were forced to give ground. Here the Burgundians remained until the beginning of the present era, when they were affected by the arrival of the Goths. Eventually the Burgundians were forced westward to Brandenburg which was their new home in the third and fourth centuries.[10] West Germanic peoples were to the west of them, Rugians to the north, Goths to the northeast and Vandals to the southeast. Under these conditions pressure was inevitably exerted by the Burgundians on their neighbors. The West Germanic *Semnones* were the ones who suffered most, who in turn crowded their neighbors, and the restlessness started by these movements resulted in the outbreak of the Marcomannic war.

The next move of the Burgundians brought them to the upper and middle Main river. Here and at the border, the *limes,* the boundary between the Empire in Gaul and *Germania,* the Burgundians came into conflict not only with the Romans but also with the *Alemanni* in territorial disputes, and in their efforts to establish themselves across the border on the left bank of the Rhine. In their newly acquired lands Worms and Speyer were the principal cities.

This was in the reign of King Gundahar (Günther) of *Nibelungen* memory. Gundahar's territorial ambitions soon brought the Burgundians again into conflict with the Roman power, the representative of which at that time was Aetius. In the year 436 Aetius sent some of his Hun allies against the Burgundians. Then took place a great battle which later became part of the subject matter of the *Nibelungen* saga, although the motivation, the locale and the time are all changed in the epic poems. It is reported that Gundahar and 20,000 of his warriors fell in that battle.

Later Aetius transferred the remaining Burgundians on the left bank to Savoie, where, after a period of recuperation, they again played an active role in the wars which involved them, the Franks, the Visigoths, the Ostrogoths and the Roman power. The further history of the Burgundians belongs to the history of the French nation. They have given their name, Bourgogne, to one of the divisions of France (Map VI).

The most probable home of the Rugians was in the Stavanger district of Southwestern Norway. The time of their emigration was about 150 B. C. They too landed at the mouth of the Oder and moved eastward towards the Vistula. Here they came into conflict with the Vandals who were forced to give way and move further south. At the beginning of the present era the Rugians were forced westward by the newly arrived

Goths to whom they were known as the *Holmrugii,* a term which survived in tribal memories down to the time of the *Beowulf.* About 200 they occupied the island of Rügen. In the first half of the fourth century the Rugians moved up the Vistula, crossed the Carpathian Mountains and settled in the area around the upper Theiss river. There they were conquered by the Huns and somewhat later accompanied them as auxiliary troops on a raid into the territory of the Eastern Roman Empire. They also took part in the march of the Huns into France in 451. After many adventures they were eventually almost annihilated, along with the Ostrogoths, by the armies of the Eastern Roman Empire.[11]

Julius Caesar was responsible for the well-known phrase: *Gallia in tres partes divisa est.* It was quite clear to Caesar, and it was important to him from a military point of view to notice this, that the northern part of Gaul which then included much of modern Belgium, had a population which differed in many ways from the central and southern parts. This northern part had been subjected to a mixture of Celtic and Germanic peoples, which he called the *Belgae.* The language was Celtic, but there was a strong Germanic physical element present in the population. Caesar was aware of the danger of an attack from the east across the Rhine. To ward off this danger he made two raids across the river in order to display the Roman power and discourage any idea of a general attack from that quarter. For the time being, these warning raids of Caesar were successful, although help to the revolting *Belgae* was to some extent forthcoming from across the Rhine, especially from those tribes who had a feeling of relationship. The Germanic element among the *Belgae* was of the West Germanic division, not the East Germanic. Caesar was of the opinion that the morale of the northern tribes of Gaul had been strengthened by this mixture of Celtic and Germanic, since the Germanic element had not been so enervated by the urban life of many of the Celts and their trade relationships with Roman merchants, who supplied them with many luxury articles.

With the gradual weakening of the Celtic power in the South the way was open to the expanding Germanic tribes. The *Cimbri* and *Teutones,* whose names have come down to us in Latinized-Celtic forms, were the first to try their fortune. These people left their homes in North Jutland about 120 B. C. and, according to their own reports, as the result of severe storms and floods which made part of their homeland uninhabitable.

The Germanic form of these names must have been *Ximbroz* and *Theudonez,* the latter having the same root as Theodoric. When the Celts borrowed these names they changed the consonants to conform to the Celtic speech, just as the Romans did with so many Germanic tribal names. That was how these names sounded to Celtic or Roman ears, or at least they were convinced that is how the names ought to sound. The same linguistic process is at work today.

The *Cimbri* and *Teutones* followed a rather irregular route. They left their home in the Jutish Peninsula, and along with the *Ambroni,* proceeded up the Elbe river to Bohemia along the ancient amber route. Defeated by the Celtic *Boii* they marched through Silesia, Moravia and Hungary and appeared at the Danube in 114 B. C. In 113 B. C. they were in the Eastern Alps (Steiermark and Carinthia). A battle took place here with the Romans under Papirius Carbo which ended in a decisive victory for the *Cimbri* and *Teutones.* They then proceeded to Gaul where they remained for eight years. Between 109 and 105 B. C., they defeated five Roman armies. This aroused great apprehension in Rome. Finally, however, the inevitable happened. It was much too early for unsupported Germanic tribes of the strength of the *Cimbri* and *Teutones* to succeed in destroying the Roman power. The Romans sent out a general of great tactical ability and in 102 B. C. Marius completely defeated the *Teutones* at Aquae Sextae in South Gaul, and in the following year the *Cimbri* at Vercellae in Upper Italy. Those who were not slain in the battle were carried off to Italy as slaves. The only survivors of the whole movement were some who had remained in Gaul, the *Aduatuci* on the river Maas, where they still were in Caesar's day.

So ended the first clash between the Germanic tribes and the Romans. This was before the Roman power had established itself in Gaul. The Empire was not yet in existence.

The man who was to lay the foundation of the Empire was soon to appear on the scene. This man was Julius Caesar. And it was Julius Caesar who had to meet the next challenge from across the Rhine in the person of Ariovistus at the head or a Swabian confederacy. Ariovistus had been invited to cross the Rhine in 71 B. C. by the leaders of the *Sequani* to help them in a war against the *Aedui*. He had been promised land in payment for his help. Ariovistus was by no means unwilling to take advantage of this opportunity. He crossed the Rhine with a large body of followers, settled the dispute, and then found that he and his army were no longer welcome in the land.

As Caesar tells of these events, Ariovistus was an invader, but Caesar can scarcely be called an impartial witness. Actually, they were both trying to do the same thing; namely, to take advantage of the lack of unity among the Celtic tribes to establish themselves securely. An understanding was clearly impossible, as it was no part of Caesar's plan to divide the authority in Gaul. In the battle that followed the breaking off of negotiations Ariovistus was completely defeated, his army shattered, and he himself was barely able to escape across the Rhine to safety.[12]

So ended the second clash. If Ariovistus had been successful the career of Julius Caesar would have been checked, the destiny of Rome might have been changed as well as the subsequent history of the Western Hemisphere. Rome still had stout native troops, even though many of them did come from the Celtic districts of Northern Italy.

Not much of a reliable nature was known by the Romans about the Germanic people before the time of Tacitus. The North of Europe was a *terra incognita,* a land about which many wonders were told, as is evident in some of the remarks of Homer and in the strange tales of the kind of which Herodotus was so fond. It is difficult to recognize in the "hyperboreans" of the time of Herodotus the Germanic people of the Bronze Age. Nor did other Greek writers, such as Eratosthenes (276-196 B. C.) or Polybius (204-122 B. C.) have much more exact information. The Greek historians did not seem to be able to distinguish between the Celts and the *Germani,* or for that matter, between either and the Scythians, since the term Celto-Scythian or *Keltoi* was applied indiscriminately to all the people of the interior and the Far North.

In the year 325 B. C., or about that date, Pytheas of Marseilles, a Greek colony of the sixth century, made his celebrated journey through the Straits of Gibraltar northwards along the coasts of Spain and France and then proceeded to circumnavigate the island of Britain. It was a daring voyage of discovery and Pytheas has never been given proper recognition for his imagination and courage. This was perhaps because the geographers and historians of his day and the succeeding generations considered that the account which he wrote of his voyage was a travel romance. In other words, they thought that Pytheas was a fraud as a geographer and a prodigious liar. But there can be little doubt that Pytheas really made this journey, and it can scarcely have been the first of such expeditions, at least as far as the Cornish tin mines. It is most likely that many of the preceding ones were distinctly 'top-secret' journeys by Phoenician and Carthaginian merchants engaged in the trade with Cornwall, and they were not at all desirous of having their trade routes opened to competitors.

Pytheas, as reported by Pliny,[13] (for the account written by Pytheas has not survived), believed that the *Guiones* (for *Gutones*) dwelt along the borders of an estuary of the ocean by the name of *Mentonomos,* at a distance of six thousand stades from the mainland. From here the island of Abalus was a day's journey. Thither electrum (the Greek name for amber) was carried by the spring tides. Pytheas describes the sea in the far north to which he claimed to have sailed as a *mare mortuum.* It would appear that Pytheas had encountered pack-ice, as already described in Petterson's explanation of climatic cycles. Such a condition would be sure to make a marked impression upon a southerner.

According to Detlefsen,[14] Pytheas passed along the coast of Schleswig among the Northern Frisian islands, and his use of the term 'estuary' refers to a condition prevailing there at that time. Pliny describes this as *aeternum rerum controversia dubiaque, terrae sit an pars maris,* referring to the marshland and the ebb and full tides.[15]

Detlefsen interprets the *Guiones* as *Inguioni* or *Ingvaeoni* who are mentioned by Tactitus as being in this area.[16]

Pliny mentions other geographical features of the North which Detlefsen interprets as referring to the Kattegat and South Sweden (Scania), also referred to as Scatinavia.

Schneider is of the opinion that Pytheas had been sent on this journey to find a new way of transporting amber to the markets of the south, because the regular trade routes overland had been disturbed by the Celtic expansion. A maritime route would not be subject to Celtic control.[17]

It seems certain that Pytheas found the source of the native amber, since he speaks of Abalus as being one of the main supply centres. On this island the amber is washed by the waves, he is reported as saying, and the inhabitants use it as firewood and also sell it to the neighboring *Teutones.*[18] The island of Abalus is thought by some to have been Helgoland.

Before the war with the *Cimbri* and *Teutones,* the knowledge which the Romans possessed of the Germanic peoples was to a great extent based on hearsay and very inaccurate descriptions which are to be found in the rhetorical writings. These descriptions were apparently copied by one author from another and in this way a certain tradition was established.[19] But with the multitude of slaves which were sent to Rome after the final battles with the *Cimbri* and *Teutones* the Romans could no longer be in error as to the difference at least between the *Germani* and the Celts. This difference was also emphasized very decidedly at the time of the Slave War led by Spartacus (73-71 B. C.), since the *Germani* and the Celts were in separate groups and under separate leadership.

In his account of the Gallic war Caesar includes some interesting remarks about the territory occupied by the *Germani* beyond the Rhine. He speaks of a forest which it would take a lightly equipped traveler nine days to cross, extending from the frontiers of the *Helvetii* to the country of the Dacians. This should be the *Erzgebirge*. There are some peculiar animals in this forest, he says. There is an ox which looks like a deer and has a single horn in the middle of its forehead. At the top this horn branches out like a tree. He speaks of elks which look like goats but are much larger. They have legs without joints. They can not lie down, and if they fall, they are unable to get up again. When they sleep they support themselves against the trunks of trees. Hunters capture them by sawing through the trees so that the slightest pressure will cause them to fall down and with them the resting animals. He also reports the presence of the aurochs, and says that the young men hunt these animals in order to obtain the horns which they exhibit as proof of their hunting prowess. The horns are mounted with silver and are used at banquets as drinking-horns. Caesar nowhere guarantees the truth of these reports.[20]

Gradually the Roman world acquired a more extensive knowledge of the customs, peoples and country of the *Germani*. Caesar's raids across the Rhine must have made it possible to obtain valuable information. Then, too, Caesar would not have missed the opportunity to obtain information from the prisoners taken in the battle with Ariovistus.

Apart from Caesar, during the latter half of the first century of the preceding era and the first century of the present, there were many others who wrote accounts of the times. Some of the more important writers who helped to spread a more accurate knowledge of the Germanic tribes were: Poseidonius (end of second century B. C.) whose works have not survived; Pliny (A. D. 23-79) in his account of the Germanic wars and *historia naturalis;* Strabo (63 B. C.-A. D. 21); Pomponius Mela (about A. D. 43); Plutarch (A. D. 50-120); Tacitus (A. D. 60-117) and Ptolemy's map of *Germania* (about A. D. 150).

In 12 B. C. Drusus with a fleet in the North Sea, began a campaign to subject the Frisians and the Saxons and thus outflank the Germanic tribes in Northwestern Germany. He was successful in making a treaty with the Saxons, as a result of which they remained friends and allies of the Romans for a long time. The Romans rounded the Cimbrian Peninsula, passed through the Kattegat and to the amber supplies in the East Baltic. From this time on a regular supply of amber went from the East Baltic to Rome.[21]

The story from Tacitus about the origin of the three Germanic cult-groups is well known. These were the *Ingvaeoni,* the *Irminoni* and the *Istvaoni.*[22]

The *Ingvaeoni* included the Frisians, the Saxons, *Anglii, Harudi, Cimbri, Teutones, Eudosii, Heruli* (on the Danish Islands), the Danes (in South Sweden) and the Swedes. Of the *Irminoni* the *Semnoni* seem to have been the most important. They were originally *Suebi* and eventually all bore this common name. Other tribes were *Quadi, Marcomanni, Ermunduri, Chatti, Cheruski,* and *Batavi.* To the *Istvaoni* belonged the *Bructeri, Chamavi* and the *Agrivari.*

These three major groups are not to be regarded as political units. They were cult-groups, and to that and to a common feeling of origin may be attributed any concept of unity that existed. All three groups, with the exception of the tribes from Denmark and Sweden, belonged to the West Germanic division.

Under the Emperor Augustus (30 B. C.-A. D. 14) there were many raids of Germanic tribes into Gaul. None of these were successful in establishing permanent settlement. Tiberius forced the *Marcomanni* and the *Quadi* to retreat from the Danube into Bohemia and Lower Austria. In the North, as long as the *Chatti* (Saxons) remained allies of the Romans, it was quite impossible for other tribes to cross into Roman territory over the low-lying land, often subject to tidal overflow. This danger from flooding caused the erection of a large number of artificial mounds upon which settlements were established (*Wurten*).

The campaigns of Augustus did not set up a *provincia germanica*. Beyond the Elbe river a group of tribes opposed to Rome was organized under the leadership of Maroboduus. But before Augustus could come to grips with the confederation, a revolt broke out among the Illyrians further east and he had to change his plan of campaign to suppress this revolt.

In A. D. 9 Arminius, who had been trained in the Roman service, headed an anti-Roman group of *Cherusci* and this led to the disastrous defeat and annihilation of three Roman legions under the command of Varus in the famous action of the *Teutoburger Wald.*

That ended for the time being all Roman attempts to establish permanent control beyond the Rhine and north of the Danube. From now on a policy of defense was in order. It was then that the *limes* along the Rhine and Danube were established to keep the Germanic tribes out of Roman territory. These *limes,* boundary lines, were protected at intervals by fortified posts and a wall with a deep ditch, in the manner of Hadrian's wall in the north of England.

There followed a period of relative quiet in the West. Further expansion by the Germanic tribes was checked, and this check lasted until about A. D. 200. This probably resulted in the formation of larger Germanic groups, combinations of tribes, and many of the smaller units disappeared. It was in this way that the Frankish confederacy was formed, and also the *Alemanni.*

But while the *status quo* was being maintained in the West the background was being prepared for a flank attack on the Empire in the East by East Germanic peoples, and especially by the Goths.

The Roman Iron Age

We first hear of the Goths in the work of the Greek geographer Ptolemy about A. D. 150, who tells about the *Gutai* in Scandinavia which, he says, lies opposite the mouth of the Vistula. He is also aware of the presence of the Goths in the area around the mouth of the Vistula. Tacitus also places the Goths in this region but does not mention their Scandinavian origin. According to the sixth century *History of the Goths* by Cassiodorus-Jordanes, the *Holmrugii* and the Vandals were displaced by the arrival of the Goths in the area around the mouth of the Vistula. There appears to be some recollection of this event in the story of Hilde and Hetel in the Middle High German *Volksepos Gudrun*, since Hilde's father Hagen was prince of the *Holmrugii* on the Baltic coast.

The main difference of opinion in respect to the original home of the Goths revolves about the question of whether they came from the island of Gotland, from Götaland in South Sweden or from both. Almgren holds that they came from the mainland and Nerman agrees with this conclusion, the time of the migration being the beginning of the present era.[1] The decisive point in Nerman's opinion is that inhumation burials appear in Scandinavia and in the area around the mouth of the Vistula at approximately the same time. There is also a decided poverty of artifacts in the South Scandinavian area at this time, which might indicate migration.

It seems clear that the Goths, coming from Götaland, with perhaps a detachment from Gotland, came across the Baltic in boats, landed at the mouth of the Vistula, and after driving out the *Rugii,* settled there and began to expand both east and west. One group, the *Gepidae,* settled at the beginning of the second century in the area east of the Vistula.[2] Later on the *Gepidae* played a fairly important role in the history of Eastern Europe.

The migration of that branch of the tribe which constituted the Goths proper began about 150, but it is not likely that the area was depopulated. The route taken by the Goths was along the valley of the Bug, the Pripet and the Dnieper into Southern Ukraine, and perhaps also some of them took the alternative route: the Vistula-San-Dniester. The first detachments arrived in the Black Sea area about 170 and settled between the Don and the Dniester. More groups arrived between 200 and 230. In 257 there took place a series of raids, partly for booty and partly in the search for land, into the territories of the Eastern Roman Empire. They also occupied the Roman Province of Dacia, roughly modern Roumania. This indicates an extensive western expansion from the Dniester along the western shores of the Black Sea and westward north of the Danube river. By 260 the Goths had split into two groups: the Ostrogoths (East Goths) and the Visigoths (West Goths). The reason for the division is not known. It was perhaps owing to internal strain or the rivalry of the two leading families, who from this time on provided the kings for both Visigoths and Ostrogoths: the *Amalungi* and the *Greutingi*[3] (Map VI).

In 264 there was a Gothic landing at Trebizont and a raid through Cappadocia, Galatia and Bithynia. Taken with the Christian prisoners were the grandparents of Wulfilas on his mother's side, who were brought into Visigothic territory. This was a very important event for the future history of the Goths.

Wulfilas received his training in Constantinople at a time when a heretical sect, following the teaching of a bishop, Arius, was temporarily in control of the church organization in the East. Violent controversies followed the spread of this heresy, and the Church was split into two confessions: the Arian and the Athanasian (after a bishop named Athanasius). The Athanasian creed was approximately the same as that of the Church of the present day, both Catholic and Protestant, as detailed in the creed beginning: "I believe in God the Father...." The Athanasian creed insisted upon the belief in the triune God and the divine and human nature of Christ, the second person in the Trinity. The Arians, on the other hand, no doubt more under the influence of the philosophy of the Eastern Mediterranean, rejected the double nature of Christ and consequently the idea of the triune God. This was a form of monotheistic belief, a point of view which is still represented in the modern Christian Church by the Unitarians.

When Wulfilas had completed his training he returned to his Visigothic people with the mission of converting them to the Christian faith. At the beginning he was only partially successful, mainly because of the violent antagonism of one of the Visigothic leaders, Athanaric. Athanaric was convinced that the change from the heathen worship of his ancestors to the new belief would be the beginning of the end for the Gothic people. He believed that the new religion would weaken their martial morale and opposed its spread even to the point of persecution of its adherents.

As a result of Athanaric's opposition some of the Goths under the leadership of Frithigern were granted permission by the Eastern Roman Emperor to settle south of the Danube in an area which is now called Bulgaria. This was the group with which Wulfilas was associated. Wulfilas realized that if he was to have any chance of success it was necessary to present the new belief to his people not only in the spoken language but also in written form. There was, however, no written form of Gothic; there was not even an alphabet, apart from the runes, some of which he used. The basis of his alphabet was the Greek of those days.

Wulfilas translated most of the Scriptures into Gothic, although it is said that he omitted the Book of Kings, since the Goths were warlike enough without any further scriptural encouragement. Most of the New Testament has been preserved and parts of the Old. The manuscript is a sixth century copy, and is now preserved in the Royal Library at Stockholm.

In the course of time, in less time than one would expect, all the Goths were converted, at least nominally, to the new faith. The new doctrine was also accepted by the Vandals and Burgundians when they came into close contact with the Gothic missionaries and Gothic political power.

About the middle of the fourth century there occurred a disturbance of peoples on the Central Asiatic steppes which had a profound influence on the future of Europe. Probably on account of increasing aridity there was a westward movement of a warlike, mounted, nomadic people called the Huns. In the early years of the century this people appeared on the horizon east of the territory controlled by the Ostrogoths. At this time the Ostrogothic king Ermanaric, better known in saga than in history, had built up a kingdom of tremendous extent, all the way across European Russia and Eastern Europe to the Baltic. This meant at least a nominal suzerainty by the Ostrogoths over a great variety of peoples and over a great extent of territory. Ermanaric's fame must have been very widespread; he appears in the poems of the Scandinavian *Edda*, in Western Germanic saga, and some of the events with which he was immediately and personally concerned seem to have been transferred to Theodoric in the celebrated *Nibelungenlied*. But Ermanaric's kingdom was a personal creation, in 375 and when he had grown old (the saga gives his age as over one hundred), the Huns descended upon the East Gothic territory with the devastating speed of a modern blitz war. The kingdom collapsed. Ermanaric in despair fell upon his own sword in good Biblical fashion, although popular tales soon supplied a much more personal and intriguing motive for his death, in which faithlessness, betrayal, jealousy and revenge play their roles to the tragic end. The majority of the Ostrogoths now came under the domination of the Huns.

This disturbance in the Black Sea area may have been in part responsible for the return of some of the Goths to their former home on the Baltic, thus spreading to the West and North a knowledge of a new type of ornamentation based on intertwined animal forms; and, according to older theories, also a knowledge of the runes.

Most of the Visigoths under pressure from the Huns crossed the Danube and were settled in parts of Thrace. Athanaric, as intransigent as ever, retreated with a part of the Visigoths into the Carpathian mountains. Misunderstanding soon arose between the Visigoths under Frithigern and the Eastern Roman Empire. In 378 at Hadrianopolis the Goths won a signal victory: the Emperor Valens in an unguarded moment was slain in the battle. This secured the Visigothic hold on their new territory for some time, and it was not until 395 that the Visigoths under the celebrated Alaric again became restless. After an ineffectual move against Constantinople, they turned ·westward, crossed Thrace, Macedonia and Thessaly, entered Greece, captured the Piraeus, Corinth, Argos and Sparta. But by this time help had arrived from the West, and Stilicho, a Vandal in the service of Rome, arrived with an army in 397, and the Visigoths barely succeeded in escaping encirclement and annihilation.

For a few years the Visigoths remained quiet in the neighborhood of Epirus. In 401, however, Alaric made his first raid into Italy. Stilicho checkmated this move and Alaric was forced to retreat. He made a second attempt in 408. Rome was besieged and after the payment of a ransom the Visigoths discontinued the siege and retreated into Tuscany. After unsuccessful negotiations with the Emperor the Visigoths again besieged Rome, stormed the city and remained in the capital for three days. Reports are to the effect that very little damage was done to life and buildings, but the Goths must have carried away a considerable amount of loot.

From Rome the Visigoths moved south with the intention of crossing through Sicily to Africa, but Alaric's fleet was destroyed by a storm and he marched again to the north. He was taken suddenly ill and died on the way. Legend has reported that he was buried in the bed of the river Busento, and if this is true, his remains are still reposing there in the silt of the river, since they have never been found!

In 412 Alaric's successor Atawulf led the Visigoths into Southern France and then into Spain. In Southern France they occupied large areas and several important cities. Pressure from the Roman armies, however, finally forced them to cross the Pyrenees into Spain, where as *foederati* of Rome they came into conflict with the Vandals. In 451 the Visigoths participated as allies of the Romans in the great battle of Troyes where Attila was defeated and forced to retreat.

After many vicissitudes in Southern France and in Spain, now as allies of the Romans, now as enemies, at one time holding large tracts of Southern France, at another being reduced to the control of a few main cities, they finally settled permanently in Spain. There they were torn by doctrinal disputes between the Arian and Athanasian creeds, by frequent persecutions, by ineffectual rulers, by internal jealousies, and perhaps by a too-willing surrender to the easier life of a southern climate. In any case, they rapidly declined in military strength and in both tribal and individual morals. In 711 the Moorish invasion of Spain put an end to the Visigothic power in Western Europe. After a weak resistance they retreated to the mountains in Asturia in Northwestern Spain, and when they emerged again to stage a counterattack they were no longer Visigoths but Spaniards.

As we have seen, the Ostrogothic power under Ermanaric fell a sudden victim to the onrush of the Huns. The inevitable dislocation of peoples; the loss in life and property; the strange appearance of those mounted warriors from the steppes who seemed to be like the centaurs; and the fear engendered in Central and Western Europe, all combined to give the Huns the unenviable reputation which has clung to them ever since.

Jordanes relates a belief that the Huns were the offspring of devils and humans and that this accounted for the terror they inspired. Of course, the monkish chroniclers made the most of the "Scourge of God" idea, and no doubt the monasteries suffered from the Hunnish depredations, as they did later from the Viking raids, but the association of the Ostrogoths and other Germanic tribes with the Huns would indicate that, generally speaking, the Hunnish practice of war corresponded fairly closely to that which was prevalent everywhere at the time. If one can judge from the account of a contemporary witness, the Greek Priscus, (secretary to the East Roman emperor's ambassador), the life at the court of Attila somewhere in the neighborhood of Vienna was barbaric, it is true, but by no means degraded. A later saga, the *Nibelungenlied,* shows that Gothic influence played a considerable role at the Hunnish court.

In 451 the Ostrogoths furnished large contingents to Attila's army when he invaded France. And so it happened that there were Ostrogoths on one side and Visigoths on the other, and indeed other Germanic tribes also participated in the momentous battle on both sides.

In 488-489 the Ostrogoths were led into Italy by Theodoric the Great. But Odoacer, who seems to have been a Herulian, had already established himself there, much to the annoyance of the Emperor at Constantinople. The last of the Western Emperors had been forced to abdicate in 476 by Odoacer. The Eastern Emperor, desirous of expelling Odoacer from Italy, and also probably not unwilling to get the Ostrogoths away from the East, is said to have commissioned Theodoric to maintain the authority of the Empire in Italy. Theodoric never took the title of Emperor of the West, nor even of King of Italy, but contented himself with the title of King of the Ostrogoths. His own people were not ready for any such drastic change as that involved in a meaningful alteration of the status of the Gothic king.

After a series of battles Odoacer was defeated, and, according to the record, was slain by Theodoric himself, thus effectively preventing any renaissance of power from that quarter. Unfortunately it is also reported that Odoacer was treacherously slain while attending a banquet of Theodoric's.

Theodoric exercised a tremendous influence on the Western Europe of his day. He had alliances with the Lombards, with the Franks, with the Burgundians and dealings with the Visigoths in Spain. On the whole his influence was a beneficial one. He attempted to establish a *pax gothica,* and apart from minor outbreaks and the customary tribal wars and rivalries, raids and breaches of the faith, there was no general outbreak of war. He was quite successful in holding the balance of power.

Theodoric, justly called the Great, in spite of certain weaknesses and mistakes, was a far-seeing man, far in advance of his time and his people. He could see clearly enough that the Goths could not remain permanently in Italy as a separate power, occupying the usual one-third of the land; that could be only a temporary policy. Theodoric was greatly impressed by the grandeur of the Roman Empire, its past and even its present and realized that a combination of Roman culture with Gothic energy and physical power represented the only satisfactory solution.

In this policy he was aided by many who had served at the Imperial Court before the coming of the Goths: such men as Symmachus and Boethius, Cassiodorus and others of foresight and vision. But the Goths of Theodoric were stubborn and were determined to cling tenaciously to their traditional customs; they were not ready for the culture of the Mediterranean, or perhaps like Athanaric, had a feeling that becoming too deeply involved with the civilization of the Empire would mean their disappearance as a people. In this they were correct; a Gothic-Roman power would have meant the eventual amalgamation of the two peoples, highly desirable from almost every point of view, except from that of the tribal, or the ecclesiastical, as long as the Ostrogoths clung to their heretical doctrine. All the authority which the Roman See could exert was directed against the adherents of the heresy, and this had no little influence on the final defeat and extinction of the Gothic power, not only in Italy, but also in Spain.

It appears to have been in connection with some suspected plot hatched by Theodoric's enemies, political and clerical, that Boethius, the last of the pre-Mediaeval philosophers, was charged with treason, tried before a subservient Senate, condemned to death and executed. It was while waiting in prison for the day of execution that he wrote the memorable work *de consolatione philosophiae,* a consolation which he urgently needed, since from a modern point of view he was probably innocent of the charge. This philosophical work, in verse, had such a wide vogue that it was translated into Anglo-Saxon by Alfred the Great as part of his program of educational improvement.

When Theodoric died he was buried in a magnificent tomb erected in his honor at Ravenna. As far as Gothic history is concerned his efforts were doomed to failure. Perhaps it might have been otherwise if Theodoric's successors had been willing and able to carry on his policy. But his successors were weak, and the Goths were disunited.

In 552-553 the armies of the Eastern Empire under Narses succeeded in decisively defeating the Goths, and after 555 we hear no more about them in the history of those times. No doubt large numbers fell in the many battles that were fought;

the remainder were eventually absorbed by the native population.

It will be recalled that the *Gepidae* remained on the East Baltic shore at the time of the migrations of the main body of the Goths to the southeast. There they appear to have remained until about 300. We hear little about them during the fourth century. After the Visigoths crossed the Danube in 376 and moved into the imperial territory the *Gepidae* probably spread into the area which had been vacated. At that time everyone was preoccupied with the movements of the Huns and took little notice of the relatively unimportant *Gepidae*. In 406 a detachment of the tribe joined the Vandals in their trek to the West, but after crossing the Rhine they remained in Gaul and became *foederati* of the Romans.[4]

It was not until 418 that the *Gepidae* came under the influence of the Huns. They were forced to supply contingents for the Hunnish armies, and consequently fought with the Huns against the Roman Empire in 447-449 and again in 451 in the West when a large contingent of them accompanied Attila.

After the defeat of Attila and his subsequent death, the *Gepidae* under their king Ardaric led the revolt against the sons of Attila, who did not have the genius of their royal father. The *Gepidae* were joined by other tribes: Ostrogoths, *Heruli*, Swabians, *Rugii, Skiri, Sarmatae* and Alans. The Hunnish Empire collapsed, and this gave the *Gepidae* a considerable amount of prestige and power.

There were constant feuds between the *Gepidae* and the Ostrogoths about territory until the Ostrogoths finally departed for Italy; the animosity continued even then, as the *Gepidae* threatened to expand westward. After the decline of the Ostrogothic power a new enemy of the *Gepidae* made an appearance in the Langobards, as they too attempted to establish themselves where there was too much competition for the available land. Between 547 and 551 there were several battles between the *Gepidae* and the Langobards who usually had the support of the Eastern Roman Emperor. Finally, in an effort to prevent either party from becoming too powerful, the Emperor arranged a truce between them which remained unbroken until 565. In this year the king of the Langobards, Alboin, abducted Rosimunda, daughter of Kunimund, king of the *Gepidae.* In those days that was good and sufficient reason for starting a war, since such conduct, although common enough according to the epics, could not be left unchallenged. The Langobards were at first victorious, but in 566 the *Gepidae,* this time in alliance with imperial troops, were successful in administering a serious defeat to Alboin, who was now forced to return Rosimunda to the family circle. However, Alboin was not permanently discouraged. When the *Gepidae* were having trouble later with a tribe of Avars (Finno-Ugrians) in their rear, the Langobards fell upon them and thoroughly defeated their ancient enemies. The *Gepidae* fell under the control of the Avars, and later in the ninth century they came under the domination of the Bulgarians who destroyed the empire of the Avars. The *Gepidae* were gradually absorbed by the population out of which the modern Roumanians developed.

Langobardic and Germanic saga tells us that Alboin, after the defeat of the *Gepidae,* had a drinking cup made out of the skull of Rosimunda's father. (No doubt he displayed this with great frequency and pride at the royal banquets!)[5]

There is still another Germanic tribe which played a fairly important role in the affairs of Eastern and Central Europe during what might be called the Gothic period. This was the tribe of the *Heruli.* Schmidt is of the opinion that the *Heruli,* or rather a part of the tribe, landed at the mouth of the Vistula in the first part of the third century, coming from Southern Sweden, where they were under pressure from the Danes who were making the preliminary moves to the taking over of the Danish Islands.[6] From the Vistula area they followed the route of the Goths, arrived in the Southern Ukraine and settled in the neighborhood of the Sea of Azov. This was about 267 according to the information given by Jordanes.[7] From here the *Heruli* raided the territories of the Eastern Empire, these raids being as a rule by sea. In 350 the *Heruli* were included in the dominion of Ermanaric. When the Huns destroyed the Gothic Empire they brought the *Heruli* under their rule. As a consequence the *Heruli* were among the Germanic contingents who accompanied Attila in 451 on his march into France. The *Heruli* also participated in the great rebellion which ended with the fall of the Empire of the Huns in 453. From this time on they served frequently as mercenary troops in the armies of the Western Empire. They composed the majority of the soldiers with whom Odoacer overran Italy in 476.

As a result of an armed clash with the Langobards in 505 the Herulian power was shattered.[8] In 512 part of the tribe sought entrance into Dacian territory. Another and smaller part chose to journey back to the Scandinavian homeland. Those who settled in Roman territory moved in 536 to the district around Belgrade where their task was to protect the northern frontier. It was about this time that the *Heruli* were converted to Christianity, some of them to the Athanasian faith, among whom was the king, but the majority of the tribe to the Arian confession. This was the cause of internal trouble, and eventually led to the *Heruli* being on two sides in a war between the Langobards and the *Gepidae,* the Arians being allied with the *Gepidae* and the Athanasians with the Langobards. The Arian *Heruli* were practically annihilated in the battle and nothing more is known about them.[9] From time to time there are notices about the remainder of the *Heruli* as mercenary troops in the imperial armies where they established a very high reputation. In recognition of their services they were finally settled in 554 in the Trient district as frontier garrison troops. But after an unsuccessful revolt in 557, suppressed by Narses, the general of the Eastern Roman Empire, nothing more is heard about them.

About 400 B. C. the cult-group of the *Ingvaeoni* included the various tribes along the Dutch and Frisian coasts, in Northwest Germany and the Jutish Peninsula as well as on the Danish Islands and in Southern Sweden. Apart from the emigrations which have been described the situation had not changed very much at the beginning of the present era.

The coastal areas of the North Sea from Holland to the west coast of the Jutish Peninsula had been subjected to periods of elevation and subsidence. A period of subsidence began about the beginning of the present era and is still continuing. Under these circumstances it is easy to understand why it was necessary for some of the people to emigrate, since in addition to the unfavorable conditions, there was also the pressure of a fertile population.

There was a Saxon expansion inland, which eventually brought about the occupation of Lower and Upper Saxony, after the removal of the Frankish threat. But before this, the pressure had been relieved by expansion westward along the French coast as far as the Seine river. These raids and settlements were so threatening that the Romans were obliged to appoint a special official called the Count of the Saxon Shore, whose special duty it was to watch for and ward off these daring attempts to take booty or to effect settlement.

After the withdrawal of the Roman troops from England in the early part of the fifth century, the partly Romanized Celtic tribes of Central and Eastern England were attacked so persistently by the Picts and Scots from the North that the Celtic leaders despairing of help from Rome called upon the Saxons for assistance. The story of Ariovistus was repeated, but this time there was no Julius Caesar. According to tradition, (and the tradition appears to represent approximately what happened), the Saxons under Hengist and Horsa, with Jutish and Anglian contingents, (and possibly adventurers from other tribes), crossed the North Sea and after forcing the Picts and

Scots to return home, settled in the country in large numbers in the eastern half of the island as well as in part of the south.

Some information about these events is given in the Anglo-Saxon Chronicle and in the Latin ecclesiastical writings of those days.[10] But we are not dependent upon this evidence alone; there is no doubt that the archaeological evidence bears witness to the approximate accuracy of the Anglo-Saxon and Latin documents. This movement of the Jutes, Angles and Saxons to England continued for almost a century. By that time the whole of England up to the Scottish border had been overrun and occupied, with the exception of portions of the Southwest, that area now called Wales and Cornwall. Here the Celtic language continued to prevail.

The consolidation of the various kingdoms that were established in England; the rivalries; the wars; the Irish missions; the mission of St. Augustine and the adherence of the new settlers to the Papal See at Rome; the invasions and settlements of the Danes; the conquest of the country by the Normans under William; the influence of the French language upon English; the eventual absorption of both Danes and Norman-French by the Anglo-Saxons — all that is a part of English history as such, rather than of Germanic.

By the year 531 the Saxons had made themselves masters of the whole of the North Sea area. It was at this time that the Saxons in alliance with the Franks destroyed the Thuringian kingdom and extended their territory as far as the Saale and Unstrut rivers. For some time the Saxons were to a great extent dependent upon the Franks, to whom they had to pay tribute, and consequently had a very precarious hold on their extended territory. In 555 they challenged the Frankish suzerainty, but were defeated. In 567 they were involved in war as allies of the Langobards. Later they were in conflict with Slavic people pressing in from the East and after successfully defending the border against the Slavs, they once more became involved in war with the Franks.[11] This new Frankish-

Saxon war lasted intermittently from the time of the Frankish Martel in 718 to the time of Charles the Great who conducted a thirty years' war against the Saxons. They were finally reduced to subjection and forcibly converted to Christianity.

On the continent this was the last stand of the old Germanic religion. It still lingered on in the Scandinavian North, and in Iceland until the year 1000, but on the mainland it had to yield to the new belief which had behind it not only the former power and prestige of the Roman Empire, but also the growing influence of the Papal See at Rome. In addition, the call of the new religion was a summons to a new philosophy of life. One of the Anglian nobles is reported by Béde to have said at a conference called by the king to discuss the adoption of the new religion: the old gods had done very little for him, and he had no objection to trying the new one.

It was not only the identification of the new religion with the power and prestige of the Roman Empire, nor the ideological appeal of the new faith which brought about the downfall of the Germanic belief. The fact that the ancient beliefs and customs maintained themselves longer in the Scandinavian North, and the longest of all in the relatively isolated Iceland, shows quite clearly that the long migrations and wanderings of the peoples had brought about a loosening of the old ties, a severance from the cult-centres, from the ancient symbols, the sacred oaks and groves. This is the reason why the Germanic people adopted the new faith with relatively little friction. But neither to the Romans nor to the Germanic peoples did the new faith bring peace and the brotherhood of man.

The *Marcomanni* constituted a constant threat to the security of the southern border. From about the middle of the second century to the middle of the fifth there were constant attempts to expand beyond their Bohemian home, with varying but insignificant success. After that, for some time nothing is known about their movements. When they reappear they have a different name. They are now the *Baiuwari* or modern

Bavarians. The name itself is an ancient Celtic designation, meaning the men of the *Boii,* and the Germanic tribe which settled in Bohemia, presumably the *Marcomanni,* brought with them to Bavaria the name of their former home. In the early part of the sixth century the Bavarians, expanding south of the Danube, became neighbors of the Alemannian-Swabians. And that is approximately where the Bavarians are at the present time in spite of all the wars and occupations which they have endured.[12]

Hessen lies between the Elbe and the Rhine rivers. This is the former homeland of the *Chatti* in the days of the Roman wars. The consensus of opinion is that the Hessians are the lineal descendants of the ancient *Chatti,* one of the tribes of the *Irminoni* group. The *Chatti* played quite an important role in the wars with Rome and are often mentioned, especially by Tacitus, who takes pains to describe their characteristics. Later they became a part of the Frankish Empire.[13]

The Franks belonged to the western branch of the Germanic peoples and were, according to Much,[14] a confederacy comprising a great many tribes; mostly units of the *Istvaeoni* cult-group. This confederation took place about 240. The collective name 'Franks' did not make its appearance until 258.[15] Opinions differ as to the meaning of the name 'Frank.' The theory that it means 'free' has been widely accepted, but there are other interpretations such as: defiant, bold, ferocious; and Grimm derived the word from 'framea' meaning spear.[16] Schmidt places the starting-point or nucleus of the confederacy on the lower Rhine.[17] Sargeant gives the Thuringian forest as the homeland, although this explanation is not generally accepted.[18] For Gregory of Tours, the historian of the Franks, there was a connection between the Franks and the Trojans, since for him the Franks could not have a less ancient and noble origin than Virgil's Romans.[19]

In respect to the Germanic tribes beyond the Rhine the defensive policy of Julius Caesar and Augustus continued to prevail for a long time. Members of various tribes did succeed in crossing the Rhine from time to time, but the Romans would either force them back or, allowing them to remain, colonize them, and often enroll them in the Roman legions. This policy was frequently applied by the Romans in the case of adventurous Frankish groups, who from time to time engaged in either raiding or land-seeking. The numbers of such parties were probably not very large and were often exaggerated by the Roman writers for very obvious reasons. It was not until the formation of the "universal monarchy" by Chlodwig in 486 that any imperialistic policy could have been formulated.

From the time of the formation of the Frankish confederacy there was no permanent peace along the frontier. A slow and steady enlargement of Frankish territory took place at the expense of their Thuringian and Alemannian neighbors as well as of the Romans or Romanized Celts. The towns and cities were the chief objects of attack since they were the centres of wealth.

Some very strange and interesting events took place in the years before the Frankish unification. In 259, for instance, a large number of Franks made their way through Gaul and into Spain where they captured and destroyed Tarragona. After wandering about in Spain for twelve years, they seized a number of Spanish ships and made their way to Africa, where they seem to have disappeared.[20] Again in 278 a number of Franks had been taken prisoners and had been sent to Thrace as colonists by the Emperor Probus. But about 280 they apparently became thoroughly "fed up" with their new home, seized some ships and made their way across the Mediterranean, through the Straits of Gibraltar and so back to their northern home.[21]

The constant raids and troubles at the border were no doubt very irritating to the Roman Emperors and their representatives in Gaul, and often they acted in a very barbarous manner. Shortly after the accession of Constantine the Great to supreme power there was a Frankish attack in the lower Rhine area. In 310 the Emperor made a counterattack, and, after devastating the country, brought a large number of prisoners back with him who were thrown to the wild beasts in the arena of a local Gallic city, for the amusement of the populace.[22]

By about 400 the Christianization of Gaul had been almost completed. The Christianity of Gaul took the orthodox form. The Germanic tribes, however, with the exception of the Goths and those more immediately associated with them who had been converted to the Arian form of Christianity, were still pagan, including the members of the Frankish confederacy.[23] This created a religious barrier to any long-term policy of settlement and assimilation of the Franks and the native population. But this barrier was soon to be removed.

Early in the fifth century the internal weakness of the Roman Empire began to reveal serious breaches in the defensive system. In the East the Goths under Alaric were on the move towards Italy and the West. Hordes of Vandals, *Suebi* and Alans were pouring across the border into Southern France and into Spain. These moves could no longer be described as raids; they were migrations of peoples, the uprooting of whole tribes, bag and baggage, with wives and children, cattle and all possessions, with long trains of ox-drawn wagons, extending for miles.[24]

It was at this time that the Romans were compelled to withdraw their garrisons from Britain, and that Stilicho struggled so desperately to hold the Empire together, which he might conceivably have been able to do, if intrigues at the Imperial Court had not brought about his dismissal and death. It was at this time too, that the Burgundians of *Nibelungen* fame were establishing themselves on the left bank of the Rhine. The Franks also were on the move.

The vultures were indeed gathering for the feast. But in

spite of the Vandals in Spain and the Visigoths in Southern France; in spite of the occupation of England by Germanic tribes; in spite of the devastation in Italy; in spite of the internal apathy, corruption and jealousy, the Empire was still able to make one last glorious stand in defense of the ancient Mediterranean centre of power.

It was not Stilicho who led this defense; he had been "liquidated." It was Aetius, who seems to have been a man with a strong sense of duty. After all, with the authority he exercised he might very easily have set himself up as Emperor. But Aetius had very few really Roman troops. He had contingents from practically all the Germanic tribes in the West under his command, and for the time being he succeeded in holding them together.

It was the march of Attila in 451 against the weakening Empire that brought about this temporary union of so many divergent forces in Western Europe. The great battle took place between Troyes and Chalons-sur-Marne. According to the chronicles the hordes of the Huns and their allies were as the sands on the seashore. The battle lasted all day, and it seemed to be indecisive, the losses on both sides being great and serious. Aetius prepared to continue the battle on the following morning, but Attila had withdrawn to the east, and Aetius was not strong enough to pursue successfully. So ended the threat of Hunnish domination of Western Europe. But that was also the last great stand of the Roman Empire in the West. Only a few years later in 476 the last weakling Emperor was forced to abdicate by Odoacer.

In 481 Clovis, or Chlodowech in the Frankish form, succeeded to the throne of the Franks. At this time the Frankish monarchy was elective, not hereditary, although it was customary to choose the king from one particular family. There was, however, more than one Frankish king at the time of Clovis' accession; there were four.

The Franks had a most peculiar custom of a division of the kingdom among the sons, at the death of the ruling king. It is evident that there must have been a great deal of jealousy and a very decided lack of unity. Clovis found himself in this unenviable position, and he proceeded to do something to remedy the situation. He treacherously killed one after the other with his own hand or had all three of his fellow-rulers dispatched by others, after which he incorporated their territories into his own kingdom. He was the first universal monarch of the Franks. Clovis was not only a most unprincipled politician; he was a very able general, and a very far-seeing and clever international manipulator.

In 493 Clovis married Clothilda, the niece of the Burgundian king, who was an orthodox Christian, in spite of the fact that most of the Burgundians were of the Arian confession. Clothilda determined to convert her husband to her faith. About 496 during a battle against the *Alemanni,* Clovis, as reported by Gregory of Tours,[25] when the battle was at a critical stage, began to pray to the God of the Christians, promising to become a Christian if the victory were granted him. 'Immediately,' says the pious Bishop, 'the *Alemanni* turned and fled.' Clovis was so impressed that he and three thousand of his soldiers were immediately baptized. Clovis was an astute man; he knew how to seize the psychological moment, and he was far-sighted enough to see that the support of the Papal power would be of inestimable value in his plans for Frankish supremacy in the West. His judgment proved to be correct; the Franks succeeded where the Ostrogoths failed.

At the death of Clovis the kingdom was divided according to custom among his four sons, and the same struggle for supreme control began again.

The expansion of the Frankish kingdom from the time of the death of Clovis to the end of the Merovingian dynasty was at the expense of the Visigoths, the Burgundians, the Alemannians,

Bavarians and Thuringians. This meant almost continual warfare, new alliances and broken treaties.

In the North also there was continual conflict. The Saxons were land-hungry. They were being pressed by the steady advance of Slavic peoples from the east, who were occupying the sparsely populated territories along the Baltic.

Clovis had established a united kingdom in 511, but this ceased at his death, and it was not until 558 that the kingdom again came under the control of one ruler. This ruler was Clotair who died in 561. But at his death the same old routine began again.

In the year 567 there appeared upon the Frankish scene two forceful women who had great influence upon Frankish affairs: Brunhilda and Fredagonda. The marriage of Siegbert, one of the Frankish kings, to Brunhilda, daughter of the Spanish Visigothic king, brought the Frankish king much honor, for the Visigothic court at Toledo was considered by the Franks as being most brilliant.[26] Siegbert's marriage was all the more imposing when compared with those of his brothers, especially Chilperic, who had repudiated his wife in favor of her servant, Fredagonda. Jealous of his brother's success, Chilperic asked the Gothic king for his elder daughter, Galeswintha, and consent was readily given. Chilperic, on marrying Galeswintha, had to send Fredagonda away. One morning Galeswintha was found strangled in her bed, and a few days later Chilperic married Fredagonda.[27] During the years that followed there was an undying hatred between Brunhilda and Fredagonda, and it is possible that this hatred is reflected in the Brunhild-Kriemhild strife in the *Nibelungenlied*.

From 561 to 613 was a period of almost constant civil war, in which Fredagonda played a major role. And it was during this period that the decadence of the Merovingian dynasty began to be most marked. This was accompanied by the increase of power in the hands of the nobles, until finally the power of the king was reduced to a nullity, and a mayor of the palace was appointed, usually from among the most powerful of the nobles, to perform all the duties of the sovereign, except that of having the title. From the year 639 on began the period of the *rois fainéants,* the 'sluggard kings.'[28]

In 717 Charles Martel, the mayor of the palace in the eastern part of the Frankish territory, Austrasia, succeeded in establishing his position on a secure basis, and he was soon able to extend his authority over Neustria, the western part.

In 711 the Moorish Saracens began their invasion of Europe by moving into Spain, where, as we have seen, the Visigothic power after an ineffectual resistance collapsed. In 716 the Saracens entered Gaul, and in 720 they had captured all of the old Visigothic territory in Southern France. The Moslems gradually moved further north until they constituted a very definite threat to the continued existence of the Frankish power. Charles proceeded to take an active interest in this Moslem advance. He collected his forces and in a great battle fought on October 17th, near Poitiers, the Moslem army was so severely handled that it withdrew during the night.[29]

After the death of Charles his authority was divided among his three sons, but one of them, Grifo, was soon set aside, and after an interval of activity one of the others, Carloman, became weary of the continual strife, entered holy orders and became an inmate of the monastery of Monte Cassino.[30] This left Pepin in control. Pepin was ambitious and moreover he could not see why the one who had to bear all the responsibility for the conduct of the realm should not also have the royal title. He sent an embassy to the Pope to ask for his opinion on the matter, and the Pope, realizing the advantage of an alliance with the Frankish power, gave a favorable reply. Pepin thereupon had himself elected to the position of king at an assembly held at Soissons in November, 751. The last of the Merovingians was sent to a monastery. This was the beginning of the Carolingian dynasty. Pepin rendered sterling service to the Papal See in the quarrels with the Langobards.

On the death of Pepin in 768 the kingdom was divided between his sons, Charles and Carloman, but Carloman died in 771 and Charles became sole ruler. This is the Charles called Charlemagne or Charles the Great, who left such a definite impression upon Western Europe that his influence is still felt. Charles continued his father's policy of supporting the Papal See against the Langobards. He established his power securely in the south of France. He made several incursions into Spain, possibly with the main purpose of discouraging any further Moslem attacks on the West, and in this he was successful, although his campaigns can scarcely be called decided military victories. It was on the return from one of these campaigns that the rearguard of his army was suddenly attacked and annihilated by the Basques, who attacked the Frankish detachment in a narrow defile of the Pyrenees. This was the basis of an epic cycle, the first of which was *La Chanson de Roland*, centering on Charlemagne in much the same way as the Arthurian stories center on Arthur.

Charles successfully put down all revolts against his authority, and challenges were frequent. One of the most noteworthy events of his reign was the long campaign against the Saxons, which began in 772 and lasted for over thirty years. Time after time the Saxons appeared to have been reduced to submission, but soon after the departure of the Frankish forces some Saxon leader would stir up a new revolt, especially after it had become known that Charles had left for a campaign in Spain or elsewhere. Perhaps the best known of these Saxon leaders was Widukind, an intransigent pagan, as it seemed, but eventually in 785 he did surrender to Charles and was duly baptized and hospitably treated. Yet Charles had to adopt severe measures to reduce the Saxons to submission and he promulgated very stringent prohibitions.[31]

It was on Christmas day in the year 800 while Charles was attending mass in the basilica of St. Peter at Rome that Pope Leo III placed the imperial crown upon the head of the

Frankish king, thus declaring him Emperor of the Romans. Irene, mother of the Eastern Emperor, made this possible by deposing her son and declaring herself Empress. It was not considered legal for a woman to occupy this position, and the throne was therefore declared vacant. This act of the Pope welded securely for some time the alliance between the Papacy and the Frankish power. It also established a precedent for the claim of the supreme authority of the Church over the civil authority: the right of the Church to depose a monarch or to release his people from the obligation of obedience.

Charles was a most remarkable man, and justly called the Great. He was a fervent adherent of the Church. He was an ardent advocate of educational reform and brought scholars from many monasteries and countries, among them Alcuin from England, to establish a Palace School for the children of the court nobles. He himself is reported by his biographer as attempting to write a grammar of the Frankish language. He was in correspondance with the celebrated Haroun al Raschid of Bagdad, who sent him a present of two elephants. He was indefatigable in enlarging the boundaries of the kingdom and defending what he had won. He seemed to be continually on the move, and although he suffered many setbacks and temporary defeats, was nevertheless completely successful in carrying out his policies.

On the death of Charles his son Louis became emperor. Louis was not very successful in the government of his realm. He appeared to be more interested in the performance of devotional exercises. At his death the usual division was made, one part to each of his three sons: Lothair, Pepin and Louis. Pepin died before he could take over his inheritance, and his share was given to another young son by a later wife. This was Charles, surnamed 'The Bald.' Lothair was the eldest son, and by virtue of that succeeded to the title of Emperor. Louis received the eastern part of the Frankish territories and Charles the western.

This divided the empire of Charlemagne into three parts, the western part corresponding partly to what is now France, the eastern to what is partly modern Germany, and the central strip as far south as Switzerland being an area which has been in dispute ever since. This division was agreed upon in the Treaty of Verdun in 843, the decision being forced upon the older brother by the alliance of the other two against him. This alliance was arranged in 842 at Strassburg, the scene of the swearing of the famous Oaths of Strassburg cementing the alliance.

The document which contains the Oaths shows that there was also a linguistic difference at that time between the eastern and the western parts of the kingdom. The Oaths had to be prepared in three languages: Latin, the Frankish of that time which was spoken in the eastern part, and the *lingua romana* of the western area. This *lingua romana* was an intermediate stage between the Latin of the earlier centuries and the Old French of the twelfth. It is clear that the Frankish invaders had mixed with the native population, the Frankish warriors had married non-Frankish speaking women and these had taught their children their native language. The Franks, a group of Germanic tribes, were responsible for the foundation of the French state, but the Frankish language did not survive in the western part of the domains of the empire.

The origin of the Germanic people out of the bearers of the Indo-European, Corded Ware culture of the Neolithic and the pre-Indo-European Northern Megalithic culture of Northern Europe has been described. The development of a distinct Germanic culture during the Bronze Age has been established. The expansion of the Germanic people has been traced from the end of the Bronze Age to the end of the Age of Migrations. Let us now see what can be said about their way of life.

The Culture
of the Germanic People

1. CLOTHING

The practice of cremation during the Middle Bronze Age and throughout the pre-Roman Iron Age has made it much more difficult to obtain the evidence to enable us to give a completely satisfactory account of the styles of clothing during the first part of the Iron Age. With the beginning of the Roman Iron Age, however, the burial practice began to change again in many parts of the Germanic world. There is more evidence, although it is very seldom indeed that clothing has been preserved in the regular burials. The practice of burying criminals in the moors has been responsible for furnishing a considerable amount of material, since the process of disintegration was checked by the tight packing of the water-logged soil and the exclusion of air. In addition to this we have the contents of some of the Roman histories, and what is perhaps more valuable, the representations of Germanic prisoners on the columns erected to celebrate and commemorate some of the victories of the Roman emperors.

It is natural that the style of clothing should change with the years, partly owing to the dictates of fashion, partly to influences from the outside, and partly to climatic changes, which made alterations in the type of clothing desirable. If the style of clothing for both male and female in the early centuries of the Roman Iron Age is compared with that of the Early Bronze Age, it will be seen that in respect to the male clothing at least, certain major changes have taken place. The men are now wearing long-sleeved jackets which reach almost to the knees; the woolen or skin mantle held at the neck by a brooch or safety pin is, however, much the same, but trousers have now made their appearance. This sartorial custom was taken over from the Celts, who in turn had it from the Eastern European, or Asiatic horsemen of the steppes. It is obviously a very satisfactory article of clothing for the horseman, and this may have been the main reason for its adoption by the Germanic peoples; although deterioration of climate may also have played a part, since the trousers are clearly much warmer than the dress of the Early Bronze Age. Judging from the illustrations on the monuments, the trousers were narrow at the ankles, a very practical arrangement in a cold, damp climate.

Whereas in the Bronze Age a helm-like cap was worn, the Iron Age practice seems to have been to leave the head uncovered. The warriors at least, and particularly those of certain tribes, such as the *Suebi,* wore the hair in a knot at the side of the head.(Fig. 13).

On many of the Roman monuments the Germanic warriors are represented as naked from the waist up, apart from the mantle worn over the shoulders. The explanation seems to be that the warriors divested themselves of all excess clothing in action in order to have more freedom of movement.[1] The customary time for warlike operations was the summer season. Some of the illustrations from Roman times show long sleeves. The mantle was either of wool or fur, and sometimes fur was used for trimming.[2] From about the third century on, linen clothing was also often worn;[3] this was no doubt regarded as a sign of comparative wealth.

Caesar's statement that the *Suebi* wore only skins is not in agreement with the statement of Tacitus at a later time, towards the end of the first century of the present era. There may have been a change of custom or Caesar may have noticed only the clothing of the warriors. The evidence of the column illustrations and of the moor burials would not substantiate Caesar's statement as referring to the generality of the *Germani.*

The jacket or coat from about the third century on was worn over a linen garment the *hamithia* or *camisia* of Latin, whence the modern French *chemise.* According to Schneider[4] short knee trousers were also worn, the evidence for this being not only moor burials, but also the fact that the short trousers were adopted by some of the Roman soldiers on the Rhine, presumably in imitation of the Germanic style. The wearing of trousers was not a Roman custom, although later adopted. The shoes were of the sandal type (Fig. 15).

The custom of wearing the hair long must have changed for the great majority since in some tribes, especially among the Franks, long hair was a sign of high birth in certain families, and shorn hair meant ineligibility for kingship. This was the reason why the last of the Merovingian kings was sent into a monastery, since, according to rule, his head would be shorn. In many cases illustrations on the Roman columns show that beards were worn, but no doubt the practice varied from tribe to tribe and from century to century.

The women, according to Tacitus,[5] were more accustomed to wearing articles of linen than the men. They wore long dresses, which were often dyed red and other colors.[6] This dress had a high waist, was of a chemise-like construction, reached down to the ankles, and as a rule was sleeveless. Judging from some of the Roman illustrations the upper part of the breast was partly exposed, but this may have been the artist's symbolism for mourning. Perhaps the chief difference between the womens' clothing in the Iron Age and the Bronze Age is in the fact that the Iron Age skirts were more ample and free-flowing. Then too the Bronze Age girdle-ornament was no longer worn.

General statements, however, which cover a period of hundreds of years are misleading. The fashions changed. What was worn in the time of Tacitus was not necessarily true for the third century. The moor burials show jackets with and without sleeves, long trousers and trousers of knee-length. If one were to judge from the Roman illustration of the mourning woman[7] one would say that the women regularly wore trousers. This, however, was not the case, as other illustrations and the moor burials show. The Roman sculptor was evidently using this female figure as a symbol of *Germania,* not of the Germanic women.

The clothing worn shows that the women of those days had attained to a fairly high degree of practical knowledge of the nature and use of materials. The preparation and weaving of wool had been known ever since the Neolithic period. The preparation and use of hides had been known for countless millennia, ever since man first emerged from the completely uncultured state. Linen from flax was also quite old, possibly Neolithic, but certainly Bronze Age. From early times weights used for weaving-frames have been found, and quite elaborate frames from the Roman Iron Age have been reconstructed. The women must have had a knowledge of dyeing; colors were doubtless natural colors obtained from plants, the most obvious source of coloring substances.

The women wore various kinds of combs, hairpins and head decorations varying with the times and the fashions. It was customary for the women to wear the hair long or plaited, often with some form of ornament around the forehead. Judging from later tradition it was considered a mark of disgrace to have the hair cut short.

From the very earliest times man has attempted to improve upon an often miserly nature by adorning himself with colored stones and shells, and by painting his face and body with a variety of colors. This desire for bodily ornamentation varies in its form of manifestation from time to time, but in all periods and in all countries the custom has survived.

We have seen how the Germanic people of the Bronze Age adorned themselves. Much of their excellent technique was handed on to the artisans of the Iron Age.

Many passages in the older epics testify to this love of display and the value attached to some of the outstanding products of the workers in bronze, gold and silver, and other precious substances. We hear of the celebrated and fabulous Brising necklace, for instance, worth far more than the ransom of a king, and one of the most treasured possessions of the Goddess Freya. And the choice jewels of the *Nibelungen* Hoard; as well as the priceless store of ancient heirlooms which Beowulf in his dying moments so delighted to see.

2. WEAPONS AND WAR

Most of the historical accounts which have survived from early times have something to say about the Germanic manner of carrying on war. There is a fair amount of information on general matters in the works of the Greek and Latin historians, and in the works of those who, although neither Roman nor Greek, wrote in Latin and discussed the movements and fortunes of many of the Germanic peoples. Such works are: Bede's *Ecclesiastical History of the English People,* Jordanes' *History of the Goths,* Paulus Diaconus' *Story of the Langobards,* Gregory's *History of the Franks,* Saxo's *History of the Danes* and many others. In addition there are many passages in the ancient Germanic epics, in the Heroic Ballads, in the Icelandic Edda and the Sagas which depict most vividly the warlike nature of the people, the principles by which they lived and the way in which they warred and fought. Hundreds of graves, too, have yielded up their buried treasures, and have shown actual examples of the swords, the spears, the daggers, the shields and other war-gear of the times.

On the whole the latter part of the Neolithic period seems to have been a period of migrations, land-taking and war. In Northern Europe, in the ancient Germanic home, after the initial shock of the arrival of the Single Grave People had worn off and a cultural and physical assimilation and amalgamation had taken place, the North would appear to have enjoyed several centuries at least of comparative peace. Although bronze swords, daggers and other weapons are common enough throughout the Bronze Age, there is no evidence of any forcible penetration of the North by a foreign people, and the expansion along the North Sea and along the Baltic does not appear to have caused any general disturbance. Nor is there any evidence of any general exodus from the North which would set many tribes in motion. The conclusion then must be that there were no wars on a large scale in the Germanic North during the Bronze Age, and that whatever war was carried on was rather in the nature of tribal wars, caused by local disputes and ambitions.

But the situation changed with the beginning of the Iron Age. Tribal migration on a vast scale can only take place peaceably if there is plenty of unoccupied land, but if the supply of land is limited there will be friction between those who are already settled in a district and those who desire to settle there. And so for over a thousand years the Germanic youth, and in fact all who could bear arms, were accustomed to the prospect of war and violence.

There does not seem to have been any general training system as there was in the Roman army; the individual learned the practice of arms and the art of war at an early age in common with his fellows and under the instruction of his immediate male relatives. The original and basic principle of the Germanic armies was the organization by "hundreds," as they were called, that is, on the basis of family relationship. It was essential for the elders to see to it that all the younger members of the family became adept in the use of weapons. This organization by hundreds was the common practice in the time of Tacitus. This system undoubtedly had its advantages, not only making it easier to call up the armed strength of the tribe in case of danger, but also because there would develop in the individual units that feeling of *esprit de corps* which is so necessary in an efficient army. In the Roman armies this *esprit* was attained by training and discipline and the prestige of the legion.

Actually there were three forms of war during the Germanic Iron Age: feuds, raids and wars involving whole tribes and larger organizations. Feuds were no doubt common and universal. The Icelandic Sagas, the Heroic Ballads and epic poems, such as the *Beowulf,* would certainly show that these private quarrels were very frequent. There was at that time no common tribal law for the regulation of quarrels between individuals, and consequently feuds were the only method of obtaining satisfaction for injury.

Raids were organized for two purposes: for booty, but also to spy out the land for future operations. These were organized by individual leaders who wished to repair their fortunes or seek adventure and who invited all those interested to join them in an expedition. In later times it was called going a-viking. Tacitus relates[8] how the chieftains would keep their followers in training by engaging in these raids, and Caesar[9] tells us how such chieftains would announce a contemplated raid in the popular assembly and call for volunteers. These raids were private war expeditions, and the tribe as a whole was not necessarily involved.

Some of these raiding expeditions eventually led to the migration of whole tribes. An example of this is the mass migration of Angles, Jutes and Saxons from the continent to England in the fifth century. This mass movement had been preceded for generations by individual raids on the English coast during the time of the Roman occupation. Similar raids by Saxons took place on the Northern French coast. These raiding expeditions were practically always by sea, since a relatively small body of men could carry out a surprise attack, proceed quite a distance inland, collect the booty, retreat to the shore and be off again before effective resistance could be organized. Alfred the Great of England eventually had to create a fleet to ward off such sudden raids. At times the raiders made use of horses, but their real element was the sea, not, however, for sea warfare, but as a means of rapid and secret transportation.

Wars in which all the able-bodied men of the tribe were engaged were not common until the beginning of the migrations, early in the Iron Age. One such tribal movement was that of the *Basternae* who appear to have come into violent conflict with the Illyrians as they moved eastward along the Baltic. We are told by Jordanes that the Goths arrived at the mouth of the Vistula under the leadership of kings, but we cannot be sure that these kings had the authority of the later leaders such as Ermanaric, or Theodoric.

In later times, in the campaigns of Theodoric, for instance, unitary command of the army was necessary to ensure cohesion and success in the full-scale battles which were waged. Such an army as that of Theodoric was not composed exclusively of Ostrogoths. It is known that the army led by Attila into France was composed of contingents of many peoples, as was also the opposing army commanded by Aetius.

These campaigns had got beyond the stage of tribal or folk-wars. Generally speaking, however, the earlier migrations of the Vandals, Langobards, Burgundians, Goths and the West Germanic tribes were of the nature of tribal movements; the most mobile part of the tribe packing up bag and baggage, with the women and children and moving in long trains of ox-drawn wagons, much in the same way as in the covered wagon period in the earlier history of the Western States of North America, but on a larger scale.

At first the place of the leader, *Herzog,* or king, was at the head of the battle, the usual battle formation being the wedge. This was the most dangerous position, and sometimes when the leader fell, the whole organization was thrown into confusion. In any case after the initial attack, the wedge formation was very difficult to maintain, and often the battle became a series of fights between individuals or small groups of contestants. In the case of retreat or panic, it was clearly impossible for the leader to exercise proper authority over such a mass of struggling men.

If the initial attack was not successful and retreat became necessary, it was usually every man for himself. We know that this was the case in the battle between Caesar and Ariovistus, in spite of the fact that Ariovistus had taken every precaution to make retreat difficult. Ariovistus was forced to abandon the wagon-train with all the supplies, women and children, which fell into the hands of the Romans. In one case we are informed, the women of the *Cimbri* after the battle slew their children and committed suicide in order to avoid the fate of slavery.

These were really tribal wars, but in later times it was no longer possible for the king himself to lead in the forefront of the army; he had to control operations from a place of vantage. The Germanic leaders had also learned, in some cases at least, the advantage of having reserves, instead of throwing the whole weight of the army into the struggle at the beginning. It was because Caesar had reserves that he was able at the crucial moment to turn the tide of battle against Ariovistus.

The general practice, however, seems to have been a wild enthusiastic attack, with much shouting and noise, trusting to the effect of the first shock to cause the enemy to give way. This often happened too, but in other cases the strict discipline of the Roman army withstood the initial attack and was able to create confusion among their opponents by the solidity of their line and the stubbornness of their resistance.

The tribal armies of the Germanic people were mobile. They either took with them all their possessions, if on a migration move; or, if the operation was a temporary one, they planned to live off the country, and so had no need of cumbersome supply trains, which the Romans found so necessary. We continually hear of the Roman anxiety about *impedimenta* and the risk of making an advance without assurance of sufficient food. The Germanic soldiers, however, did not seem to lay the same stress on this aspect of war, no doubt on occasion suffering severely for want of proper provision for supplies.

Defended camps in the Roman sense do not appear to have been customary among the Germanic peoples in the pre-Roman Iron Age and in the early centuries of the post-Roman Age. We know that the Goths in Southern France took possession of several key cities and defended them stubbornly, although instances are known where the leaders had difficulty in restraining their men from opening the gates and rushing out to attack the enemy. The Germanic peoples had a strong disinclination to be shut up within the walls of a city in war time, especially those who lived some distance away from the cities of the *limes* of Roman-Celtic nature. The fortification of a camp which was to be occupied for only a short time was definitely contrary to their custom and inclination. The digging of the defensive trench, the erection of structural defenses, such as was customary in the Roman *castra* required greater cohesion and greater discipline than the majority of the Germanic warriors were willing to adopt. The normal procedure for the Germanic folk-armies on the move was to arrange the ox-wagons at night in a circle around the camp, just as was done by the western pioneers of the covered-wagon days when attacked by Indians. And if there was a battle, the women and children remained there, anxiously awaiting the outcome, imploring the men not to allow them to be carried off into slavery.

Nevertheless, fortified places were known. Several such forts, probably places of refuge for the non-fighting population have been found and excavated. They are usually encampments of approximately circular nature with a trench and a double earthwall.

Their village communities appear to have been undefended, and the only artificial defense of the tribal territory was to maintain a wide strip of wasteland between them and their neighbors.

Military campaigns were timed to take place during the summer months, since campaigning in the winter under prevailing conditions was much too difficult. Even the Romans, with all their organization, found winter campaigns very arduous, and Caesar undertook them in Gaul only under extreme necessity. He continually reports preparations for going into winter quarters. Of course, when the Germanic armies were engaged in military operations in the southern lands, there was no such climatic barrier to continuing the campaign during the winter, and that appears to have been done in such countries as Italy and Spain.

Just as every soldier was responsible for providing himself with weapons, so he was responsible for his own commissariat when at war. This is no doubt one reason why we hear so much about devastation of the enemy's country. If an army, even a relatively small one, must live off the country through which it is passing, one can readily understand that the writers of the chronicles of those days could speak bitterly of the destructive barbarians. Some of the devastation, of course, was planned to strike terror into the hearts of the population and so lower their power of resistance or desire to attack.

The customary procedure after a battle, if successful, seems to have been to attend to the wounded and to bury the dead of one's own side only, the enemy dead being left a prey to the birds and beasts of prey, and some grimly descriptive lines of such scenes occur in the ancient epics and sagas.

It was during the Roman Iron Age that the Germanic armies became intimately acquainted with strongly fortified towns and cities. At first, as in the case of the Goths in the East, for instance, they had very little success against these fortifications, and were usually forced to bypass the cities and devastate the countryside. Eventually, however, they learned from the Romans how to overcome the barriers of the strong walls, by undermining and thus causing them to collapse; by the building of towers on wheels from the top of which bridges were thrown onto the walls; and also on occasions by bribing some of the inhabitants to open the gates. As a rule they attempted to reduce such fortified places by blockade. This required patience and discipline, and the temper of the Germanic warriors was not always equal to the task.

Booty belonged to the army as a whole and was divided among the troops, usually by the casting of lots. In certain cases the total booty, including the prisoners, (as happened after one of the battles of the *Cimbri*), was sacrificed to the god of war.

The rapidity of movement of the Germanic armies is rather surprising, when one considers that so often the movement of the army was also a tribal movement. On the raiding expeditions the bands were naturally unencumbered and extremely mobile, could travel either by land or water, as occasion demanded. At times they marched with great rapidity over Greece and Asia Minor, sometimes with success, sometimes being severely handled, but in some way or other the survivors appear to have made their way back home again. Some of these expeditions were raids in search of booty, some of them scouting parties in search of land for settlement. The Eastern Roman Empire seemed better able to ward off the attacks than the Western, for no permanent Germanic settlements were made in the Eastern Roman Empire, apart from those on the northern border along the Danube. Nor were these permanent settlements, although they might have been, if the Goths had not suffered from that incurable sickness of the times: the urge towards Rome.

One is filled with astonishment when one thinks of long marches of the Vandals, the Burgundians, the Langobards and the Goths. Back and forth across Eastern, Central and Western Europe they marched, some of them, the Vandals, for instance, crossing over to Africa and extending their power as far as ancient Carthage. The Goths under Alaric left Eastern Europe, marched all the way to Italy from north to south and back again to the north, all within the lifetime of any individual soldier, and they must have had with them all of their earthly possessions. That was no raid; that was a tribal trek; there was no turning back when the die was cast. They would have had to fight to regain their former home, if they had returned, since even though some of the Visigoths had remained behind, a vacancy was created which was soon filled up by other Germanic peoples, in this case, by the *Gepidae*. And these same Visigoths in Italy, after the sudden death of Alaric, marched all the way from Southern Italy to Southern France, and from France to Spain. Similarly, with the many raids and campaigns of the Ostrogoths, until they were finally also led into Italy, there to found a temporary kingdom, as has been described.

During these strenuous days the Germanic peoples might be called agricultural peoples on a more or less continual war footing. The search for land; the pressure of neighboring tribes; the increase of population; possibly the exhaustion of the inadequately cared-for soil; the restlessness of the warriors; the hope of getting rich quickly by the acquisition of booty; the overpowering impulses of the military life for which they had been trained from early youth; all the customs, traditions and necessities of life combined to set the whole of the Germanic peoples into motion and commotion and to send them in wave after wave against the Roman frontiers until, as we have seen, they finally burst through and changed the destiny of Europe.

Every age produces its great leaders, and the Age of the Migrations was no exception, except that then most of the great leaders were on the sides of the attackers. The defense was weary, and would have collapsed earlier if it had not been bolstered by Germanic mercenary troops, and led by outstanding men such as the Vandal, Stilicho. With few exceptions, Aetius, Belisarius and Narses, for example, the Romans were woefully lacking in energetic leaders and strategists. On the other hand, among the Germanic people we find such men as Ermanaric, Alaric, Theodoric, Odoacer, Gaiseric, Gundaharius the Burgundian, Alboin the Langobard, Atawulf the Visigoth, Merovech, Clovis, Pepin, Charlemagne of the Franks, Widukind of the Saxons. All of these are historically substantiated, not to mention the great figures of the Germanic epics who are partly historical and partly legendary, but who nevertheless show the same great qualities of leadership, ambition, imagination and daring which actuated the more historical characters in their military exploits. Without these great leaders in whom often the subconscious wishes of their peoples were made manifest, the Great Migrations could not have taken place.

We are reasonably well-informed about the later phases of the *Völkerwanderung* of the Germanic people, those which were loosed by the Hunnish attack on the Goths, and the final phase in the Viking period. But apart from what information the Roman historians have preserved for us about the *Cimbri* and the *Teutones,* the campaign of Ariovistus in Gaul, the few remarks by Caesar and others, we are left completely in the dark about the great movements of the earlier phases of the Great Migrations, those which took place at the time of the transition to the pre-Roman Iron Age. For information about these migrations we have to depend on the investigations of the prehistorians.

For the latter part of our period, from that time when the Germanic people came into contact with the Romans, we have some written descriptions of the way in which the Germanic soldiers were armed. In addition there is the evidence of a vast number of graves. For the earlier part of the period the only evidence is from the graves and buried hoards, merchants' supplies, probably hidden in time of war. The practice of cremation which persisted generally among the Germanic peoples until the end of the pre-Roman period has not helped in obtaining a clear picture of the life of the times, even though the burial fires did not destroy the weapons which were given to the fire along with the deceased.

The magnificent swords of the Bronze Age, with their highly ornamented sword-grips and the beautifully finished blades, the bronze axes of the different periods and the exquisitely shaped daggers were the products of the highly developed technique of the Bronze Age smiths, who made the moulds, poured the metal and polished the weapons with the greatest care. Seeing that all the metal had to be imported, it is clear that in addition to bronze axes, stone, bone and horn must still have been in use for the making of many of the work tools at least. Probably only the wealthier, the leading men of the family and of the community carried the expensive swords and axes of bronze. It was a long time before the sword became a common weapon in the hands of every warrior, for even in early imperial Roman times the chief weapon of the Germanic soldiers was the spear, not the sword. Tacitus is witness to the use of the spear, the javelin or the throwing-spear, and the shorter weapon which was called the *framea*.

Since, however, iron ore was available in many areas and did not need to be imported, in the centuries following the time of Tacitus the sword became the chief weapon of offense of the Germanic warriors. The iron sword became a relatively cheap product. Yet the smiths had not acquired the art of making iron weapons which would stand up against hard usage. The swords wore out or were damaged especially when used against opponents wearing armor and helmets. This can be said in spite of the lavish terms bestowed upon certain well-known swords of Germanic story, such as Siegfried's sword, the ancient heirloom in the *Beowulf,* and the celebrated sword of Roland. It is rather significant that the swords of epic story were in most cases the work of elves and dwarfs who were supposed to have an intimate knowledge of the secrets of nature. In other words, these were swords of wish-fulfillment, not the swords in the hands of the ordinary warriors. The representation of a Swabian warrior, although somewhat idealized, gives an approximate idea of the military equipment of that time (Fig. 13).

There were many varieties of swords, and the fashion changed from time to time. There were long swords and short ones, one-edged and two-edged, hewing swords and stabbing swords. The handles of the swords of the leaders were often inset with gold and silver. The sword was carried in a sheath of wood, leather or even iron fastened to the girdle or suspended from the shoulder.

The shafts of the spears were usually of ash and the spearheads were of iron. Some of them were designed for throwing, and evidently great skill and accuracy was attained in the art of throwing the spear. One is reminded of the spear-cast with which Hagen slew Siegfried in the *Nibelungen* story and the spear-throwing competition in which the wooers of Brunhilda had to engage.

Axes were also often used as weapons, and in some cases the wooden club, later provided with iron spikes. The bow and arrow, although used in hunting, does not seem to have been a favorite weapon until later times. The Vikings used it freely.

The main defense weapon was the shield, which varied from the oval to the round shape. The shields were usually of wood, often with a hide covering. The edge was made firm by an iron band and in the centre was the iron shield-knob, the purpose of which was to protect the hand of the holder, and also to serve as a ward against sword thrusts. Helmets and armor are sometimes found from the beginning of the present era, usually belonging to the leaders. The armor was of thousands of small rings, called ring-mail, and we hear of it frequently in the *Beowulf* epic, since by that time it had become much more common. Usually, however, the main body protection was made of leather, or, as in the time of Tacitus, there was no body protection at all, apart from the shield, the upper part of the body being completely naked. One is reminded of the Bersekers of Icelandic story who worked themselves into a state of mouth-foaming frenzy and fought in a partly or wholly naked state.

It is evident that the equipment of the Germanic warrior was intended to emphasize attack rather than defense, and was also designed to provide freedom of movement during the battle. On the other hand, the Roman soldiers were often burdened with quite a weight of equipment. Apart from the throwing spear, the weapons of the Germanic warriors were designed for close combat. A large Germanic army would no doubt be armed in a rather varied manner, according to the predilections of various tribes which composed the army. With the practice of painting the shields with tribal symbols, the wild shouting which was intensified by holding up the shields, an army about to attack must have been rather an awe-inspiring sight, and one can well understand the anxiety which some of Caesar's soldiers showed before the meeting with Ariovistus; an anxiety which Caesar was at some pains to dispel by a speech of encouragement to his soldiers.

For the period under discussion most of the movements of the Germanic tribes were by land; if by water, boats were merely used for the purpose of transportation. However, tribes along the North Sea coast were quite expert in the use and manipulation of boats as is shown by the Saxon depredation along the coasts of Northern France and along the

English coast. There were some sea battles, but at this time
the Germanic peoples had not developed the art of maritime
warfare to the same degree as the Romans. The Nydam
boat is an example of the larger type of boat used, and this
led to the building of very efficient warships in the following
centuries among the peoples of the North Germanic branch.

Although the Germanic peoples placed the chief emphasis
on the infantry, they by no means neglected the training and
use of cavalry, which was used for reconnaissance and flank-
guards on the march and for certain specific tasks during the
battle and pursuit. We hear from Caesar that the *Suebi* had
the custom of attaching a fast-running, foot soldier to each
mounted warrior, who was able to keep up with the horse and
assist in both defense and offense. We also hear from Caesar
that the Germanic tribes across the Rhine with whom he had
contact were excellent riders, and Caesar, to remedy his
inferiority in cavalry, sent across the Rhine to these Germanic
tribes for recruits. Caesar does not seem to have had a very
good opinion of the horses ridden by the Germanic cavalrymen,
since he mounted these recruits on horses requisitioned in the
territories under his control, instead of allowing them to ride
their own. Presumably, the horses ridden by the Germanic
peoples were of the smaller, native variety, closely related
to the Upper Palaeolithic wild horse.

For proper protection on the march a long wagon train was
accompained by mounted men, and this was no doubt the
rule among the Germanic tribes. All of the important leaders
were mounted, the chief evidence being that in many cases
the bones of horses have been found buried with their masters
in the same grave.

Spurs were in common use and the bridle-bits which are so
essential for the proper control of the horse. It was only much
later that the stirrup was introduced. The stirrup has two
functions: to assist in mounting and to provide a more secure
seat on the horse's back when in action. It seems   strange

that such a simple aid to stability was not utilized much earlier. It certainly indicates excellent horsemanship on the part of the riders.

The number of the personnel of the Germanic tribes on the move would appear to have been exaggerated, something which could very easily happen in estimating the number of people in a long wagon-train winding over the ill-conditioned roads or paths, and stretching for miles in a seemingly endless line. And fear, too, would tend to exaggerate the reports of the number of people involved. The numbers of those who fell in battle must also have been greatly exaggerated, since, in spite of the large families and the rapid rate of reproduction, the Germanic peoples would have been exterminated if the casualties as announced represent the actual losses. The total number of the Germanic people at the time of the beginning of the main phase of the Migration could scarcely have been more than about 4,000,000. There were many Germanic tribes and divisions of tribes, and in the fourth century they were scattered over an immense territory; some in Eastern Europe or on the way there; some remaining in the area of the Eastern Baltic; some surging southwards into Central and Southern Germany; some steadily driving across the Rhine and the Danube; some crossing the North Sea to the British Isles; some remaining in the Scandinavian homeland.

3. FERMENTED DRINKS

The word 'beer' would seem to be of distinctly Germanic origin, as is also the word for 'ale.' There are no cognates in the other Indo-European languages. That does not mean that only the Germanic peoples were acquainted with beer and ale; there were other names for beer as, for instance, in Gaul *cervisia* and in Spain *caelia*. It is altogether likely that soon after the introduction of agriculture the principle of fermentation was discovered by those who had to do with the making of bread, and chemical analysis of matter adhering to some of the drinking vessels of the Neolithic period shows a knowledge of fermented drinks. It is scarcely likely that there would have been such a variety of drinking vessels, or that so much time and artistry would have been devoted to the making of them if they had been intended to serve merely the prosaic task of holding water!

Tacitus gives the first written evidence of malted intoxicants among the Germanic tribes, when he reports that their drink "is a liquid made from barley or wheat fermented into a faint resemblance of wine."[10] There were two designations for this fermented drink in Germanic: beer and ale. The latter word has survived only in English and the Scandinavian languages; ale and öl. The probable difference between the two is that the word 'beer' referred to a sweetened form achieved by the addition of honey, while 'ale' was made from grain alone. If this is correct, it means that beer came to Northern Europe later than ale, since the honey for the making of beer had to be imported. Both were known long before the time of Tacitus.

Mead is probably the oldest alchoholic drink known. The basis is honey, of which there has always been an excellent supply in those countries whose climate is favorable for bees. Far back in Upper Palaeolithic times we have a rock-painting in Spain of a woman gathering honey, but whether the principle of fermentation had been discovered at that time is not known. The Sanskrit word for honey is *madhu* which is a cognate of the English 'mead.' When the climate of Central and Western Europe had warmed sufficiently to permit the existence of bees, honey soon became known to the inhabitants, and the making of the fermented drink would in all probability have soon followed since fermentation was such a common phenomenon in household activities that its occurrence and effect could scarcely go unnoticed. Mead was known in classical times in Greece and Rome, but the oldest literary mention of its presence among the Germanic tribes comes from a much later period, from the fifth century A. D., when Priscus, who accompanied an ambassadorial mission from Constantinople to the court of Attila, attests to its use there. The preparation of mead was very simple: a water and honey mixture was boiled and then left to ferment; in later times the drink was "fortified" by the addition of wine.

The idea that mead was the special drink of the Germanic tribes is founded on Anglo-Saxon and Norse sources. There is a wealth of compounds of *medu* and *meodu* in the Anglo-Saxon epics: mead-hall, mead-bench, mead-cup, mead-path, mead-joy, mead-house, and in the Poetic *Edda* mead is the favorite drink of the gods and heroes. In Scaldic poetry too, there are many similes which make poetic use of the word for mead, such as the "mead of Odin," and of a woman as "the pine tree of the mead," the meaning of which is somewhat obscure and forced, as is quite often the case with Scaldic metaphors. Perhaps this special value placed on mead in Northern Europe can be explained by the fact that honey at that time had to be imported, usually from England. Just how common mead was in the Scandinavian countries before the days of the Vikings is not known.

Ticknor Edwards gives an interesting account of bee culture in the British Isles in early times.[11] According to him, Pytheas found the people in England brewing a drink from wheat and honey. And in old Celtic legends Britain was called "the Isle of Honey," because of the abundance of wild bees in the primeval woods.

Wine seems to have been introduced to the Germanic peoples relatively late. Northern Europe is not a wine-producing area, and it was only later when the Germanic peoples came into contact with the more southerly districts that they became acquainted with the product of the vine. The date of the origin of wine is unknown; it seems to have been definitely pre-Homeric. It was known to both Indo-Europeans and to the Semites, and both peoples appear to have borrowed the word for wine from some other source. The word for this product in Germanic languages is of Latin origin: *vinum*. In 129 B. C., according to Cicero, an order was passed with intent to prohibit wine culture in the Transalpine provinces, to protect the monopoly of the Italian wine growers.[12] This policy in the long run could not have been successful, since it would be very difficult to enforce. It seems quite certain that wine was made in Provence and in the Rhine districts at an early date, and that the Germanic peoples obtained their knowledge of wine from these sources through the intermediacy of Gallic and Roman merchants. Caesar is responsible for the statement that the *Nervii*, a Germanic tribe on the right bank of the Rhine, did not admit traders into their country and would not allow the importation of wine or other luxuries, because they thought such things made men soft and took the edge off their courage.[13]

Tacitus was of the opinion that the *Germani* did not exhibit much moderation in their drinking. He says "in drinking they are less temperate. If you pander to their intemperance by supplying as much as they want, their vices will conquer them as effectively as any troops."[14] According to Tacitus, these strange people often drank from dawn to dawn, a literary metaphor which may be forgiven the author of the *Germania;* he probably meant until the "wee small hours." He reports that there were frequent quarrels, and brawls and also bloodshed, which is extremely likely. Yet they had one good custom, he says, namely,

> that on the next day, when sober, they discussed the question of the preceding banquet again, thus preserving the advantage of either state, drunk and sober; they debate, while incapable of deceit, and decide when they cannot be misled.[15]

Tacitus, in spite of his tendency to moralize had a sense of humor.

There is evidence from the later centuries of the part that the drinking of beer, mead and wine played in the banquets in the Germanic halls, such as is described in Priscus' account of the court of Attila, the *Beowulf,* the *Nibelungenlied* and the Poetic *Edda.* In *Beowulf* is the passage:

A henchman attended,
carried the carven cup in hand,
served the clear mead. Oft minstrels sang
blithe in Heorot.[16]

We also hear of the hero who "full oft the mead-bench tore from the hall of his foes." Hrothgar's complaint about how his men boasted when in their cups and failed afterwards to perform, gives us a picture of some of these banquets:

Boasted full oft, as my beer they drank,
earls o'er the ale-cup, armed men,
that they would bide in the beer-hall here,
Grendel's attack with terror of blades.[17]

This boasting when under the influence was quite a common occurrence, and there are humorous and also tragic instances of the consequences of liquor, for the boasters were expected to perform what they so rashly promised when they were sober again. And that was the cause of much grief.

The description in the epics and in the Eddic poems of the huge quantities eaten and drunk are, of course, not accurate descriptions of what actually took place; they are rather in the category of 'poetic exaggeration.' A good example comes from the Icelandic *Thrymniskvitha*:

Early it was to evening come,
and forth was borne the beer for the giants;
Thor alone ate an ox, and eight salmon,
all the danties as well that were set for the women;
and drank Sif's mate three tuns of mead.[18]

After, however, making allowance, for exaggeration on the part of the Roman historians and the poetic license of the epics, there can be very little doubt that there was a great deal of intemperance among the Germanic people during the period

under consideration. But we are confronted with special circumstances and the descriptions are scarcely universally applicable.
The Roman historian, Tacitus, for example, was acquainted
mainly with those Germanic tribes beyond the Rhine who were
restless and on the move in one of the greatest and longest
migrations which has taken place within historic times. Under
these circumstances the able-bodied men of the tribe were
almost continually on a war footing; and it is well known
that the established codes of conduct and habits of hard and
regular labor are as a rule discarded, and a much more
liberal code prevails. Then too many of the descriptions are
of the followers of a king or chieftain, the *comitatus*, the
band of faithful followers which the ambitious leader gathered
around him, and which as a rule ate in common in the great
hall, and even slept there during the night. Under such conditions the banquet would naturally be attended by a considerable amount of hard drinking, for after all, these followers
were not expected to engage in manual labor; they must have
had a great deal of spare time between the occasions when
they were actually engaged in the serious business of fighting;
plenty of spare time in which to drink deeply of the (no
doubt) potent mead and beer of the day.

Those were unsettled and unsettling times. In more peaceful periods the great majority of the Germanic people were
busily engaged in the more prosaic business of making a
living from the soil. They were farmers, and there never
has been a farming population which could continue to survive
without hard work; and such hard work definitely forbade
spending half the night in the royal hall quaffing deeply of
the mead, ale and wine from the horns, beakers and carven
cups. The idea that the men of the Germanic tribes, as Caesar
relates, had a hearty dislike for work is probably quite true;
there are very few men who do not share this dislike; but that
they could spend their time in the pursuit of hunting and
lying on the bear-rugs telling tall stories and gambling away

their farms, even clothes, wives and children, as a regular form of life, is beyond comprehension, and cannot be made to fit into the agricultural form of life which can be proved to have been the norm; not even if it is assumed that the grown-up children and the women were also engaged in labor on the land which of course they were, and still are in all areas where farming has not been mechanized.

Even though the times are later, we can still see some of the old traditions in many of the characters appearing so vividly in the Icelandic sagas; these men may at times have gone a-viking, but they were primarily farmers, and they did not forget it; moreover they worked on the land along with other members of the household, free and unfree. It is consequently not advisable to generalize too hastily from the sensational news which gets into print. The normal life of quiet, sober hard-working people is seldom "news."

4. HALLS AND HOUSES

These royal halls, the mead-halls of the epic, should not be regarded as representing accurately the normal living quarters of the Germanic people. They were built for a special purpose: to serve as a dining-hall and also a sleeping-room for the leader's followers. They were designed also as assembly halls where the king or chieftain could preside at the feast. We have some very accurate descriptions of the halls of the seventh century. The royal hall of the *Beowulf* epic was a quadrilateral wooden structure, with a raised platform along either side within, and in the centre on one side a high-seat, the royal throne, and a secondary high-seat on the other side opposite. This was for the guest of honor. In front of these and along the length of the hall were long tables made of trestles and heavy planks were laid upon them. These tables were easily removable. The chief's retainers slept at night on the raised platforms, with their equipment hanging above

them on the wall ready for instant use. The king himself had
a separate house and sleeping-place. In the centre of the hall
was the blazing hearth, and the dogs who fought for the
remnants of the feast. It must have been a stirring scene
when the carven cups were being freely filled and the great
horns were being emptied and the *scop* was relating the deeds
of some mighty hero amid the loud applause and the thumping
on the wooden tables. It is no wonder that the poets were
enthusiastic when describing such a scene; it is no wonder that
even the Christian poet of the *Beowulf* is carried away in
his enthusiasm for the good old days and becomes really eloquent,
with an apparent disregard for the more sober practices and
teachings of the new religion. This royal banquet hall, this
Heorot of the *Beowulf*, was not an Anglo-Saxon hall; it was
of Denmark, and probably of the sixth century.

Many of these halls, such as that described in the *Lay of
Finnsburg*, were eventually destroyed by fire in the continual
tribal wars and feuds of those days. One of the most dramatic
tales of a house-burning in a family feud is that of the burning
of Nyal's house in the saga of Nyal. But that was a dwelling
house, not a hall; yet the action can be taken as a model
for the story of the burning of another hall, a most capa-
cious structure, large enough to hold a thousand men. That
was the huge banquet hall of Attila when the Burgundian
brothers with Hagen and a small group of followers fought to
the last rafter on the roof of the burning hall and literally almost
to the last drop of blood, for the survivors in the agony of
thirst were brusquely told by the dour and fated Hagen to
quench their thirst with the blood of the dead. That was a
mighty hall and a mighty combat! True, it occurs in an
epic poem, but there must have been many models which
the poet could use as a guide. We have also the story of
the burning of the house of Signy's husband and Signy's
self-immolation after her work of revenge was accomplished.

That too was poetry, but the burning of the house of Nyal was a brutal fact. There were plenty of models.

The problem of the nature of the dwelling-houses of the Germanic people during the pre-Roman and the Roman Iron Ages is complex; there was a great variety of structures. These varied with the times and the locality. They have had to be excavated and reconstructed, and naturally there is some variation of opinion on the matter.

Generally speaking, the presence of the forest in the North determined to a very great extent the nature of the construction of the dwelling-houses, at least in respect to shape and material. The typical Northern house was of rectangular construction, with walls of upright posts, the intervening spaces being filled with interwoven branches and twigs, and then smeared with clay which when dry had about the same effect as the modern stucco. The roofs were thatched with grass or straw. Some of these houses, those belonging to the wealthier and more important members of the community, were fairly commodious and were certainly far beyond the dug-out shelter with the dung-covered roof. These do seem, however, to have continued to be built[19] and were probably used as store rooms for a winter supply of food, surplus accommodation, work-rooms, and possibly as dwelling-places for the less fortunate of the population.

One method of house construction was that of the house or group of houses, constituting a farm housing-unit, for both human occupants and stock, a type which can still be seen in Northern Europe, especially in Lower Saxony. Sometimes houses of this nature were built on artificial mounds, in Germany described as *Wurtensiedlungen.* It was made of spaced, upright posts with a steep, thatched roof borne by long rafters, with walls of woven branches or reeds and covered with adhesive clay. These structures had to be roomy enough to shelter all the cattle, provide storage facilities and living quarters, since they were built with regard to the possibility of the surrounding land being flooded by storm-waves from the North Sea. It will be recalled that there was considerable variation in the relative levels of land and water in Northern Europe after the beginning of the recession of the ice. In the North Sea coast area the eustatic and isostatic conditions did not remain the same; at times a sinking of the water level or a rise in the level of the land had a very serious effect upon the inhabitants of these areas. Towards the end of the former era and during the early part of the present, the coastal districts in this part of Europe were often subjected to severe flooding, which made it necessary, when there were no natural mounds available, to construct artificial mounds on which the dwelling places were erected.

Another type of house of a unitary nature, that is, designed to provide accomodation for both man and beast, is dated about the beginning of the present era. The construction principle is that of upright logs or posts for the walls, long rafters crossed at the top, thatched roofs, with the main entrance at the side, accommodation for the cattle in one part of the building and the living quarters in the other part, with an exit in the roof for the smoke from the hearth. These houses appear to have had saddle-roofs, the interior area being divided into three parts by two rows of upright posts. The side areas contained the stalls for the cattle. The living room was divided off from the remainder by a wall. This tradition of house construction has survived right down to the present in parts of Northwest Germany (Fig. 14).

The round-house was not unknown, but appears to have occurred more frequently in Western and Southern Europe. It seems to have been a type of house favored by the Celts, or possibly by the pre-Celtic population, since similar structures have been found from Neolithic times. In that case this method of construction would have been taken over by the Germanic intruders, such as the *Marcomanni,* from the local inhabitants. A scene on the Marcus column depicts Roman soldiers setting fire to a Germanic village composed of houses of this round type.

A simpler construction than some of the houses described above is that of Burgdorf, a Saxon settlement. This is a plain log hut with a thatched roof at an angle of about 45 degrees, designed as a simple accommodation for a family of no great pretensions. Roman writers, such as Strabo and Pliny, speak of a type of Germanic house which could be loaded on wagons and set up in a new place. These were undoubtedly of very simple construction, and only the basic material would be moved. Such houses would be used for temporary residence, mainly during time of war or temporary tribal settlement. They are clearly not farm houses.

5. STATUS OF WOMEN

The position of women as individuals in the Germanic society of the Iron Age is in many respects not clear. Even as regards the position of women in the community there are many complicating factors. It is true that the woman had no political rights, that is, she could not claim the right to participate in the popular or tribal assemblies which were called together from time to time to decide upon matters of importance to the community as a whole, such matters as war and peace, for instance. In this respect the woman was represented by her father, brother or husband, as the case might be, and the only influence which she had was exerted behind the scenes.

Yet we are told by some of the Roman writers that the Germanic peoples had a very great reverence for women, considering that there was an aura of mysticism about them, which made them especially suitable for prognosticating the future and serving in the capacity of priestesses, as among the *Cimbri* and *Teutones,* and apparently also in the camp of Ariovistus, who refrained from a general attack because the sooth-saying and lot-casting women had declared that the time was unpropitious.

There were Germanic goddesses of fertility-cult origin also who were highly revered, such as Nerthus of the *Ingvaeoni,* and Freya. According to the Eddic poems it would appear that at least the supernatural element claimed and took quite a number of liberties. It is misleading to draw conclusions as to the attitude towards women in Germanic times from the instances which have been recorded when they acted as priestesses. One suspects that later such women would have been called witches.

Women's rights as individuals within the home are in a somewhat different category; they are partly legal and partly traditional. There is no doubt that legally the woman at marriage came under the guardianship of the man, and before marriage, and when unmarried, under the guardianship of the father or other senior male member of the family. This legal authority of the man over the wife was a survival of the practice of wife purchase, according to which the man theoretically could dispose of that which he had purchased in any way he saw fit. It was not, however, quite so simple as that. If he were proved guilty of any act of violence against the woman, he had to reckon with his wife's relatives, and a deadly feud could easily arise, if we may judge from the Icelandic sagas. Perhaps experience had taught the Icelandic husbands that it was better to leave the women alone to do as they wished, even if they acted in a belligerent manner. Poor Gunnar of the Nyal saga discovered this when he made the mistake of slapping his wife in anger at the trouble she had caused. Years later in a moment of dire need this cost him his life. But conditions in the Icelandic sagas probably cannot be taken at their full value for much earlier times.

Theoretically it was possible for a man to give away or sell both wife and children, but it is very doubtful whether this right was often exercised. Theoretically also the parents had the right to arrange the marriage of the daughter, and no doubt this was the practice, but the wishes of the daughter were often taken into consideration. There are plenty of instances of this in the Icelandic sagas, and the poet of the *Beowulf* comments doubtfully on the wisdom of giving the daughter in marriage to an enemy with the hope that in this way peace would be established. Yet the synonym for woman in the poem is 'weaver of peace.'

Insofar as the *Nibelungenlied* reflects earlier times it is quite clear that some women at least excercised a very great personal influence. We have seen the same phenomenon in Frankish Merovingian history. In the *Beowulf,* Hrothgar's queen is granted social equality and she further takes it upon herself to express opinions on matters of tribal and political import. The following passage from the *Beowulf* illustrates this attitude:

Came Wealhtheow forth,
Queen of Hrothgar, heedful of courtesy,
gold-decked, greeting the guests in hall;
and the high-born lady handed the cup
first to the East Danes' heir and warden,
bade him be blithe at the beer-carouse,
the land's beloved one......

. . . .

through the hall then went the Helmings' Lady,
to older and younger everywhere
carried the cup, till came the moment
when the ring-graced queen, the royal-hearted,
to Beowulf bore the beaker of mead.[20]

From what evidence is available, and here it is necessary to lean rather heavily on the Icelandic sagas, it would appear that the married woman had the keys of the house, and was allowed almost complete control of everything connected with household management. It is reasonably certain that this represented the practice of earlier times also, a practice which usually prevails in any well established and flourishing agricultural community. It is doubtful that the practice of *suttee,* the immolation of the woman, willingly or unwillingly, on the bier of the dead husband, was anything but a poetic motif, except in very few and exceptional cases of renowned leaders of the people. The motif occurs in literature; we find it in the *Nibelungenlied* matter, and also in the poetic *Edda*. No doubt many a Germanic warrior dreamed of such devotion, and the poets encouraged him, but it is not likely that many of the women followed the poetic examples. The self-destruction of the women after a lost battle and the death of the male members of their families is in an entirely different category. This self-destruction was to avoid the horrors of slavery, a fate always worse for women than for men.

In the Icelandic sagas the "purchase price" paid for the bride often had to be returned to the parents of the woman in case of a separation. And any property which the woman legally owned she could take with her on separation from her husband.

In the remnants of ancient Germanic literature there are many sarcastic references to the mischief caused by women, and there are also many eulogies. A great deal depends on the poet's experience. On the one hand we have the spitefulness of Gunnar's wife and her refusal to render assistance in a moment of peril, and on the other we have the fidelity of Bergthora, wife of Nyal, who would not be parted from him or the home in which they had lived. On the one hand we have the revenge of Brundhild on Siegfried for what she believed was his infidelity, and on the other hand her self-immolation to follow him to Valhalla. It is impossible to generalize. Human nature has at all times been much the same!

It used to be claimed that the change in motivation of the later form of the *Nibelungenlied* whereby Kriemhild avenges the death of her husband at the hands of her brothers as compared with an earlier version where she avenges the death of her brothers at the hands of the hoard-seeking Attila was caused by the higher conception in the twelfth century of the obligations of the marriage vow. This was an unjustified generalization, made on the assumption that the marriage state under Christian belief was more binding and sacred than among the pagans. There is no foundation for such an assumption. The regard for the marriage state among the Germanic pagans, in so far as there is evidence, was just as high as after the acceptance of Christianity.

6. FEUDS AND PUNISHMENTS

The blood feud has already been mentioned in connection with the practices of war. To allow private war to go on unchecked would soon have brought disaster upon the community. One means of avoiding the ultimate consequences of unlimited feuding was the establishment of the *wergild,* a sum of money which could be paid to the injured party for the damage done to person or property, originally to person only, as the word indicates, actually 'man compensation.' The *wergild* was regulated according to a fixed scale, so much for a free man, so much for a slave, so much for an arm and so on. The amount of money compensation, (for such it was, rather than a fine,) varied according to place and time. Damage or destruction of property was also regulated according to a fixed scale, or according to a sum determined by the local or the general 'Thing' or assembly of free men. This arrangement appeared to work fairly well as a general rule, although we hear much more about it in the writings of the Anglo-Saxons and the Icelanders.

The Icelanders seem to have developed a passion for "going to law" and most of the time of the general assembly was spent straightening out quarrels and disputes, not always successfully either, for the parties to the dispute could refuse to accept the decision and could then take the matter into their own hands, which usually meant an outbreak of violence.

When the private feuds could not be settled by arrangement and payment of money, and when they threatened to involve whole communities in conflict, the general assembly took the matter in hand, and often one of the two parties, the one held responsible for the trouble, was declared an outlaw and was forced to leave the country. This was of very common occurrence in Iceland. Eric the Red, the discoverer of Greenland, was required to leave Iceland. Outlawry among the Germanic peoples must have had about the same devastating effect upon the individual as excommunication in the Middle Ages.

Outlawry, *wergild* and private feuds were all means of settling quarrels. There were also crimes against the community, and in any community which is not anarchic there are ways and means of dealing with such deeds. Certain offences were punishable by death: such were treason, cowardice in the face of the enemy, desertion, secret murder, injurious magic practices, robbing of one's fellow tribesmen. The expression "secret" murder requires comment. In the case of a private quarrel which resulted in the death of one of the parties, the survivor was not accused of murder, if he at once announced what he had done. That was a private act of revenge for injury, or an act of justice according to established custom. But a secret and unannounced murder was in an entirely different category and became a crime against the community. The severe punishment for robbery is quite understandable, since there was no police force and private property was completely unguarded. Treason, cowardice in the face of the enemy and desertion from the ranks in time of battle require no explanation, since modern practice differs little from that of former times.

There were various ways of proving the guilt or innocence of the accused. One way was for the accused to get a sufficient number of relatives and friends to swear an oath to his innocence. This was not as simple as it seems; the swearing of this oath meant a sharing in the responsibility, which might be, and in the Icelandic chronicles often was, a very serious matter indeed. Perhaps the classical example of this sharing of the responsibility by oath-taking is the *Chanson de Roland,* where the relatives of Ganelon are involved in the punishment of his treason against the Emperor. There is no doubt that we have here the survival of old Frankish and therefore Germanic customs. But when both sides to the dispute had plenty of supporters who were willing to be sworn, then other means of settlement had to be devised.

The later trial by ordeal may have been one method to which recourse was had, but the individual who was accused had to be in desperate circumstances to appeal to this judgment, or had to be able to make quite sure that the ordeal could be undergone without fatal results. Common forms of ordeal, if one can judge from later practices, were by water and by fire. If the accused, for example, could plunge his hand into boiling water without injury, or could pick up a rod of red-hot iron, it seemed to be quite evident that the tribal gods were not offended and that therefore the accused was innocent. If the accused, when thrown into water, sank, as was normal, then he was innocent; if he floated, he was guilty, the idea being that the waters refused to take a guilty man. Prompt measures presumably had to be taken to rescue the innocent man who sank, before it was too late, but we are not told what happened in such cases.

Another method was that of trial by combat. This was a community-regulated matter. The theory was that the gods would grant the victory to the innocent party, not to the one who was the stronger and more adept in the use of arms. This practice was continued into the days of chivalry, and even then received the blessing of the Church, again acting on the principle that right will prevail. Ganelon's final doom was sealed, it will be recalled, when he lost in this trial by combat. In some cases the gods made the correct decision, but we can only indulge in speculation as to how many times justice was blind.

Crimes against the community were regarded as crimes against the tribal deities, and it was therefore quite logical that the representatives of the deities, the priests, should take charge of the determination of guilt or innocence and should also carry out or supervise the carrying out of the punishment. According to Tacitus, the usual punishments were by hanging or burial in the moors.[21] The moor burials of the third and fourth centuries would indicate that this form of punishment was still in force in later times. The hanging of the guilty was regarded as an offering to the gods, and the burial in the moors was also evidently a symbolic act, the complete removal of the criminal from contact with the living. This would also be the reason why in the moor burials the victims were so often bound, to prevent the spirit of the dead from further troubling the living. Whether these unfortunate individuals were put to death before burial or whether they were buried alive is an open question; many of them were probably buried alive. In some cases the accused were buried fully clothed, and this has been of great value in determining the nature of the clothing worn and the technique of manufacture, since the water-logged moors made preservation much more likely than in ordinary graves (Fig. 15).

7. SLAVERY

Slavery was a common institution among the Germanic peoples of the Iron Age, as it was among the Romans and the peoples of the Near East. The slaves were acquired by purchase or were captives of war. Sometimes also the slaves were those who had lost their freedom by reckless gambling, although these unfortunate individuals were in most cases no doubt sent out of the community. The slaves were used for both domestic and farm labor. Tacitus seemed to think that the lot of the slaves were not as bad as among other peoples.[22] At least there are no surviving accounts of serious misuse of slaves; they were apparently regarded as members of the household, as part of the necessary equipment. The master had the power of life and death over the slave, but here again what information is available would indicate that the life of the slave was infinitely better than on the industrialized farms of Italy. Undoubtedly the more attractive of the female slaves frequently became the concubines of the wealthy landowners or those in positions of authority. Whether this was to their advantage or not is a matter of opinion. If one can judge from the Icelandic sagas the children of the slaves and the children of the masters played and were brought up together. The practice of bestowing freedom on the slaves for meritorious service was also prevalent, as among the Romans.

With the almost continual raids and tribal wars there was a cheap and constant supply of slaves, and it is only under these circumstances that slavery in an agricultural community is economical. But even so there is no reason to believe that slavery ever reached the same height as in Italy. The degrading games of the circus in which slaves played such an important role were not practiced among the Germanic peoples. It is, however, quite possible that many of the Germanic people, who in the early centuries of the Roman Iron Age had settled in the cities along the Rhine and had become celticized or romanized, participated in the shows offered in the arenas of these cities, modelled after the much greater attractions of the Roman capital.

8. GAMBLING

The Roman writers report the Germanic warriors as being inordinately fond of gambling. However, the people with whom the Romans came in contact were as a general rule those who were on the war-path and living an unsettled life, in an atmosphere of movement and war. And soldiers of all nations and of all times have been addicted to gambling. It is extremely doubtful that the Germanic people as a whole were more addicted to the practice of gambling than the Romans themselves. Really serious gambling belongs to the crowded cities and the war-camps, not to the settled agricultural communities.

9. RELATIONS BETWEEN THE SEXES

The Romans who came into contact with the Germanic people or who had their information from those who had such contact, such as officers and merchants, can scarcely have failed to notice a striking difference in the attitude of the so-called barbarians in such matters as the relations between the sexes. Caesar, or his informants, was greatly impressed when he wrote:

They spend all their lives in hunting and warlike pursuits, and inure themselves from childhood to toil and hardship. Those who preserve their chastity longest are most highly commended by their friends; for they think that continence makes young men taller, stronger and more masculine. To have had intercourse with a woman before the age of twenty is considered perfectly scandalous. They attempt no concealment, however, of the facts of sex; men and women bathe together in the rivers, and they wear nothing but hides and short garments of hairy skin, which leave most of the body bare.[23]

This must have seemed quite strange indeed to the sophisticated Romans of Caesar's day, when the old and severe customs and traditions of the more primitive Republic had broken down and Rome had become a metropolis and a centre of world power with all the attendant vice and corruption of morals. The much simpler and primitive life of the Germanic peoples was not owing to any consciously accepted set of rules of social conduct, but to the lack of sophistication of their community life. It is a serious error, and one that has been all too frequent, to conclude that primitive people with entirely different customs of social conduct do not have high social standards. Caesar's informants at least recognized that the promiscuous bathing of the Germanic youth did not mean what it evidently would have meant in the sophisticated society of Rome. That these people wore very scanty garments was probably quite true, but the passage has been frequently misinterpreted. Caesar was writing a treatise on his Gallic campaigns, not on the habits and customs of the *Germani.* In this particular passage he tells us in an aside, as it were, about some of the Germanic customs which he had noticed or which had been reported to him by others. The time would also be summer, as indicated by the remark about the community bathing; Caesar might almost have been describing the apparel or lack of apparel of a modern bathing beach. Such conduct would have been scandalous in Rome, but what went on behind the scenes, in the palaces or at the banquets would have been far more scandalous in the Germanic settlements. Caesar was perhaps in his own mind making some such comparison, and took this indirect way of expressing his opinion of the contemporary code of his fellow Romans. Caesar was also quite correct in his conclusion that the outdoor life of hunting and the inurement to hardship was a very practical way of ensuring a restraint in sexual matters. It does not follow that continence as an aid to growth and strength is an actual fact.

10. IDEALS AND PATTERNS OF THOUGHT

The Germanic people were divided into the free and the unfree. The unfree were the slaves, thralls, as they were called. There were two classes of the freemen: the great mass of independent landowners and the wealthier or more aristocratic class of certain recognized families, which might be called the nobility. The difference between the two was partly a difference of wealth and partly one of birth. However, there was, at least in the olden days, no difference in respect to social equality. The state, if one may use that term, was composed of all the free men of the community. On certain occasions all the free men were called together, to give assent to certain projects which had already been considered by the council of elders and leaders. The assembly had the power to reject such proposals, and instances are known when such assemblies forced on the leaders a policy of war, because peace had become monotonous, and the hope of booty was a strong lure.

These assemblies also had the power to elect the leaders in time of war, who for the time being had almost dictatorial power. The position of the leader eventually became hereditary in certain families, and kingship resulted. It is impossible to determine definitely just when the institution of kingship began among the Germanic peoples. According to Jordanes the Goths were led across the Baltic by kings, but these may have been simply chosen leaders, to whom the title of king was given by Jordanes at a later time when kingship was well established on an hereditary basis. By the time of Alaric of the Visigoths and Theodoric of the Ostrogoths, the title of king had been definitely established in their respective lineages. We have noted the rise of the Merovingian dynasty, and how it was supplanted by the Carolingian. Odoacer bestowed upon himself the title of king; Alboin of the Langobards was king; Gaiseric of the Vandals; and Günther of the Burgundians. Hengist and Horsa of the Saxons appear to have been chieftains (*Herzöge*), but kingship was developed in the new territories. Whether this was imitation of the practice in Mediterranean countries or whether the role and title of king grew naturally out of the environment of the migrations it is impossible to say; perhaps both factors played an important role. Kingship spread to the Scandinavian countries, although not without considerable strain and strife. Only in Iceland did the old form of democratic community rule survive, but Iceland was comparatively isolated and besides, the original settlers of Iceland had left their homeland, Norway, in order to escape the imposition of Harald's kingship. Such movements as those of the main phase of the *Völkerwanderung* required a leader with more authority than could be claimed by one who had been elected for a period of time to perform a specific task, and not only more authority, but more prestige, the prestige of inherited authority. And this, after all, was perhaps the chief reason for the establishment of kingship among the Germanic peoples.

Never at any time does there seem to have been a Germanic state, in which all the Germanic peoples were included in a closely knit political union. Perhaps the nearest approach to any such universal Germanic kingdom or empire was that of Ermanaric before the attack of the Huns; but this, as we have seen, although of vast extent, was a very loosely organized kingdom, and at the first attack from without it fell to pieces almost immediately. Theodoric the Ostrogoth may have had ambitions to form a Romanic-Germanic empire, but was unable to accomplish this in his lifetime, and he had no successors who were strong enough or far-seeing enough to carry his policy to fruition. The kingdom of the Carolingian, Charles the Great, was also an attempt to establish an empire, but neither did Charles have successors who could hold together the realm which he had created.

But there were other more fundamental reasons why it was not possible to create a unified Germanic state. These reasons are intimately associated with the inherent Germanic love of independence, the spirit of individualism and the respect for personality. These are all highly desirable qualities, but in an exaggerated form they do not facilitate the formation of political unity beyond a limited geographical area. Love of independence, individualism and respect for personality are the products of a life of toil and struggle for existence under circumstances which present a never-ending challenge to the individual; a challenge which is never so strong as to force the acceptance of a political or environmental totalitarianism, but yet is always strong enough to encourage individual activity. Such was the environment of the Germanic people, from the very beginning of their existence as an ethnic unit; such was the environment of the people of the Northern Megalithic culture and the Corded Ware culture out of whom arose the Germanic people; such was the environment of the Mesolithic and Upper

Palaeolithic ancestors of these Neolithic peoples. It is no wonder that these Germanic peoples developed a stubborn love of independence and individuality which often led to extremes and to disaster.

Moreover, as far as Northern Europe was concerned, there must be added the environmental influence of the sea and the forest. The earliest settlers of the North were in close contact with the sea; it provided food, it was a highway; but it also demanded its sacrificial victims. The sea has ever been a harsh mistress, and it produces a dour, stubborn people. But it produces courage, encourages adventure and inures to hard and arduous labor. Since the time when the Mediterranean ceased to be the centre of political power on the earth, all of the great empires have been based on control of sea power. Many brave hearts indeed lie asleep in the deep. This close connection with the sea was brought into the Germanic social complex by the native people of Northern Europe, by the pre-Germanic, pre-Indo-European population, some of whose ancestors first reached the North in pursuit of the retreating reindeer after the beginning of the melting of the ice. The following extracts from Anglo-Saxon poetry will illustrate this attitude towards the sea:

> And yet my heart is now restless in my breast, my mind is with the sea-flood over the whale's domain; it fares widely over the face of the earth, comes again to me eager and un-satisfied; the lone-flyer screams, resistlessly urges the heart to the whale-way over the stretch of seas.[24]

> The hail flew in showers. I heard nought there save the sea booming, the ice-cold billow, at times the song of the swan. I took my gladness in the cry of the gannet and the sound of the curlew instead of the laughter of men, in the screaming gull instead of the drink of mead. There storms beat upon the rocky cliffs; there the tern with icy feathers answered them; full oft the dewy-winged eagles screamed around.[25]

* * * * *

In the road-stead rocked a ring-dight vessel,
Ice flecked, outbound, atheling's barge.[26]

* * * * *

A stout wave-walker he bade make ready.[27]

* * * * *

Then moved o'er the waters by might of the wind
That bark like a bird with breast of foam ....[28]

And the influence of the forests! Anyone who has lived in a pioneering settlement in a heavily forested area knows the enduring effect of the forest upon the character of the inhabitants. It produces the conviction that the individual must depend upon his own efforts, and these efforts will tax all his strength. It produces a feeling of isolation and aloneness, the *Waldeinsamkeit* of the German Romantic poets. It produces a feeling of mystery, and then too a feeling of oneness with nature. This close contact with the sea and the forest are indelibly impressed upon the character of the ancient Germanic peoples.

The family group and the wider relationship, the sib, was basic to the organization of Germanic society. The family group consisted of the parents, the grown-up children, their wives and children. Theoretically the *paterfamilias* exercised considerable authority over the other members of the family group, and practically also as long as he was sound of mind and limb, but when he became feeble with age the eldest son took over the responsibility of direction of the homestead and family matters. This closed family group belonged to a larger unit, the sib, consisting of the various relations of the head of the family. This was the basis for the formation of the "hundred" organization for purposes of war, and it also played a very important role in the demanding and receiving of *wergild*.

This naturally tended to bring about a close-knit unity of the larger group, the sib. The totality of sibs in turn con-

stituted the tribe, and the tribe was the basic political unit.
In course of time, and as necessity demanded, various tribes
were united in a larger cult-group for religious purposes, as
in the *Ingvaeoni*. There were also the combinations in the
main phase of the Migration period, combinations such as
the Frankish confederacy which included a large number
of originally distinct tribes. The same is true to some extent
of all the other large groups of this period, such as the Goths
and the *Suebi*.

An outsider could become a member of the tribe by adoption,
and this was frequently done, just as one who was not a
blood relative could be adopted into the family. The household
is a wider term than the related family group. The household
consisted of all the inmates of the house or all those who
worked on the estate, and that would include all the unfree,
the thralls, as well as other freemen who for one reason or
another, although not blood relations, had associated themselves with a particular household. And, if one can judge from
the Icelandic sagas, the head of the family was responsible for
all these various members of the household.

The *comitatus* has already been mentioned in connection
with the organization for raids and war. The *comitatus* also
witnesses to an outstanding ideal among the Germanic peoples,
the ideal of fidelity. Joining the leader's personal following
was a purely voluntary matter, and the individual could also
sever his connection with the group if he wished to transfer
his allegiance. As long, however, as he was a member of the
personal following of the chieftain, he was expected to remain
absolutely loyal, to be ready at all times to defend his lord,
to guard him in battle, and to perish with him as a matter of
honor, or if not to perish, to avenge his death: "Yea, death
is better for liegemen all than a life of shame."[29] It will be
recalled that Beowulf had but one faithful follower who dared
to assist him against the fire-breathing dragon, and who had
courage enough to avenge his death. It will also be recalled

what bitter words of scorn were directed against the rest of the group who had accompanied Beowulf to the fatal encounter, but who failed their master in the moment of danger. That attitude towards the faithless follower can be taken as characteristic not only for the sixth and seventh centuries but also for earlier times. On the other hand the chief was expected to reward his followers liberally, to provide them with food, shelter and weapons.

These members of the personal following were not always of the same tribe as the lord; in many cases they were young men of other tribes who were in search of honor and adventure, and who were attracted to the service of a particular individual by the fame which he had achieved among the peoples. The attainment of honor, fame and recognition was a driving ambition. These members of the personal following were professional soldiers, professional adventurers, and they found their opportunities for the acquisition of reward, honor and fame in the constant tribal wars and feuds of the time. Absolute fidelity on the part of the followers, princely liberality on the part of the chief; these were the ideals of the day. After Beowulf's successful combat against the monsters Grendel and his mother, he is liberally rewarded by Hrothgar and his queen Wealtheow, and the poet speaks in glowing terms of their generosity and holds it up as a model for others to follow.

Time and again throughout the poem examples are given of chieftains who failed in their duty, who were mean and cowardly and who failed to retain the loyalty of their followers. The poet is particularly contemptuous of both followers and chieftains who fall short of the high ideal which he portrays in the character of his hero.

The poet, obviously a Christian, is nevertheless enamoured of the ideals of his pagan ancestors, and he finds it impossible sometimes to restrain his enthusiasm when describing some of the more exciting events. His admiration reaches a high peak

when he is describing the grim old warrior stirring up the
young man to avenge his father:

> Then over the ale, on this heirloom gazing,
> some ash-wielder old who has all in mind
> that spear-death of men, he is stern of mood,
> heavy at heart, — in the hero young
> tests the temper and tries the soul
> and war-hate wakens, with words like these:
> Canst thou not, comrade, ken that sword
> which to the fray thy father carried
> in his final feud, 'neath the fighting-mask,
> dearest of blades, when the Danish slew him
> and wielded the war-place on Withergill's Fall,
> after havoc of heroes, those hardy Schildings?
> now, the son of a certain slaughtering Dane,
> proud of his treasure, paces this hall,
> joys in the killing, and carries the jewel
> that rightfully ought to be owned by thee![30]

The Christian poet of the Old Saxon *Heliand* was also so
full of admiration for the pagan virtues that he describes Christ
and his disciples in terms of the chieftain and his band of
personal followers. He even uses the old alliterative verse, and
many of the old descriptive terms. No doubt the intransigent
Saxons who had been so forcibly converted by Charles were
particularly susceptible to this kind of appeal.

These ideals and the troublous times developed in the par-
ticipants in these events a belief in fate, "Fares Wyrd as she
must" is a favorite expression in *Beowulf*. If a man was 'fey'
there was nothing which he could do to avoid his fate. Many
instances of this kind occur in the Icelandic sagas, and this
attitude can be regarded as typical of the earlier times. The
mental and physical environment tended to produce this acceptance and yet stubborn defiance of fate, the determination
not to lose caste by a weak surrender to overwhelming odds, but
to struggle to the last breath of life. We are reminded of the

defiant Hagen of the *Nibelungenlied,* who, convinced of the accurate prophecy of the mermaids that the Burgundian party on the way to the court of Attila will never return to their own land again, transports the little army across the Danube, and then in a grand gesture of defiance destroys the boat. And his last stubborn refusal to reveal the whereabouts of the *Nibelungen* Hoard, although he knows his refusal means certain death, is a typical example of this death-defying attitude of mind; this stubborn adherence to a principle and to an ideal; this courageous assertion of individuality and personality which was the very life and breath of the leading spirits of the ancient days of Germanic history. Nothing but the retention of the sturdy individual and communal self-sacrificing spirit of the ancient Roman Republic could have withstood the ardor and the violence of the advance of the Germanic peoples against the frontiers of the Empire. And that spirit of the ancient Republic had perished.

To be sure, ideals are not always lived up to, and there is the reverse side. The physical environment, the mixed cultural inheritance of the Germanic peoples produced a conflict in the minds of many of the people. They could have said with Faust: *"Zwei Seelen wohnen ach in meiner Brust."* There was this idealism, this defiance of fate, this exaggerated respect for personality, this striving after the unknown and the unattainable, this innate romanticism on the one hand, and on the other hand the realization of the stern practicality of existence, a realism that often led to an excess of cruelty and violence. Possibly this conflict between the two extremes had been more manifest in the Germanic peoples, as their literature plainly shows, than in any other, and it is a conflict that cannot be resolved, for it is of the North and ever will be. There is the beauty and the mystery of the Northern Lights and the harsh and cruel reality of the frost. No wonder the poets of the *Edda* pondered about the fate of the mighty gods in their Valhalla and the ever-enduring inevitable threat and hostility of the frost-giants. And the end: the *Götterdämmerung*, the Twilight of the Gods. Romanticism and Realism inextricably intertwined!

It would not be fitting to conclude this brief description of some of the more important habits and customs and ways of thought of the Germanic peoples without some reference to a quality of mind which is the saving grace of any individual or people, the quality of humor. The above paragraphs give too severe a picture of the Germanic people; one would think they never had time for anything but feuds, land-seeking, wars, weapons, banquets and high ideals. This is the impression one gets by reading most of the descriptions of ancient Germanic life and literature. It is strange that this quality of humor is so seldom noticed, or if noticed, so seldom emphasized. It is at times a grim humor, as in the Icelandic sagas, when a man who has suddenly lost his leg as the result of a sweeping blow from his opponent's sword, remarks: "Well, the leg is off", or when met at the door of his house by an enemy who without a word thrusts a spear through his body, remarks: "They make the spearheads wide these days." It is immaterial whether these remarks were ever actually made by individuals under these circumstances or not; it is quite sufficient that the saga tellers could think of them and that the hearers could appreciate them. Then there is the defiant and sarcastic humor of many of the Scaldic poems. Poems written by men of action, poems sometimes written in defiance of death, poems which had a bite and a sting, poems which caused men to laugh at the unfortunate individual who was thus lampooned. These people were not lacking in a sense of humor.

There is also the grim humor of the *Waltharius* ballad. Waltharius and Hildagunda have been surprised in the mountains by Günther, Hagen and a small band who are intent upon seizing the booty which Waltharius has brought away with him in their flight from the court of Attila. Waltharius has slain all of Günther's men, and there now remain only Günther and

Hagen. By a ruse they entice Waltharius out of the narrow mountain defile which he has so successfully defended with the enthusiastic encouragement of Hildagunda. Out in the open now the fight is renewed with great vigor and with considerable success, for they are all three severely mutilated by the loss of limbs during the combat. At last they are forced by exhaustion to make an end of it, which they do in a most amicable manner by all sitting down on the turf and partaking of a very hearty meal prepared and served by Hildagunda from supplies brought from Attila's court. That is all; they eat and drink and shake hands in reconciliation; the bearer is left to wonder how they survived their terrible wounds; the poet is, however, sure of his effect; the guests around the banquet table at the conclusion of the narration would all raise their flagons and drink deep draughts to the three mighty heroes and the impossible situation in which the poet has left them. And the shouting and the laughter at this tall story!

Then there is the gentler humor of the *Beowulf*, where the poet is describing the actions of Hrothgar's retainers when they heard of and saw the ravages of the dreaded Grendel in the royal hall:

> They were easy to find who elsewhere sought
> in room remote their bed at night,
> bed in the bowers, when that bale was shown....[31]

And again the *scop* would attain the desired effect. The listeners at the banquet table would laugh quietly and appreciatively, not uproariously this time, as the poet would pause long enough to give his audience an opportunity to appreciate the point. Just as with modern audiences!

There are two outstanding examples of uproarious humor in the *Beowulf*. The poet has been telling about the raid of Hygelac on the Frankish coast, on which raid he was accompanied by Beowulf. Hygelac himself was surprised by a large party of Franks and was killed in the fight that followed.

Beowulf, however, who had the strength of thirty men in his arms, was able to escape:

> Thence Beowulf fled
> through strength of himself and his swimming power,
> though alone, and his arms were laden with thirty
> coats of mail, when he came to the sea.[32]

All he had to do was to swim from the Frankish coast back to Denmark with the thirty suits of armor in his arms! Quite an easy task!

The other incident takes place shortly after the arrival of Beowulf at Hrothgar's court. A banquet is held in the evening and at this banquet Unferth, one of Hrothgar's men who seems to be jealous of Beowulf, makes the unfortunate error of trying to haze the visitor. Then Beowulf spake:

> Beowulf spake, bairn of Ecgtheow: —
> what a deal hast uttered, dear my Unferth,
> drunken with beer, of Breca now,
> told of his triumph! Truth I claim it,
> that I had more of might in the sea
> than any man else, more ocean-endurance.
> We twain had talked in time of youth,
> and made our boast — we were merely boys,
> striplings still —, to stake our lives
> far at sea: and so we performed it.
> Naked swords as we swam along,
> we held in hand, with hope to guard us
> against the whales.........
> ....
> ....
> together we twain on the tides abode
> five nights full till the flood divided us,
> churning waves and chillest weather,
> darkling night and the northern wind
> ruthless rushed on us: rough was the surge.
> Now the wrath of the sea-fish rose apace;

yet me 'against the monsters my mailèd coat,
hard and hand-linked, help afforded,
battle-sark braided my breast to ward,
garnished with gold. There gripped me firm
and haled me to bottom the hated foe,
with grimmest gripe. 'Twas granted me though,
to pierce the monster with point of sword,
with blade of battle; huge beast of the sea
was whelmed by the hurly through hand of mine

. . . .
. . . .
. . . .
And so it came that I killed with my sword
nine of the nicors. Of night-fought battles
ne'er heard I a harder 'neath heaven's dome,
nor adrift on the deep a more desolate man!
yet I came unharmed from that hostile clutch,
though spent with swimming, the sea upbore me,
flood of the tide on Finnish land,
the welling waters. No wise of thee
have I heard men tell such terror of falchions,
bitter battle, Breca ne'er yet,
not one of you pair, in the play of war
such daring deed has done at all
with bloody brand, — I boast not of it![33]

No, no, certainly not! Just a little spent with swimming, with
a sword in one's right hand and fighting not only the cold and
the storm but also the terrible sea-monsters for day after day.
Nothing to boast about, just a little exercise!

All around the banquet table sit hardened warriors, drinking
deeply of the mead and ale that was so freely served. Of
course they knew they were listening to a fish story, to one of
the best fish stories since the poet Homer told of the wanderings of Odysseus, and they were waiting for that climactic
punch-line: "I boast not of it." And then the wild cheering
and the shouting, the emptying of the flagons and the calling
for more! What a wild tumultuous scene! And how the

scop must have grinned in satisfaction at the applause and the success of his *tour de force!* Now everybody is in good humor, and will be prepared to listen to the rest of the story, even if it isn't all quite so funny as this fish story. Is it not just like Shakespeare, who filled the theatres with people who wanted to listen to his jokes and his merry quips, and who then were forced to listen to his sublime poetry?

11. AGRICULTURE

Caesar writes:

The Germans are not agriculturists, and live principally on milk, cheese and meat. No one possesses any amount of land as private property; the magistrate and tribal chiefs annually assign a holding to clans and groups of clansmen or others living together, fixing its size and position at their discretion, and the following year make them move on somewhere else. They give many reasons for this custom: for example, that their men may not get accustomed to living in one place, lose their warlike enthusiasm and take up agriculture instead; that they may not be anxious to acquire large estates, and the strong be tempted to dispossess the weak; to prevent their paying too much attention to building houses that will protect them from cold and heat or becoming too fond of money — a frequent cause of division and strife; to keep the common people contented and quiet by letting every man see that even the most powerful are no better off than himself.[34]

Over a hundred years later Tacitus writes:

The country, although very varied in appearance, generally consists of rough forests or foul swamps. It is wetter where it faces Gaul and windier on the side of Noricum and Pannonia. Though fertile in crops, it bears no fruit-trees; it is rich in flocks, but they are generally stunted ... They take pleasure in the size of their herds: these are their sole form of wealth, and they are very proud of them.[35]

It has been one of the chief merits of the investigations of the prehistorians to have shown that this picture as given by Caesar and Tacitus is not entirely correct. Unfortunately these passages from the Roman writers have in the past been taken at their full value by many modern historians and in consequence a false picture has been established in the minds of the readers.

What is wrong with the picture as given by Caesar? In the first place, Caesar can scarcely be regarded as an authority on the nature of the vast areas east of the Rhine or of the people who inhabited them. His personal knowledge of the country and people was extremely limited; there can be very little doubt that he copied to some extent from other writers who knew even less about the subject than he did. No doubt he had made very careful observations on his two raids across the Rhine, and had obtained information from prisoners and from those Celts in his camp who presumably had some knowledge of their Germanic neighbors. But even so there is something wrong with the picture: it has been definitely proved over and over again that the Germanic people were agriculturists, that they had been so from the very beginning of their existence as an ethnic unit in the Early Bronze Age, and that the constituent parts of this ethnic unit in the preceding Neolithic were also agriculturists. It is then impossible to accept Caesar's description as an accurate representation of conditions among the Germanic peoples in the first century of the former era. The usual explanation and excuse for Caesar is that he was describing customs and manner of living of tribes who were for the most part on a war footing, often on the move and consequently forced to depend to a great extent for food on their flocks and herds, which they could take with them when they moved from the temporary place of settlement. But if that was the case, why does Caesar go on to tell us about the method of land division, the yearly change-over, the strip-farming procedure? Why was such a division necessary if they were not agriculturists? For pasture land, for the raising of herds, such a method is surely out of the question. The answer, of course, is that the land was so divided for agricultural purposes, and that the Germanic peoples even of Caesar's time and in the neighborhood of the Rhine were engaged in the raising of crops, and were not restricted principally to a diet of cheese, milk and meat.

Caesar's description of the method of land division may be accurate for those limited areas with which he was acquainted, although it does not follow that the reasons given for the adoption of this method were the real ones. It sounds like an explanation after the fact, whether devised by Caesar's Celtic or Roman informants or by some of his Germanic prisoners. Whatever we may think of the system as an economic policy it apparently met the local needs, at least for the time being. It could have been a local custom; it could not possibly have been a universal practice, since in many areas of Northwest Germany the only system for which there is any evidence is that of individual farms (*Einzelhöfe*), a system of settlement which still persists in those districts as compared with the farm-village system, which obviously could lend itself more readily to the practice of yearly land distribution described by Caesar.

It seems very strange that the Germanic tribes were always clamoring for land on which to settle if they were not interested in agriculture, that is, in grain production, and only in the raising of cattle. The limited areas available for settlement in Western and Southern Europe are more suitable for intensive agricultural production than for the exclusive raising of herds. The fact that wealth may have been counted in terms of cattle is no proof of the universal nature of the economy. Is not our modern currency supposed to be based on gold, a substance which very few of us ever see these days except in the windows of the jewelry shops? And if there was such an extreme dependence for food on meat and milk products, how did it happen that the Germanic tribes, as for instance the Goths in Eastern Europe, so often asked for supplies of grain when settling in a new area, sufficient supplies to last until the harvest was ready?

Tacitus' description of *Germania* as a country consisting generally of rough forests and foul swamps leaves a great deal to be added. Swamps undoubtedly did exist in some areas, especially in the area of the Lower Rhine, but many excavations have conclusively shown that Tacitus' description is an exaggeration even for this region.[36] And as for the Middle and Upper Rhine, there were few swamps there in the first century. There were in many districts, it is true, rough forests, and these forests probably seemed very terrifying to the southern mind, but it is surely obvious that if *Germania* at that time had been so covered with swamps and forests, as Tacitus thought, it would not have offered the attraction as desirable land which it plainly did. Nor could it have provided food for the constant stream of land-seekers from the North. It should also be kept in mind that these areas had been occupied by the Celts before the southward movement of the West Germanic peoples, and before that by Neolithic agriculturists. A casual glance at the map of Europe will show innumerable river valleys which were eminently suited to agricultural settlement, and had been ever since the loess deposits of the Ice Age. Actually Tacitus' description is more accurate than that of Caesar's. However, the scarcity of fruit trees was not because the climate was unfavorable for their culture. A fruit tree is not like a crop of wheat; it is many years before a fruit tree will bear fruit, and after all when Tacitus was writing, the Germanic settlement of Central and Southern Germany was just beginning. That the cattle of the Germanic tribes may have seemed to Tacitus to be stunted is quite natural, since he was comparing the breed with that of the Italian, where the cattle were larger and where the selective breeding practice was probably more advanced. It has already been noted that Caesar considered the native horses of the Germanic cavalrymen too small for his purpose. Perhaps Caesar, however, was wrong. The Western cow-pony is not a large animal, but certainly excellently suited for the purpose for which it is employed.

Archaeological investigations have made it quite certain that two forms of settlement existed among the Germanic peoples[37]: the farm village (*Haufendorf*) and the individual farm (*Einzelhof*). The prevalent form of settlement depended chiefly on the nature of the land. The individual farm is the prevailing type in certain areas, not because, as sometimes stated, the Germanic love of independence was so extremely developed that the desire to live apart overruled all other considerations. The Celts also had this form of rural economy. The Germanic peoples, however, did not take over this custom from the Celts in the northern part of Germany, since the Celts had never settled there. The reason for the holding of individual farms was partly the nature of the soil and partly a plentiful supply of water. Where there is a plentiful supply of water it is not necessary to settle in villages. Then too in those areas which are low-lying and on the heath, larger farms were necessary because the soil is not so rich, and this encouraged the practice of individual settlement. In other areas where the land was broken up by hills, it was also advantageous to have individual farms. These individual farms seem to have been the rule at the time of the settlement of Iceland, for we hear nothing about village settlements there. The same appears to have been true of Norway at that time, from whence most of the Icelandic settlers came. But the nature of the soil in both countries is such that the individual farm is almost an economic necessity.

The establishment of the agricultural village, on the other hand, was to a large extent dependent upon the scanty supply of water and upon a richer soil. Under these circumstances smaller plots suffice, and the dwellings are grouped around a common water supply. Hundreds of such farm villages can be seen at the present time scattered over the rural areas of Britain and Europe, although they have been considerably enlarged by the addition of shops and public buildings. Perhaps the desirability or necessity of communal effort also played a part in the original establishment of these farm villages. It is clear that if the annual redistribution of the land, as described by Caesar, was at all general, this communal effort would be essential, since it is difficult to see how the strips could have been tilled and planted if each individual worked according to his own ideas. Such a system requires some form of community organization and supervision.

The Germanic peoples placed the emphasis on cereal production or cattle raising according to the nature of the district, or according to the necessities of local and temporary conditions. It is quite likely that in those areas of the North Sea coast where the mound settlements were the custom, the emphasis was on cattle raising, since, even if infrequent, the flooding of the land by salt water would certainly render it unfit for grain production for some time. The emphasis would also naturally be on cattle raising in more mountainous districts where there is excellent pasture, but not always good agricultural land. In the coastal areas fishing was then and still is a major industry.

The cereal products were not as a rule sold or exported,[38] but were used for home consumption. Cattle hides on the other hand were a major article of the export trade, and no doubt many of the merchants came to the conclusion that the main industry was cattle raising. That agriculture was the basic industry is shown by the fact that a crop failure was always a serious matter for any of the Germanic tribes. Caesar tells us that the *Usipeti* and the *Tencteri* were eventually forced to migrate, because the *Suebi* had seriously interfered for years with their agricultural operations and crop failure had resulted.[39]

The main cereal grains were wheat and barley, but in the post-Christian Iron Age oats and rye also were cultivated. Both flax and hemp are quite old. The garden products: peas, beans, turnips and beets were well known. Even though the main emphasis may have been on cattle, yet sheep, hogs, goats and the horse played a very important role in the economy, and had done so since early in the Bronze Age at least. It was from the sheep that the wool was harvested which was used for the clothing. Oxen were used for ploughing and for drawing the wagons which were the main means of transport. The horse was used for riding, and only later as a draught animal. The Bronze Age custom of using horses for the drawing of the two-wheeled war-chariot seems to have been given up during the Iron Age. Chicken, geese and ducks were plentiful in the farm yards. The dog was everywhere.[40]

At this time the plough was the most important of the agricultural implements. The economy had long since developed beyond the hoe stage of Neolithic times. Both the words for plough and for furrow are Indo-European. The rock carvings from the Bronze Age show ploughs drawn by oxen. The wheel plough seems to have made its appearance first in the Alpine area among the Rhaetians, and spread then to the Southern Germanic peoples, and very slowly to the North and to England.[41] The Goths appear to have retained the more old-fashioned kind of plough. The main difference between the two types of plough was that the wheel plough turned over the soil, as is customary with modern ploughs, whereas the older type merely hacked up the soil, and presumably cross-ploughing was necessary for efficient cultivation. This new form of plough must have made quite a difference in agricultural methods. It was a definite advance towards mechanized agriculture, and, as a matter of fact, very little improvement was made on this type until comparatively recent times.

The harrow is a very old implement, since the word is Indo-European. There was not much improvement on the sickle for the reaping of the grain and the old practice of beating out the grain with sticks or tramping it out still prevailed. These methods also lasted down into comparatively recent times.

On the whole, during prosperous times the Germanic people had a fairly varied and healthy diet. But when the harvests failed over a period of years because of exhaustion of the soil, or when climatic deterioration reduced the yield, or again when the land was rendered unsuitable for agriculture by floods in the coastal areas, then the pressure of population and the lower standard of living was such that migration was the only solution. Conditions described in the *Beowulf* and on the farms in Iceland would indicate a plentiful supply of food, although few of the luxuries of the banquets of the Roman world were available.

Although there are examples of well-constructed roads across moors,[42] the Germanic peoples were not road-builders. There were paths and wagon tracks, but they learned the art of road building from the Roman engineers. The rivers were not bridged; they were crossed at fords (hence such names as Frankfurt), or by boats, as in the *Nibelungenlied.*

Where possible settlements were made on the coasts or beside lakes and rivers. They utilized the forests for many purposes, but they did not live in them. The fact that the settlements were necessarily scattered is perhaps one of the reasons why the Germanic peoples failed to come together into a larger political unity. The area occupied by one tribe would be quite distinct from that occupied by another. Caesar noted this peculiarity. He reported that:

the various tribes regarded it as their greatest glory to lay waste as much as possible of the land around them and to keep it uninhabited. They hold it as a proof of a people's valor to drive their neighbors from their homes, so that no one dare settle near them, and also think that it gives them greater security by removing any fear of sudden invasion.[43]

The latter was probably the chief reason for the practice. It shows a mutual suspicion and a lack of feeling for the common weal, outside of the narrow confines of the tribe. Even tribal feeling was not always sufficient. We have seen not only East Goths fighting against West Goths, but also one part of a tribe fighting against another part, especially if divided by confessional differences.

12. TRADE

At no time since the beginning of the Neolithic period was Northern Europe completely cut off from the Mediterranean world, either culturally or in economic relations. The intensity of these relations varied from time to time according to circumstances and according to the possibilities of trade relationships. The trade in amber, and the presence of North Sea amber in the Mycenean graves shows that trade relations existed in the Early Bronze Age, although they may not have been direct. Then too Italian bronze daggers may have influenced the form of the stone daggers of the Late Neolithic and the Early Bronze Age of the North. That these trade relations were continued and enlarged during the following centuries is apparent, since the trade in amber increased in volume and the North had to import the bronze it required from further south. Imported Italian swords and daggers in the Early Bronze Age show that the trade was not restricted to raw materials alone. Trade relations between the North of Europe and Ireland brought large quantities of Irish gold across the North Sea. The introduction of and the lasting popularity of the spiral ornamentation of the Danubian culture would indicate relations with this centre also.

During the Hallstatt Iron Age the amber trade continued to flourish, since Hallstatt received extraordinary amounts of amber. Hallstatt was near the southern trade route from the North.[44] The graveyard at Hallstatt has yielded such great quantities of amber, in such a variety of forms from the richest to the poorest, that it is obvious that amber at that time was common and not expensive. Trade for salt must also have played a role in bringing the amber there, since Hallstatt means 'the place of salt,' and salt has always been eagerly sought after as one of the necessities of life.[45] Beads, rings and pendants are among the finds. The Villanova culture in Italy was strongly influenced by the Hallstatt culture, and amber is next to glass in importance in the graves of Villanova and Bologna.[46] Amber has also been found in the oldest Greek graves of Southern Italy.[47]

The full import of the impact of the new metal was late in reaching the North, and when the Iron Age does at last begin, it coincides with a period of climatic deterioration and an early phase of the *Völkerwanderung*. The result was at least a partial collapse of the brilliant artistic and material culture of the Northern Bronze Age.[48] In the La Tène period amber was not so popular as it had formerly been. In Northern and Middle Europe only scattered examples of beads, rings and pinheads are found. Finds are somewhat more numerous in the Etruscan graves of the fifth and fourth centuries. Little is found west of the Apennines. In the classical period the Greeks had very little use for amber.[49]

The city of Massilia (Marseille) was founded by the Greeks about 600 B. C. The merchants of Massilia received amber by way of the Rhone route from the North, and about 320 B. C. they financed the expedition of Pytheas to the North to explore the possibilities of the Phoenician ocean route.

Changes in fashion can have a tremendous influence on the channels of trade and upon the industrial success of certain localities. During the Roman Republican period amber was not a popular ornament in Rome, but the fashion changed towards the end of the first century of the present era. Amber then became very fashionable in Roman Imperial society. Its peculiar character of acquiring an electric charge and attracting bits of lint and straw may have caused people to attribute to it magical properties.[50] It was worn in districts where the water was bad (perhaps deficient in iodine) to ward off swellings of the throat.[51] The Romans preferred a transparent golden variety of amber, and it was the fashion in high society for women to dye their hair to match the color of the amber.[52] Its electrical properties also made it useful for spindles.

By this time the Romans had conducted their Germanic campaigns, had taken their fleets into the North Sea and even into the Baltic and had acquired considerable information about the geography and natural resources of that area. It was about this time also that the source of the amber was in the East Baltic instead of in the North Sea. Either the amber of the North Sea had become exhausted or the great storm-floods had had a deleterious effect. There was at this time an extensive trade between Rome and the North. The routes are well marked with Roman goods of various kinds: glassware, silverware, weapons, beads and coins. Besides amber the Romans obtained slaves, fur and cattle from the North. In Nero's time a Roman knight was sent to the source of amber by Julianus, the manager of the imperial gladiatorial contests. His task was to bring back quantities of this substance. The knight was most successful; he reached and explored the amber coast, and brought back so much amber that at the next games the nets that hung before the imperial boxes at the arena as protection against the wild beasts, were studded with pieces of amber. The costumes and weapons of the gladiators were also ornamented with the same substance. The knight brought back one piece weighing thirteen pounds.[53] There appear to have been two trade routes between Rome and the Baltic, one of which was the maritime route, and the other by way of Caruntum at the head of the Adriatic to the river March, thence to the Vistula.

With the main phase of the migration period the hey-day of the amber trade had passed. The spread of Roman coins among the Germanic peoples reduced the significance of amber as a medium of exchange. As the Germanic peoples came into closer contact with the products of Roman industry, they acquired greater confidence in the value of the Roman coins, both gold and silver. There was a considerable increase in trade relations. It was now much easier for Roman or Romanized Celtic merchants to do business with the Germanic tribes. There was also a greater cultural contact between the Romans and the *Germani,* either in the normal ways of peace, or as the result of raids and wars. Moreover, there was a large number of soldiers of Germanic origin serving in the Roman army, some of them in high positions, and many others had received their military training in the Roman service. In addition, from the fourth century on there were Germanic tribes occupying parts of the former Roman Empire, almost continually or even, as in the case of the Ostrogoths, being settled in the heart of the Empire itself. Under these circumstances it was natural that the Germanic territories should be flooded with Roman trade-goods and Roman influence.

From the fourth century on wine was an important article of commerce across the boundaries of both the Eastern and the Western Roman Empire. This was regarded as a special delicacy and was used in considerable quantity by the wealthier leaders, chieftains and kings. The wide distribution of Roman drinking glasses is evidence of this acquired taste. That only those Germanic peoples who had come into direct contact with the Romans were affected is contradicted by the large number of Roman coins which have been found in the Scandinavian North. According to Wilke, 6400 Roman coins had been discovered in the North up to 1906, dating from the first two centuries of the Roman Iron Age, most of them from Gotland, Öland and Scania, very few in Norway, about 600 in Denmark and in addition a considerable number in Silesia, Posen and West Germany.[54] This distribution points to three important trade routes: the Vistula, the Oder and the Elbe.

That the metal workers of the North, and especially the ironsmiths played a tremendously important role in the life and thoughts of the people and soon divorced themselves from the necessity of copying the important wares, is shown not only by the artifacts which have been excavated, but also by the emphasis placed upon the work and art of the smith in Germanic saga. One thinks at once of Wayland the Smith, and the smith who forged the celebrated sword of Siegfried. In both cases an aura of magical power seems to surround the art of the smith, a connection with the mysterious powers of the dwarfs and of the fire.

13. BURIAL CUSTOMS

In the early Bronze Age the practice of cremation gradually replaced the previous inhumation of Neolithic and earlier times in Northern Europe, as well as elsewhere. During the Middle and Later Bronze Age in the North cremation was practically universal. This practice was associated with various kinds of burial. Usually after the deceased had been burned on the funeral pyre the remains, with weapons and private possessions, were placed in an urn for burial. The practice arose of establishing burial grounds. In these burial grounds the urns were without the accompanying mound. In the pre-Roman Iron Age, however, there are cases where everything that the fire had not consumed had been deposited in a hollowed-out grave without an urn.

In the early Roman period while the practice of cremation was still in vogue, the rule was flat graves in which the remains were buried in urns. Mound graves with inhumation are reported by Tacitus.[55] But this passage of Tacitus can scarcely be taken to refer to the Germanic tribes as a whole; the archaeological evidence does not support that interpretation. The burning of the body on the funeral pyre appears to have been much more common in the Scandinavian North in the post-Christian Iron Age than further south, and cremation was also practiced longer.

In the North among the coast and island peoples the body was placed with all the owner's personal possessions on his boat which was then often set on fire. Examples of this are the descriptions of the boat-burial of Scyld Sceafing in the *Beowulf* and the funeral of Balder. Later when inhumation again became the prevailing practice the body was often placed in a boat over which a mound was erected, or in a boat-shaped grave.

Inhumation gradually became the prevailing practice again during the main phase of the Great Migrations. The graves are often arranged in long rows, which is why they have been called row-graves. These graves were not distinguished by mounds. Usually they were arranged on either side of a highway, a practice which had survived from Neolithic times. Wars were frequent, and battle losses were heavy. It would seem natural under these circumstances to dig the graves in rows. With the body was buried the warrior's sword, personal adornments and various other belongings, sometimes also the warrior's horse, and before the conversion to Christianity servants were sometimes slain and buried with the master to serve him in the next life. But this would only be done in special cases.

14. GERMANIC PHYSICAL CHARACTERISTICS

Tacitus appears to have had quite definite opinions about the physical appearance of the *Germani,* and some of the reasons which he gives for the support of his views are not particularly flattering to the climate and landscape of the country east of the Rhine. But, of course, Tacitus was a Roman and an inhabitant of the sunny Mediterranean. He says:

The Germans are, I am inclined to believe, an indigenous people, very little affected by admixture with other races through immigration or intercourse. For in old days emigrants travelled not by land but in ships, and owing to the limitless extent of the sea beyond our ken, and what I may call its inhospitality, Germany was seldom visited by ships from our clime. Besides, to say nothing of the dangers of the rough and unknown sea, who would leave Asia or Africa or Italy and sail for Germany, with its grim scenery and severe climate, ill to visit and ill to live in — unless of course it were his fatherland?[56]

Tacitus evidently thought it quite unlikely, and if he had lived long enough he would have found it perfectly reasonable that hundreds of thousands of *Germani* made every effort to leave this land *informen terris, asperam caelo, tristem cultu aspectuque* and establish themselves in the sunnier and more climatically hospitable South, much to their eventual disadvantage and ultimate extinction.

In respect to the physical appearance of the *Germani* there are two passages in Tacitus which are of interest. The first is in the *Agricola*: "The inhabitantts of Caledonia have red hair and large limbs; this betrays German origin."[57] As a matter of fact there is reason for believing that a settlement of Germanic people had taken place in some parts of the British Isles before the migration of the Anglo-Saxons. These large-limbed Caledonians could conceivably be descendants of the Neolithic Bronze Age Beaker people, but Tacitus could not be expected to know anything about that. They could of course, also have been Celts. In another passage Tacitus remarks:

> Personally I incline to the opinion of those who hold the peoples of Germany are not contaminated by intermarriage with other tribes, but have remained a race peculiar, pure-bred, and unique. This accounts for their physical type, which in spite of their numbers, is universally the same. They have fierce blue eyes, red hair, and large frames, only capable of sudden effort. They endure labor and service less patiently than we, and cannot support thirst and heat. But their climate and soil have accustomed them to cold and hunger.[58]

That all of the *Germani* whom Tacitus or his informants had seen appeared to have the same physical type is substantiated by modern investigations, if one disregards the extreme type-inventing of some of the experts. One can pardon Tacitus for the expression "fierce blue eyes." After all, the eyes of the

Germanic warriors probably did appear to some of the Roman soldiers as being fierce, all the more so because blue eyes were not a part of their everyday experience, especially when associated with tall stature. The expression "red hair" is to some extent at least a way of describing *rutilae comae* which we moderns so often call 'golden-haired blond.' These things appealed to the Romans as being something out of the ordinary run of experience. What Tacitus has to say about the Germanic incapacity for endurance, except of cold and hunger, can probably be better explained by his geographical and climatic preconceptions than by accurate observation. If the country was so inhospitable, as Tacitus has described, it would require more than a capacity for sudden effort to survive, especially among those who lived along the sea coast and were dependent on the sea for a living and for transportation. But we should not be too critical of Tacitus; he was not a trained anthropologist; he was writing an historical treatise on the *Germani* based on information at his disposal, and he did quite well, all things considered. But what about the remark of Tacitus that the Germanic people were unique *tantum sui similem gentem.*

The physical characteristics of the constituent parts of the Germanic people during the Bronze and earlier periods have already been described. There is an hiatus during the Middle and Younger Bronze Age periods, when cremation was the universal practice, and little more of a definite nature can be said about the physical nature of the *Germani* until inhumation again becomes general. Some deductions have been made from an examination of bones, or parts of bones, which the cremation fires had only partly consumed, but definite conclusions from evidence of this kind can scarcely be expected. However, as already stated, there is no archaeological evidence for any further immigration into the Scandinavian North after the incursion of the Corded Ware people of a nature to alter materially the physical characteristics of the people. If no further land settlement took place, and if the physical characteristics of the *Germani* in the early centuries of the present era were the same as they had been during the Early Bronze Age, we are justified in concluding that the later *Germani* were the direct descendants of the inhabitants of the North of earlier times.

Nielsen, the Danish anthropologist, has noted that the physical type in Denmark in the post-Christian Iron Age was quite different from that of Neolithic times.[59] How could this have happened, and how can such a statement be made to agree with the conclusions drawn above? The explanation is really quite simple: if the dominant type in Schleswig-Holstein, Peninsular and Island Denmark in Neolithic times in the days of the megalithic graves was the tall, sturdy and heavy-skulled Cro-Magnon, and if the dominant type among the people of the Central German Corded Ware culture was the Combe Capelle, it is quite clear that the intrusion of this latter type into Denmark and Schleswig-Holstein would materially alter the physical appearance of the people in favor of the more gracile type. This would also be true of the Danish Islands, but scarcely to the same extent, since the cultural evidence shows that the Corded Ware people did not penetrate the Islands in such numbers as the Peninsula. But even in Island Denmark the Cro-Magnon type receded somewhat into the background. The reason is that the population of Island Denmark in the later centuries of the post-Christian Iron Age and before the beginning of the Viking Age was to a very great extent changed. The Danes of this later period were not the people of the preceding centuries; they had emigrated and the sparsely populated districts had been settled by other tribes from Sweden. We get glimpses of this movement of peoples in the oral traditions preserved for us in the *Beowulf*. If the dominant form in Southern Sweden was the more gracile form and not the Cro-Magnon, this settlement of Island Denmark offers a very satisfactory explanation of the change in the physical appearance of the population as recorded by Nielsen. This is the type that is often called the "East German."

This Roman Age row-grave type was very common among the Germanic tribes who participated in the Great Migrations, because most of them came from areas where formerly the Corded Ware culture and the Combe Capelle type had made the greatest impression upon the North. It is for this reason that Tacitus could speak of a 'unique' type. But the Cro-Magnon type is also Germanic and is an important constituent of the Germanic people at the present time.

A skull from the Early Roman Iron Age of Mecklenburg may be taken as a typical example of the row-grave type. In spite of the fact that from a strictly craniological point of view there are certain Cro-Magnoid characters the "East German" type is dominant.[60] This dominance of the "East German" or the earlier Combe Capelle type tones down and ameliorates the somewhat rough modelling of the typical descendant of the Cro-Magnons. In the Mecklenburg graves of the third and fourth centuries of the present era the same type of skull is dominant, that is, the Combe Capelle-East German type with some Cro-Magnon characters in the background. The same is true for the skulls of the Merovingian graves and for the skulls of Southwest Germany.[61]

The evidence from the graves of the Roman Iron Age, and from the representations of Germanic warriors and others on the triumphal columns erected by the Romans in celebration of victories, the evidence of Tacitus and other Roman writers, is sufficient to come to a definite conclusion about the physical characteristics of the Germanic peoples in the Roman Iron Age.

15. RELIGION OF THE GERMANIC PEOPLE

A description of the religious ideas and practices of the Germanic peoples during the Iron Age is more difficult now than it was a few years ago. It was difficult enough formerly when distinctions had to be made between that which was native and that which was regarded as having its source in classical antiquity or in the Christian religion. These difficulties still exist, but in addition the new interpretation of cult-symbols has added another complication to an already complex problem.

A distinction should be drawn, as Schneider points out, between the religious belief of the Germanic people and their human relationships, customs and practices.[62] There is no necessary relationship between ethics, a code of moral conduct, and religious belief. Such connection is or was by no means universal, although many religious organizations have attempted to base the one upon the other. In this restricted sense religious belief deals with the individual's concept of some mysterious or extra-terrestrial power, his attitude towards death and survival, methods of burial, ancestor worship, methods of appeasing or indicating gratitude to these intangible powers.

Schneider has made a very fruitful suggestion for the consideration of the problem of Germanic religious belief.[63] He has compared it with a two-act drama, with a prologue and an epilogue. The prologue takes place during the Bronze Age and the pre-Roman Iron Age. The first act begins about 100 B. C. and continues for several centuries. Then there is a long pause; the curtain falls for half a millennium, and when it rises again we are in the Viking period for a few more centuries for the second act. The epilogue is still being played.

Schneider is of the opinion that the main traits of Germanic religious belief had already been established by the time of Tacitus, that is, that it had by that time reached its climax, *Hochform,* as he expresses it.[64] This does not mean that evidence from the Viking Age is to be entirely disregarded. A distinction, however, should be made between the religious belief of the Germanic people and the romantic extras which were added by the Scandinavian poets, a distinction which at times is very difficult to make.

The attitude towards the acceptability of the Icelandic poems as evidence of Germanic religious belief sways from one extreme to the other. Formerly, and possibly under the influence of Romanticism, the *Poetic* and the *Prose Edda* were regarded as wells of information about the religious ideas of the earlier centuries. Then came a reaction; a great deal of the contents of these works dealing with the gods and religious belief was explained as foreign matter which had been introduced into the Germanic North as the result of contact with the world of Christianity, mainly by way of Ireland, and also by contact with the ideas and myths of the antique world. This meant that it had very little value for determining the religious beliefs of the pre-Christian or early post-Christian Iron Age. The proper attitude towards this material is a middle way, avoiding extremes. It is no doubt true that the poets of the *Edda* and the author of the *Prose Edda* allowed their imaginations a considerable amount of liberty, and did a little embroidering. Yet on the other hand, it is quite clear that these poets did not invent Wodan and many of the beliefs associated with the Wodan worship. Religious beliefs and customs are very tenacious, and long after they are no longer felt as expressing the realities of belief, they continue to live as traditional forms, and are explained as symbols, or become part of the body of superstition. Often the gods of one age are the devils of the next.

There are other sources upon which considerable reliance can be placed. In many cases Roman soldiers of Germanic origin erected stone monuments upon which they wrote votive inscriptions to their gods. Some of the charms which have survived have given indications, such as the *Merseburg Charms.* Then too the chronicles written in Latin dealing with the oral traditions and migration sagas of the Germanic tribes contain valuable information. Caesar in his passing remarks, Tacitus and Pliny and other Roman writers make some mention of Germanic religions. In addition there are many indications of Germanic religious belief in the reports of the Christian

missionaries, in their condemnation of certain beliefs as superstitions, in the confessional formulas to which the newly converted were required to subscribe, the beliefs they were required to abjure. Information is also to be found in the
heroic ballads and epics which have survived in part or in
whole, especially such epics as the Anglo-Saxon *Beowulf*.

These are written sources and belong for the most part
to the post-Christian era. But in order to avoid the necessity
of interpreting the preceding centuries entirely in the light
of the following we require a guide to the prevailing belief
of the pre-Christian era from which time there is no written
evidence. Some such evidence is to be found in the symbols
imprinted on the pottery, engraved on the bronze artifacts,
scratched on the rocks. Schwantes[65] and others have supplied
valuable interpretations of the meaning of symbols handed down
from generation to generation by the makers of brooches,
pottery, girdles, ornaments and rock drawings throughout part
of the Neolithic, the whole of the Bronze and Iron Ages into
the Viking period, and in many cases even beyond into the
present.

A result of the assimilation of two quite different cultures in
the formation of the Germanic people was a mixture of two
radically different religious systems: sun worship or the worship
of the Sky God on the one hand, and on the other the more
earthly and more mysterious worship of Mother Earth, the
Magna Mater. The religion of the Sky God is to be found
in a more or less definite form among all Indo-European
speaking peoples, and is in these cases associated with the
patriarchal form of family organization. This religion of the
Sky God was introduced into Northern Europe by the Indo-
European bearers of the Corded Ware culture. The native
culture in the North of Europe was that of the Northern
Megalithic, a culture which, if not matriarchially organized,
certainly showed signs of its influence.

The mixture of these two radically different forms of religious belief can be traced in the use of religious symbols during the Bronze Age. It appears in certain manifestations of the Iron Age, and after being for many centuries to a very great extent overshadowed and forced into the background by the more dominating religion of the Sky God, comes decidedly into its own again in a renaissance during the Viking Age. This has not been sufficiently stressed in the discussions of the religious belief of the Germanic peoples. It is because of this double origin of Germanic religious belief that a slightly different interpretation is here given to some of the symbols than is customary. In other words, there are reasons for believing that we have symbols of what might be called the submerged religion, that of the Earth Mother.

Typical symbols of a religious nature are: a simple point with the radiating beams of the sun, the indication of the four directions of the compass, either with or without the sun circle, the sun-wheel, the sun chariot, the swastika, which is a development of the sun-wheel, the cross, the radiating sun in many forms, the vault of heaven, the tree of life, the symbol of the serpent, the spiral, the concentric circle, the double-headed axe, the cup-stones and the cup-indentations on the stone-axes which represent the sun symbol of the circle, the beautifully made pins and brooches with their sun-circles and sun-spirals, the spectacle brooches with their sun-circles, the sun-boat pictured on the razors, the horseshoe labyrinthine moon-disc forms, the processions, the accompanying musical instruments, the masked figures, the votive horses, the deer horns, the dependent votive axes, the sun symbols on the pottery, on girdles (symbol of mystic strength). (Fig. 16). All these and many more appear right through the Bronze Age, the Hallstatt period, the La Tène period, the post-Christian Iron Age, and continue on through the Viking Age.[66]

The evidence is overwhelming. The new element is the demonstration of the use of these symbols on the things used in everyday life. These symbols seemed to permeate the whole life of the people. This is after all not so very astonishing; many of the customs, practices and beliefs of the modern world are survivals of older customs and cults, and new symbols are being continually created as beliefs and ideologies change. These symbols also become a part of our daily life to such an extent that we unconsciously think in terms of them. The main difference is that some of these symbols now appear in a disguised form of the written language, and so we are not always aware of their significance, but in the earlier days this expression had to take a different form, and the religious symbols became intimately associated with the ornamental and decorative arts.

Such a symbol as that of the horseshoe and its labyrinthine forms may be regarded as a symbol of the moon, and the moon is associated with the worship of Mother Earth. We have here the symbol of the practices of the worship of the symbol of fertility in the dark and mysterious depths of the labyrinth. In that case it would not be an example of the part circle representing the whole (*pars pro toto*) as sometimes stated, but a complete unit in itself, and a survival of the religious symbolism of the megalithic matriarchially-inclined Moon-Earth worship of reproduction.

The ax is usually interpreted as a symbol of the Sky God, a symbol of the thunderbolt, but this may very well be a secondary attribution. The ax symbol, and especially the double ax may also be regarded as a phallic symbol, and therefore as a symbol of the reproductive forces of the consort of the Earth Mother, an ever-present feature of the *Magna Mater* worship. Later the symbol was transferred to the Sky God when the latter became confused with the divine-human dying and reviving consort of the Earth Mother.

In a similar way one can explain the symbolism of the girdles. In mythology these are always closely associated with the earth, and it is by virtue of these girdles that the wearer renews his strength by contact with the Earth Mother. That these girdles should be adorned with symbols of the Sky God should not be at all surprising, because one could expect some such development with the mixture and confusion of cultures and religious symbols. As a matter of fact there are survivals of the ancient mystery religions and the worship of the Sky God in the cult and ritual of Christianity.

The serpent and the tree of life have both been claimed as symbolic representations of the Sky God. May they not with more right be claimed as original symbols of the Earth Mother, and then later transferred to the Sky God? The serpent is regarded as a symbol of resurrection because of its periodic shedding of the skin and its apparent resurrection in a new form. But this idea of resurrection is closely associated with the idea of the dying and reviving god, the symbol of the annual death of nature in the autumn and its revival in full strength in the spring. This surely belongs to the *Magna Mater* cycle. And the tree of life also, the tree which grows out of the Mother Earth, and produces the fruit of life and of knowledge, as we can see in the story of Adam and Eve and the serpent.

This survival of the older religious symbolism of the Northern Megalithic culture can be also seen in the emphasis in the rock drawings on the symbols of fertility, the pictorial representation of the symbolic union of the Earth Mother with her consort, the corn king of the folklorists, and the annual human sacrifice to the goddess of fertility.

On the basis of certain lines leading into circles or horseshoe moons, Schwantes suggests that we have here pictorial representations of stone or wood cult circles of the same nature as those of Stonehenge and Avebury.[67] These stone temples in Western Europe are usually interpreted as sun temples in which sacrifices to the Sun God were made on certain specific occasions. There is considerable evidence to support that view, but if the interpretation of the horseshoe half-moon labyrinths as given above is correct, we have here again a confusion of the two traditions. Perhaps after all the old tradition that these stone circles in England were Druid temples was not so very far off the mark, not only in the sense that the Druids may have used the temples which they found already constructed and surviving from a former religious practice, but that they may actually have owed their origin to the religious practices of the Druids. This would, to be sure, involve the acceptance of Hubert's thesis that the people of the Zoned Beakers were the first Celtic-speaking people to enter the British Isles. These Beaker people then would have come into contact in England, (if not already on the continent), with a culture, basically Mediterranean in respect to origin, and with a preponderance of *Magna Mater* religious tendencies. In addition to the more open daylight rites of sun worship, they would also show some of the darker and more mysterious rites of the great Earth Mother.

It is also possible that there is a double significance in the small votive ships which are so common in the cult symbols of the Scandinavian North. They have been interpreted as sun symbols, as representing the ship in which the sun rides across the ocean. This may also be a secondary attribution. The representation of the ship is also a symbol of the passing of the dead across the river beyond which lies the home of the dead, or the Elysian fields. And is not this cult in origin intimately associated with the ancestor cult which is again closely connected with the worship of the Mother Earth? Further, this symbol may have signified originally the female organ of reproduction, just as the double-headed ax symbolizes the male. Then later there is a mixture and a transference. Perhaps the artisans or artists who made use of these symbols were still aware of their significance, even if the knowledge had become vague in the minds of the great mass of the people and had become merely a traditional survival of something which formerly had magic potency. However, they should not be neglected; like carrying a lucky coin or a rabbit's foot, just in case there might be something in the ancient belief.

The horse and the deer were sacred to the sun god. The chariot of the sun was drawn by horses; horses were sacrificed to the sun. Deer horns appear in large numbers on the rock drawings, undoubtedly with a cult significance. Cattle were sacred animals of the Great Mother, as one would expect them to be, seeing that the Great Mother is in origin an agricultural goddess; or rather, having been first the goddess of fertility, she was taken over by the agriculturists as a suitable divinity.

Tacitus gives us some details of the Nerthus worship of the *Ingvaeoni* of the North. This was a goddess of fertility; once a year, presumably at the spring festival, the goddess whose home was on an island, was drawn by cattle in a cult wagon, accompanied by self-scourging priests, to bless the land and make it fruitful. After the ceremony was over the goddess was cleansed in the sea; the slaves performing the ceremony were put to death, ostensibly to preserve the secrecy of the ritual, but actually a survival of the ritual death of the male consort, the corn king, the dying and reviving god. We have here a continuation of an age-old ritual, and this confirms the suspicion that some of these symbols belonged not originally to the sun but to the Great Mother.

We also hear in Tacitus of a people in the Scandinavian North, the *Swioni,* who have a queen instead of a king.[69] There is nothing strange about this if we regard it as a survival of an older matriarchal form of society, a form of society closely associated with the worship of the Great Mother. Perhaps this tribe, owing to isolation, was not affected to the same extent as others by the patriarchal and sun-worshipping customs of the intruding Indo-Europeans. This remark of Tacitus is usually dismissed as being either unintelligible or insignificant. It may be neither; it may be an important guide-post to the interpretation of the past of Germanic religious and social usage.

The sister's son and the uncle both belonging to a matriarchal system, play an important role in the society described in the *Beowulf,* and it is significant that this mention occurs in an archaizing poem of the Scandinavian North where the Nerthus cult of the *Ingvaeoni* had survived to the time of Tacitus. Tacitus was not merely reporting an idle rumor, but the survival of an ancient custom.

Germanic mythology is full of hints of the reality of past practices and beliefs from the Sleeping Beauty to the fantastic figures of the carnivals; from popular superstitions to surviving and little-understood cult practices. The woods were filled with spirits, the fountains and the streams also; the caves of the earth with strange dwarfs; and fire and the mists of the sea and the moors were peopled with phantasms. These "little people" owed their origin not to the bright light of the life-giving sun, but to the cult of the dead, the cult of ancestors, and to the peopling of the forces of nature with animistic models of the human kind. These were not invented in modern times; they are and were survivals; they are particularly common in the more out-of-the-way and devious lanes of Germanic ways of thought, which is the reason why so much was made of them by the more mystery-loving of the Romantic poets. They are survivals from the Iron Age, and survivals from the Bronze Age.

The Kivik stone may be interpreted in the light of the above remarks. (Fig. 17). In the top row on the right there are three male figures, two of whom appear to be making appropriate music with the Bronze Age musical instruments, the *Luren.* The other is holding up his hands in the attitude of adoration. A female figure stands before the horeshoe half-moon, the symbol of the labyrinth, which is also the symbol of the place of sacrifice to the mysterious underground divinity. Within the half-moon symbol stand two more figures, one certainly a male, the other probably a female, on each side of the symbol of the double ax. It seems clear that we have here a pictorial representation of the ritual marriage of the Earth Mother and her consort. In the second row there are masked figures on either side of a large vessel, obviously a container for the blood of the sacrifice. Below again are two groups of four in front of two symbols of the half-moon labyrinthine mystery of the underworld, the two groups about to enter the unknown, from which there is no return.

If this is regarded as phantasy and exaggeration, the sceptical should read the descriptions of the rites pertaining to the Cretan Minos, and the mysteries of many of the religions of the Near East, with their esoteric rituals, their sacrifices and orgiastic rites. These mystery religions of the Near East did not derive their peculiar rites from the worship of the sun, but from the worship of the Great Mother, which permeates all of them, in spite of an overcast of sun worship. This is the Dionysian element in the religion of the Greeks; it is also present in the Germanic and for the same reason. It appears in many of the religious beliefs of the Viking Age: Freya, for example, Freyr, her brother, but formerly the consort to be annually sacrificed, and in many of the attributes of Wodan and Thor that seem to be out of place as part of the worship of the sun.

There are other traits in the religious belief of the Viking Age which seem to have been survivals of the worship of the Great Mother. The world tree, Iggdrasil, which plays such an important role in the religious concepts of this period can quite easily have been a development of the concept of the tree of life, a partly poetic and partly philosophical development of the idea, no doubt, but nevertheless a renaissance of an idea from the submerged religion. Wodan's self-immolation on the cross in order to win the secrets of the universe shows a mixture of traits from both religious beliefs. The cross is a symbol of the sun, the sun-wheel originally, the wheel standing as a symbol of the sun-wagon of which it is a part. But the cross can also be regarded as a symbol of the tree of life. This and the immolation, suggests the *Magna Mater* cult.

Many disguises in which Wodan wanders around on the face of the earth and the parades of mummified figures are suggestive of the mystery religions. Thor too performs many deeds which have a much closer relationship with the Great Mother belief than with the worship of the sun; for example, his possession of the double ax, his close contact with the things of the earth, his wooing. Iduna with her strength-renewing apples, without which the gods would waste away, belongs to the fertility cult, as does the taking of an oath from all living things not to harm the peace-loving Balder. Frija, the Frigg of the *Edda,* still remembered in the name of the sixth day of the week, and whose very name originally meant 'love,' belonged to the same submerged cult, until her status was changed and she became the wife of the All-Father, the Sky God.

Late Northern tradition, that is, the tradition of the Eddic poems, speaks of a struggle between two groups of divinities: the *Vani* and the *Asi.* In this tradition the *Asi* were regarded as intruders from southeast, which has led to some rather futile speculation about their derivation from Asia, along with an Indo-European and Germanic Iron Age migration from somewhere in the depths of that little-known continental area. The *Vani* on the other hand were the native deities. Finally a compromise is arranged between the two struggling forces, and an assimilation takes place: the highest deities of the *Vani* join the *Asi.* This ancient tradition supports the interpretation given in the preceding paragraphs.

For the first act of the drama of the development of the Germanic religion there is a considerable amount of written evidence. Our first documentary contact with Germanic religious beliefs comes from the descriptions of Latin historians of the ritual of the *Cimbri* and *Teutones.* After a successful battle in the earlier stages of the conflict with the Romans, the victors are described as sacrificing the prisoners taken in the battle to the gods. They were led up to a large cauldron and there they were held over the edge and their throats were cut by the "priestesses" of the *Cimbri* and *Teutones,* who then made their prophecies from the swirling blood in the cauldron. Rather a gruesome proceeding, but there is no reason to doubt its authenticity. Such wholesale blood sacrifices seem to be rather a part of the sun worship than of the darker and more mysterious rites of the Mother Earth.

Caesar has a brief comment to make:

> They (the *Germani*) have no Druids to control religious observances, and are not much given to sacrifices. The only beings that they recognize as gods are things that they can see, and by which they are obviously assisted; the sun, the moon and fire; the others they have never even heard of.[70]

It seems to be quite correct that there was no organized priestly caste among the Germanic peoples, such as the Celts had in their Druids, but still there were certain individuals who on the proper occasions performed the ceremonies of sacrifice and consultation with the divinities. They were in some way associated with the interpretation of the will of the gods, even though they may not have belonged to any official organization which could be described in the same terms as the organization of the Druids. We have already seen that these "priests" were required to administer punishment to those who were regarded as having transgressed against the customs of the tribe, and consequently as having offended the gods. In the later Icelandic sagas we hear of priests who had certain definite duties to perform.

When Caesar says that the *Germani* were not much given to sacrifice, he was apparently thinking of the multitudinous sacrifices common to Roman practice of his day; not only the sacrifices which pertained to the Roman state religion, but also the many rites which flowed into Rome from the mystery

religions of the Eastern Mediterranean. By comparison the
Germani paid very little attention to sacrifices; but the blood-
sacrifices of the *Cimbri* and *Teutones* show that the practice
was far from being unknown, and in addition there are many
examples of offerings to the gods in the form of huge masses
of weapons and booty committed to the earth as thank-offering
to the gods for victory granted.

That the *Germani* in their religious observances recognized
only such objects as they could see was a rather inaccurate
way of stating the facts: they could see the sun, the moon
and fire, but the Germanic religion was much more complex
than that. Unfortunately Caesar does not specify just what
divinities were worshipped under these designations. The sun and
fire are closely associated with the worship of the Sky God,
but the moon belongs to the Earth Mother.

Tacitus is a little more explicit than Caesar:

> They worship Mercury more than any other of the gods.
> They do not think it wrong to propitiate him on certain days
> with human sacrifices. Hercules and Mars they appease with
> more venial sacrifices. A portion of the *Suebi* also sacrifice
> to Isis. The origin of this foreign rite is quite uncertain:
> but the symbol itself is made in the shape of a galley, which
> shows that the worship is imported.
>
> However, they consider that it ill accords with the majesty
> of heavenly beings to coop them within walls or depict
> them in any human shape. They consecrate groves and woods
> and give divine names to that mysterious abstraction which
> they see by the eye of awe alone.[71]

It is generally agreed that under the Roman name of Mercury
the Germanic Wodan is meant, that Mars is Tiu (Germanic
Tiwaz) and that Hercules is Donar or Thor. Not that there
were exact similarities, but when the Germanic prisoners of
war or Germanic soldiers in the Roman army were explaining
these matters they recognized a sufficient number of common
traits to identify the Germanic gods to the Romans in this

manner. Already by the time of Tacitus about the end of the first century, and in the area of more or less direct contact with the Romans, Wodan had displaced Tiu as the chief god, although this may not have been general among all the Germanic peoples at this time. Nevertheless it indicates a tendency which spread widely and which, by the Viking Age, had become the cornerstone of religious belief in the North. The mention of Isis does not necessarily mean that this is a foreign goddess or a foreign rite, as Tacitus thought; this would be any of the Germanic goddesses of fertility origin, identified with Isis because of obvious similarities, and particularly so perhaps because of the symbol of the ship, a fertility symbol. This symbol does not show that the rite had been imported, since it is found in Germanic territory in the Bronze Age. Generally speaking, it is correct that the Germanic people had no temples for their gods; that they utilized the woods and sacred groves; nor as a general rule did they make images of their gods until later times; but there are exceptions.

In another passage Tacitus refers to the earth-born god Tuisto, who had three sons after whom the tribes nearest the sea are called *Ingvaeoni,* those in the interior *Herminones,* and the rest *Istaevones.*[72]

This is actually an explanation of the origin of man, rather than of the origin of the gods, except that Tuisto is spoken of as earth-born, which indicates that Mother Earth religion played a very prominent role in the formation of the religious belief of the Germanic people. It is nothing unusual to attribute divine origin to the original founders of the tribes or of royal families. That is quite a common practice in the Anglo-Saxon tradition, where the ancestors of many of the kings are traced back to the gods of heathen days, and then under Christian influence to Noah. The real importance of the passage in respect to the religious belief of the times is the reference to the origin in the fertility religion.

The three chief deities of the Germanic peoples — Wodan,

Tiu, and Thor — during the early centuries of the present era were all war gods or had assumed this status by this time. The names of these three are still preserved in the names of the days of the week, designations which appear to have been given about the third century. It is not surprising that these deities were thought of as war gods, since those were times of almost constant strife, and man always makes his gods in his own image. It does not follow that they had always been war deities, or that many of their former characteristics did not still cling to them in the popular tradition.

The identification of Wodan with Mercury was made chiefly on the basis of a comparison of the habit of both deities wandering freely on the earth among the sons of men. This trait becomes very characteristic of Wodan in the later Eddic poetry. It indicates a connection with the earth-born fertility cult. Wodan is the leader of "the hosts of the dead," the spirits which haunt the night and the storm and who can be heard in the howling of the winds. This is quite clearly an indication of the early connection with the fertility cult. Whether the eagles and the wolves attributed to Wodan in Viking days were newly acquired or whether they were attributes from earlier days can not be definitely determined. They may even have had a totemistic origin. In any case they do not belong to Wodan as the sun-god; they are symbols of the destroyer, of the return to Mother Earth; the vultures and the wolves devour the slain on the field of battle. Such concepts naturally had a strong appeal to the warriors of the Viking Age.

On the other hand, the association of Wodan with the horse, which is so prominent in the Eddic poems, is an indication of a connection with the cult of the sun, since the sun chariot is always drawn by horses, and horses are the sacrificial animals of the sun-god.

That Wodan is the god of the dead can be referred back to the fertility religion, but the Wodan of the Germanic warrior of the Migration period and of the Vikings, the Wodan of the Valhalla, the Wodan who sends his messengers, the valkyries, the choosers of the slain, to the battlefields, that Wodan is the creation of a time of war. He is a warrior's god, and Valhalla is a warrior's paradise. There the chosen of Wodan engage in battle all day long on the plains, and at the close of day are all healed of their wounds or restored to life, are seated at the banquet table, where they can eat and drink until the next day, when they once more go joyfully out to battle. They are to be the helpers of Wodan in that last battle, the Armageddon of Germanic Viking belief; when in the twilight the gods shall perish and also the heavens and the earth, and for a time the enemies of the gods will prevail. Then too this Wodan (*id est furor*) is the symbolization of the fury of the warrior in the storm of conflict, in the intoxication of destroying and of destruction, the berseker fury of the Viking days. Wodan has supplanted Tiu, who is the Zeus of the Greeks and the Jupiter of the Romans, the father of the gods, the great ruler of the heavens. This transference and development had probably taken place by the beginning of the present era, since time must be allowed for such a belief to become part of the daily life of the warrior, as appears to have been the case by the time of Tacitus. This concept of Wodan would appear to have developed in the West along the Roman frontier and to have spread from there to the North.[73]

The ancient god Tiu maintained his original status in the area of the lower Rhine, where the *Semnoni* revered him as the highest of all the gods, and where he was worshipped in the sacred grove. This Tiu who is identified with the Roman Mars was not a war-god in the same sense that Wodan was. He was the one who determined the outcome of the battle; he was the god who administered justice; in his hands lay death or life; but he remained aloof from contact with the more sordid doings of his adherents. He retained the attributes of the former Indo-European Sky-God in many respects: he was the ruler of heaven, the All Father; he was remote; he was unknowable. Wodan had been humanized; one might almost say that Tiu was the real Tuisto, the god of double origin, the sun-god and the god of the fertility cult, the god of the unknown sky and the god of the mysterious earth, a much more spiritualized form than that of Wodan. This Tiu is worshipped in the sacred grove, which is a trait of the Mother Earth cult, and this sacred grove, as Tacitus relates, can only be entered in all humility and reverence. Tiu is the product of feeling; Wodan is the product of a life of action. It is this Tiu concept which continued to live so actively among the ancient Saxons when Charles the Great had such difficulty in converting them to Christianity. Eventually the sacred oaks were destroyed, and the Christian cross was erected in their stead. But no one knew at the time that the Christian cross was a surviving symbol of the ancient cults.

For some strange reason the number 'three' has had a peculiar fascination for the human mind. Man is not satisfied with one god; he has created three; three separate gods or three aspects of the same. The Germanic people were no exception; in addition to Wodan and Tiu, they had also Thor, the god of the thunder, the god who caused the lightning to flash across the sky, and who hurled the mighty and destructive thunderbolts. This was the Vulcan of the Romans, also identified with the Hercules of the Greeks. He shares some of the attributes of the Greek Zeus who is also regarded as the Thunderer. The sign of the god of the thunderbolt is the hammer or the double ax. This Thor, who was also referred to in the Eddic poems as Asathor, is part Vanic and part Asic, as the name shows.[74] But Thor is not only the thunderer; he is also the performer of feats of strength, as was Hercules. He was the knight errant who fought against the giants with his mighty club. His strength comes from his contact with the earth. He is also the favorite god of the agriculturist. He is by no means a spiritualized concept; in later Eddic poetry he was even the butt of practical jokes at the hands of the Earth Giant.

Where there are gods there are usually goddesses either in being or in process of being. We have a survival of the chief Germanic goddess in Freya. She belongs to the fertility religion. The root *fri,* Indo-European *pri* has given the modern word 'friend,' but it is also the root of "Priapus," and to that concept belonged Freya, Isis, Cybele, Venus or under whatever other name the same principle is worshipped, ancient or modern. Among the *Ingvaeoni* she was called Nerthus; to the Vikings she was Frigg. She may have been of the ancient Idisi, those women of magic and prophecy, who tied and unloosed the bonds, the possible ancestors of the valkyries of Viking days. In the Germanic theogony she became the wife of Wodan, and the two elements of the ancient religion of the *Magna Mater* are thus brought together again. Her brother Frey, now one of the gods associated with Wodan, was formerly the consort of the earth divinity, but he plays a relatively minor role in the later religion of the Germanic people.

There is another of the deities assembled around Wodan who should be mentioned. This is Balder. Balder belongs not only to the North of Viking days; he is mentioned in the *Merseburg Charms* as one of the gods, and that would not have been the case if Balder had been a stranger; one does not bring strange gods into the magic charms which are so strict as to form and meaning if they are to have the desired potency. Schneider accepts Balder without hesitancy as one of the gods of the fertility cult.[75] He is the god who must die, but who revives; he is the symbol of death and resurrection; his name means 'the Lord' as does the Babylonian Baal, the Adonai of the Semites, and the *kyrios* of Christianity.

There are still others: Ull or earlier *Wulthus,* the Norns, who may be related to the Celtic *matronae,* (one is reminded of the Mothers in Goethe's *Faust*), Nehalennia, Hludana, Garmangabis, Vercana and others. Some of them belong to the one cult, some to the other.

If the later traditions of the *Edda* are a safe guide to follow, these gods and goddesses are not thought of as being entirely remote from their human worshippers. They visit the earth frequently; forever wandering around bent on adventure, and Wodan is called the Wanderer. Often Wodan is in disguise, and he too has adventures, as a seeker of knowledge and as a friend of women. The gods and goddesses quarrel among themselves; they also have their affairs; they act much like the Greek deities of the Homeric epic. This description is, of course, from the Viking Age, and we do not know just how much of it was invented by the poets and how much was survival of early traits. In the main it is perhaps safe to assume that many of the traits are survivals, since man does not change his gods quite as quickly as he changes other ways of living. The poets, however, dressed up the ancient stories a little in order to make them more interesting.

No system of theology has a lasting appeal to men unless there is a contrast between the good and the evil, between the principle of creation and that of destruction, between the god and the demon. God and the Devil. Germanic religious belief was no exception to this. The later Eddic story makes a great deal of Loki and the Fenris wolf. Loki is a strange character; he seems to represent the principle of opposition to the gods, and yet he is at other times one of them, as in the *Poetic* and *Prose Edda* stories of the *Nibelungen* Hoard, almost as Mephistopheles is pictured in the prologue to Goethe's *Faust* or as Satan in the Book of *Job*. It is Loki who is responsible for the death of Balder. Loki at the end, on the day of the great final battle, in the *Götterdämmerung,* is in alliance with the great Earth Serpent, with the fierce Fenris wolf, with the giants of the trackless mountains, with the giants of the regions of frost and ice. The serpent and the wolf belong to the ancient fertility cult, the frost giants may well have been a later addition after the deterioration of the climate had sharpened up a possibly long-remembered tradition of the far-off days of cold and snow and ice. This tradition now becomes embodied in the haunting fear of the *'fimbul'* winter, the period of eternal cold, which will in the future return to destroy both man and gods. Then too there may have been in this idea of the *Götterdämmerung* a symbolization of the annual struggle between the warmth and the cold, light and darkness, the Good and the Evil. That would show a mixture of concepts from both of the cults which lie behind the Germanic religious beliefs.

It will perhaps always be impossible to give a positive opinion on matters of this kind, and interpretation must necessarily be to some extent of a somewhat subjective nature. Making all due allowances, however, for the window-dressing of the later poets, most of the important traits attributed to the gods and the demons are survivals of age-old beliefs which go back to the Bronze Age, even to the Neolithic. At the same time it can be readily admitted that there is a possibility of some outside influence; the duality of the religion of the Persians, the principle of Good and Evil, had a tremendous impact upon the belief of the people of Israel, and in this way it also permeated the late Hebrew belief and Christianity. No doubt this symbolism played a role in the development of the concept of the Germanic Loki, although it would be extremely hazardous indeed to claim Christianity as the source of the Loki character. The Christian prophecies of the end of the world may have influenced the Germanic concept of the end of all things, but again the concept was present before the foundation of the Christian religion; it is a symbolism of the never-ending principle of opposition and conflict between light and darkness, between death and life, winter and summer, good and evil. And as such it is inherent in both the worship of the Sky-God and the Earth Mother.

In its finished form the precise details of the concept of the world as the tree Iggdrasil belongs to the Viking Age. According to this concept the upper part of the tree extended into the dwelling-place of the gods, with the earth in the centre and the underworld beneath where the envious teeth of Nithhogr are constantly gnawing away the roots of the Tree of Life, and where the solid earth is surrounded by the long writhing form of the Earth Serpent (Fig. 18). The serpent symbol is old in Germanic art. Many of the brooches, for example, end in serpents' heads, as do also the boats. It is even possible that there is sufficient background in the twining serpent to account for the Germanic animal ornamentation of later times without having the Goths import it from the Scythians.

The thing which is new in the Germanic religion, in its later form at least, is its inherent pessimism. There is not only a Twilight for the Gods, there is a deep, dark impenetrable night. There are two obvious explanations. It might be said that we have here symbolized the constant fear in the minds of men that the strength of the sun would not be renewed, that the Everlasting Winter would sometime rule, that the darkness would conquer the light, and that the everlasting gods as well as the everlasting hills would one day cease to be. One can imagine that as a possible belief in a northern clime, where the division of the year into a period of light and a period of darkness was not so far from being realized, and must certainly have been known to those who had been to the more northerly areas. On the other hand, one could introduce an ethical explanation. One could say, with the poets of the *Nibelungen,* that the ring-symbol of honor, of integrity, of worth and value, came into the possession of the gods in the first instance as the result of treachery and deceit; of treachery against the mysterious forces of the underground as represented by the dwarfs, and that the curse upon the Hoard by the chief of the dwarfs must be expiated not only by the gods but by all those mortals who might come into possession of the Hoard. That was certainly true of all the mortal owners from Siegfried to the Burgundian kings. But the gods too were guilty; they built the mighty fortress of Valhalla as a protection against the day of expiation and the inevitable battle, and even cheated the giant who built the stronghold for them. And thus the whole foundation of the heavenly structure was built upon deceit, and if justice were to prevail, the gods themselves must perish. Perhaps the true explanation lies in a combination of the two alternatives; a combination which was not the result of conscious elaboration or metaphysical speculation.

We must remember that the people who put the final touches to the Germanic religious system were trained from youth to the expectation of war, to the idea of death in conflict, to the belief that death in battle was rather to be welcomed than feared, for was not the afterlife a warrior's paradise? Such conditions are favorable to the development of a fatalism, whether amongst Germanic peoples or amongst the followers of Mohammed, and fatalism can very easily end up in the acceptance of negation, in the belief of the final end of all things. People in a northern clime are more likely to be vaguely conscious of these ideas than people in the softer climate of the south. The North is a land of conflict and struggle. It is easy to believe in Fate, it is easy to believe in a *Naturdämmerung,* and it is not a very long step from that to a *Menschendämmerung* and a *Götterdämmerung.*

The principle of conflict was inherent in the religion of the Germanic people. This was the never-ceasing struggle between the *Vani* and the *Asi,* between the cult of the Earth Mother and that of the Sky-God. Even within the cult of the Earth Mother there was inherent the principle of death. This was, to be sure, followed by a resurrection, but the doubt was always there, otherwise the ceremonies, the sacrifices, ritualistic practices and orgiastic rites which were necessary to ensure the revival of nature in the springtime could all have been omitted.

It is in the second act of the long drama, in the Viking Age, that one can see the complete working out of the assimilation of the two cults, and in the epilogue the falling apart, the period of disintegration. During the period of struggle, the period of the migrations, the more warlike element of the combined cults came to the fore; the times required war gods and war heroes. Later the submerged elements of the Earth Mother cult came to the fore again and had a tendency to dominate.

There were among the Germanic peoples as among the Romans two forms of worship: the domestic or household worship and that of the community or public worship. The domestic worship was not necessarily restricted to the interior of the house, but might be performed in the open in connection with a certain sacred tree, a grove or a stream. The head of the family acted as the family "priest," not only in the performance of some religious ritual but also in the casting of lots or the interpretation of the *signa* to determine the course of action of the family.

To what extent statues or models, in wood or other material, of the household gods were made before the days of direct contact with the Roman Empire is still undecided. Tacitus tells us that the Germanic peoples made no use of *simulacra*, material representations of the gods, but then in another passage he describes the Nerthus procession with a statue of the goddess. This, of course, was a public ceremony, and Tacitus may have been referring only to private worship when he made the statement about the absence of *simulacra*. However, some rather crudely made figures, presumably of the deities, have been found, but it has proved quite impossible to identify them with any particular god or goddess. It is an open question whether the *gode* or priest of Iceland was a survival of an ancient custom, with the shrine and paraphernalia of worship, or whether it was developed in later times after contact with Roman usage, with possibly some indirect influence of Christianity.

It is also known from various sources that many of the Germanic tribes, the Saxons, for instance, regarded certain trees, usually the oak, as sacred, and as being the home of the god. In order to convince the heathen Saxons of the impotency of their gods the Christian missionaries, we are told, cut down the sacred oaks. These sacred trees, sometimes also wooden pillars, were either survivals of the Tree of Life, or phallic symbols respectively, and were consequently closely associated with the worship of the Great Mother. That is why we hear so often in the ancient records of prisoners of war being hanged on the trees of the sacred grove; they were a sacrifice to Wodan, who, it will be recalled, of his own free will, hung on the tree in order to penetrate the mysteries of the universe.

In connection with the religious practices of the *Semnoni* we are told that they worshipped in a sacred grove, that they entered this grove fettered and so appeared before the sacred and invisible presence. If by any chance they stumbled and fell they were required to make their exit from the grove crawling on hands and knees.

No doubt the practice varied from tribe to tribe, but generally speaking, Germanic religious belief did not favor corporeal representation of the tribal deities, at least during the period of the high form of the Wodan cult. This is also an indication that the Nerthus cult belonged to a different religious concept.

It is impossible to say definitely whether or not the figures on the rock carvings of the Bronze Age are intended to be representations of the gods. They appear to portray certain acts of worship or attitudes towards the deities. If they had been intended to indicate the gods themselves, they would probably have been drawn with some characteristic mark by which they could be identified.

It is difficult to decide just what was the precise attitude of the Germanic people towards their gods. Usually sacrifices and religious rites are either for the sake of appeasing an angry god or for the sake of obtaining some special favor either for personal or communal advantage. No doubt both of these principles played a certain role in the attitude of the Germanic people. Humility, in certain cases, undoubtedly was there, as witness the approach of the *Semnoni* to the dwelling place of the god in the sacred grove. Generally speaking, however, it seems to be correct to say that the Germanic spirit of independence and of defiance was so strong that too suppliant an attitude towards the deities is scarcely to be expected.

There were certain festivals in the public worship that were of particular importance in the lives of the Germanic people; these festivals were in the autumn, at New Year, in the spring and on Midsummer's Day. The festivals are quite clearly connected with the rites of fertility worship and with the cult of the sun. The winter festival, the *Jul* (our Yule) or New Year's festival was intended to induce the sun to regain its former strength and return to fructify Mother Earth.

The spring festival, our Easter season, corresponded with the signs of the renewal of nature; it was a justification of the preceding sacrifices, it was proof of the revival of the god, a proof of the reality of hope. The word 'Easter' is connected with the word for 'east,' and is a very ancient word in the Indo-European languages. The sun rises in the east, and out of the mysterious depths of the unknown beyond the horizon the sun has been resurrected to greater, increasing power daily as a blessing to plants, animals and man.

The autumn festival, on the other hand, would be a period of mourning, as in the ancient records of the "mourning for Tanaros." The god has apparently lost his virility, he is dying, and there is sorrow for his death, and sacrifices and offerings of the first fruits and of the first-born to bring about a return, a resurrection.

Probably the greatest festival of all was that held on Midsummer's Day to celebrate the sun's regaining full power and virility. This was the occasion for the coming together of the larger cult-communities, embracing many related tribes, when such festivals were held as those of the Nerthus cult or the religious celebrations in the sacred grove of the *Semnoni*. On these occasions a general peace would be declared, something like the "Truce of God" in the Middle Ages, or the "Peace of Frey" which we hear about in Viking times. The memory of this festival is still preserved in the lighting of the *Johannis* fires on the night of Midsummer's Day.

The Viking concept of Wodan will give some idea of the thoughts of the Germanic people in respect to their gods in a period of strife and turmoil. The concept of Wodan was of a mighty warrior, of an imposing figure who had acquired a knowledge of the intimate secrets of nature and of human fate, and who ruled over the universe much as the Germanic chieftain or Viking leader ruled over his people. This concept was the creation of the Germanic people. Many of the beliefs of this ancient Germanic religion, in both the Wodan wargod aspect and in the aspect of the religion of the *Magna Mater* were only superficially modified by the teachings of the Christian Church. Old beliefs and customs are hard to eradicate.

16. THE RUNIC SCRIPT

When Wulfilas, about the beginning of the last quarter of the fourth centrury, translated the Bible into the Gothic language he found it necessary to create an alphabet which could be used for this purpose. This he did by making use of the Greek alphabet and using some of the runic characters. What Wulfilas created was a literary alphabet, and this alphabet should not be confused with the runic.

The runic alphabet was only used for epigraphical purposes, that is, for inscriptions, whether on stone, wood or metal. These inscriptions were used to denote ownership, or to give the name of the rune engraver, for magical purposes and for grave inscriptions. The earliest runic alphabet consisted of twenty-four characters, each of which represented a distinct sound of Germanic. But at the same time each rune had a definite name of a much more meaningful nature than the names which we now give to the letters of our alphabet, names which, however, formerly did have a definite meaning in the Semitic language from which our alphabet was derived by way of the Greek and Latin. This is the reason why single runes, in some cases the whole alphabet, are found on some of the artifacts and on some of the monumental inscriptions — to give extra potency to the magic charm.

Reicher points out that symbolic signs occurring throughout Germanic times in both the Bronze and Iron Ages and which undoubtedly had a cult significance should not be interpreted as runes;[76] there is no reason to believe that they had any phonetic significance and without phonetic significance they cannot be regarded as alphabetic characters. This does not mean that some of the runic characters did not owe their origin to the cult symbols which were in common use. In such cases phonetic values were given to symbols which had been previously non-phonetic.

The Germanic runes are not Indo-European in origin. There is no evidence of their existence at such an early period as that before the Indo-European dispersal. They are of much later origin. Any attempt to derive the Germanic runic alphabet and the signs of the Old Irish Ogham script from a common Central European basis, apart from Latin, Etruscan or Greek influence, has proved unacceptable. That the runes must have had their origin after the sound shift had been completed is obvious. All the available evidence points to the fact that the runes came into use about A. D. 200, but their origin could have been somewhat earlier. If an alphabet of this nature had existed during the Bronze Age or during the early Iron Age there would almost certainly be some indication of it along with the wealth of other characters which were used as cult-symbols.[77]

The value of some of the symbols of the runic alphabet changed with the changing language or languages. This is why the earlier 24-letter alphabet does not hold good for the whole period of time in which the runes were in use, from about the beginning of the third century until well past the Viking period. A good example of the early runic alphabet of twenty-four characters can be found in the series on the Kylver Stone, Gotland, of about the beginning of the fourth century. Another series was found on a sword from the Thames river of about 700 and gives the characters of the alphabet used at that time in England. This alphabet had twenty-eight symbols, the extra four being required by changes which had taken place in certain Anglo-Saxon vowels. Here is the alphabet from the Kylver Stone:

ᚠᚢᚦᚨᚱᚲᚷᚹᚺᚾᛁᛃᛈ

f u th a r k g w h n i j p

ᛇᛉᛋᛏᛒᛖᛗᛚᛜᛞᛟ

e R s t b e m l ng d o

There was a later Scandinavian alphabet where the original twenty-four characters were reduced to sixteen, some of them having to do double duty, such as *T*, for example, which had to be read as either *T* or *D*, as circumstances required.

There were still other varieties of the runic alphabet which were developed in the North, such as the so-called pointed runes, where an alphabet of twenty-six characters was used, strongly under the influence of the Latin alphabet. In this alphabet *B* was distinguished from *P* by the use of the dot.

The twenty-four symbol runic alphabet was divided into three blocks of eight characters:

```
f u th a r k g w
h n i j p e R s
t b e m l ng d o
```

This division was no longer possible with the twenty-eight character Anglo-Saxon alphabet. The triple division, however, was preserved in the 16-character Scandinavian series, the division being:

```
f u th a r k
h n i a s
t b m l R
```

The Icelandic word used to denote this division was *aett*, which can mean either "family" or "eight" from an older form *ahti*. The three divisions of the later Scandinavian runic alphabet were named after Frey, Hagal and Tyr, which are the names of the first symbols of the three groups, Hagal and Tyr are the names of the ninth and seventeenth runes, and with a little imagination the first one also can be made to fit. The actual name of the first rune is *fehu* meaning 'cattle' originally, later wealth, possessions. But the original meaning 'cattle' can be associated with the fertility cult, the cow being a sacred animal, and Frey was also of the fertility cult.

The runic alphabet is referred to as the *futhark* after the first six letters, *th* being one sound not two. This is the modern designation, not the original Germanic. The symbols were referred to as 'runes' by the Germanic people, and since the original meaning of this word was 'mystery,' and was so used by Wulfilas[78] we have fairly certain evidence of the magic use of the alphabet in its early stages of development.

The runes were not "written" in the modern sense, but in the earlier meaning of this word, which meant actually to 'carve,' to 'engrave,' to 'cut in.' This word *writan* (Modern

German *reiszen*) is the word most commonly used, since as a rule the characters were actually cut into the stone, wood, horn or metal by a sharp instrument. However, another word *faihjan* which originally meant 'to paint' was also used, which would indicate that the runes were also sometimes painted, or that color was introduced into the inscribed lines after the runes had been cut. The color most commonly used was probably red, that is, either blood or the color of blood to make the runes more effective in their magical properties. This was the reason why the whole runic alphabet was regarded as being so much more effective than a few characters.

If the runes were to be used effectively for magic purposes, it was important that they be given names, and this was done. There are reasons for believing that this giving of names was not a matter of accident but was consciously done, presumably by some one individual. This is the opinion held by Arntz.[79] After all it is not at all unreasonable to assume that one individual was responsible for the creation of the runic, since we know that Wulfilas created a Gothic alphabet. Further, a close analysis of the runes shows that there is some principle of order and that it is not merely a matter of accidental and random arrangement. The assigned names are given in the order of the three groups. The names of the runes are given in the common reconstructed form of the Germanic, although actually the names of the runes come from later literary sources:

First Series
1. fehu — cattle, possessions, wealth (cf. English fee).
2. uruz — aurochs, perhaps also a symbol of vitality.
3. thurisaz — demon
4. ansuz — god (cf. anses, asi).
5. raito — ride, movement, presumably on horseback.
6. kenaz — torch
7. gefo — gift
8. winjo — joy, pleasure (cf. German *Wonne*)

Second series

9. hagla — hail
10. naudiz — need, distress
11. isaz — ice
12. jera — year
13. ihwaz — yew tree
14. therthro — dance (?)
15. algiz — sign of negation
16. sowel — sun (cf. Latin *sol*)

Third series

17. Tiwaz — Tiu, Tyr, god (cf. Tuesday).
18. erkana — birch, twig.
19. ehwaz — horse (cf. Latin *equus*)
20. mannaz — man
21. laguz — lake
22. Ingwaz — Ing, a god of fertility (cf. *Ingvaeoni*)
23. tagaz — day
24. othala — possession (cf. German *Odal*)

As Arntz has pointed out there are certain peculiarities of
the order and of the naming which in the past have not
been taken properly into consideration, and consequently there
appeared to be inexplicable confusion.[80] The series begins and
ends with words denoting possession: *fehu* and *othala*. The
wild undomesticated animal *uruz* follows the domesticated
fehu. After *thurisaz* (demon) comes the designation for god.
After *gefo* (gift) comes *winjo* (joy). After *hagla* (hail) comes
naudiz (distress). After *isaz* (ice) comes the word for year
jera. *Sowel* (sun) is followed by *Tiwaz* and this in turn by
erkana which could be the symbol for the resurrection of nature
in the spring. After *ehwaz* (horse) comes *mannaz*. Some of
the other correspondences are still not clear, but the above
show that the arrangement is not a purely random one.

If the individual characters were to be given names, they
would then serve a double purpose: as names of the characters

for purposes of identification, and as indications of their magic significance. It was necessary to seek for words which appeared to be more or less suitable and which began with the correct consonantal or vowel sound. It was not always easy to do this, and the subjective judgment of the inventor must have played an important role, as well perhaps as traditional meanings which had become attached to certain words in respect to their cult or magical significance.

The question naturally arises, which was the earliest: the order of the characters in the *futhark* or the names which were attached to them? The Egyptian hieroglyphs were originally pictures of actual objects, then came representations of concepts insofar as that is possible. This is the stage of the ideogram, and by that time many of the original pictures had been generalized and simplified. These ideograms were given names originally the names of material objects represented. It is this principle which we find in the Semitic alphabets which had progressed from the ideogram through the syllabic stage to that of the phonetic, that is, the assignment of a definite character to represent each definite sound. The characters in the Semitic languages had names assigned to them, as, for instance, the character *A,* which originally stood for the head of an ox, the letter *B,* which represented the crude drawing of a house. It was in this way that the Greek alphabet acquired the names of the characters of the alphabet. And this is the origin of most of the names which we give to the characters of the alphabet. It is not at all improbable that the creator of the Germanic runic alphabet was acquainted with the principle of naming characters, and simply followed suit. It is altogether likely that the designations were given after the alphabet was actually in existence.

Wimmer, a Danish philologian, published a treatise on the runes in 1874.[81] Wimmer derived the runes from a late Latin alphabet, from the capital letters of the third century. Wimmer, however, was not able to give a satisfactory explana-

tion of all of the twenty-four characters. Moreover, the earliest
use of the runes has been dated about 200, and this does not
agree with the derivation of the runes from a Latin alphabet
of a later time. Any explanation of the origin of the runes
must necessarily fit into the scheme of Germanic historical
development, and even if it were possible to make the two
dates agree by raising or lowering one or the other, it is not
likely that the knowledge of the runes would spread with
such rapidity in so short a time, since it is known that the
runic script was not restricted to any one or to any group of
tribes.

Otto v Friesen, a Swedish scholar, attempted to derive the
runes from the Greek cursive script of the third century, and
attributes the achievement to the Goths on the Black Sea.[82]
But again this explanation does violence to the date of the
earliest runes, and it is scarcely likely that a script used for
magic, monuments and for inscriptions would be derived from
a cursive script, which was mainly designed for business
purposes.

The third basic investigation of the origin of the runic
characters was made by Marstrander.[83] Marstrander claimed the
futhark was older than the Germanic kingdoms in the Southern
Russian area, and therefore could not have been the work of
the Goths. He finds the closest affinities in the Celto-Latin
alphabets of the Alpine area. These alphabets were based on
the North Etruscan and Latin systems, and Marstrander would
make the *Marcomanni* in the first century of the present era
responsible for the creation of the alphabet and its spread among
the other Germanic tribes. This certainly gives the requisite
time for the known distribution of the runes.

Derivation of the runes from a widespread Celtic alphabet
originating in the Alpine regions and spreading over Western
Europe and the British Isles, and making this alphabet the
common source of both the runic characters and the Irish
Ogham script was suggested by Magnus Hammarström.[84] This

explanation is based upon too many unknowns. It is supposition that such a Celtic alphabet existed, and to suggest a common origin for the runes and for the Ogham script seems to be entirely contrary to probability. The basic principle of the Ogham script is quite different from that of the runes, being based upon a system of horizontal, oblique and vertical lines for the consonants and dots for the vowels: As far as is known this Ogham script was used only for monumental inscriptions, and not for purposes of magic. Further, the order of the characters is entirely different from that of the runes.[85]

In the last centuries of the pre-Christian Iron Age there was quite an active trade between Italy and *Germania,* the Celtic, Rhaetian and other tribes acting as intermediaries. It was in this area that there were at that time a great many varieties of an Etruscan-Latin alphabet. This area had been settled earlier by the Etruscans, but in the last centuries of the pre-Christian era Latin influence had become quite pronounced. Arntz comes to the conclusion that a large number of the runic characters owe their origin to one of these North Italian alphabets.[86] The North Italian alphabets because of their origin in the Etruscan area are basically left-directional, that is, the arms of the upright staves point to the left, but insofar as alphabets were under the influence of the Latin they are right-directional. Further, these alphabets can at times be boustrostrophic, that is, written in the manner of ploughing, when one line is finished the writer begins another line from right to left immediately below it. It is a fact that some of the runic characters are sometimes written left-directional, some right-directional, and also the boustrostrophic method is occasionally employed. This could scarcely have happened if the creator of the runes had been influenced by the Greek or Latin inscriptions and scripts of the third century were right-directional, not left.

The order of the characters of the *futhark* appears at first glance to be quite different from that of the Latin alphabet.

If the characters of the *futhark* are examined, it will be seen that the symbols for *F* and *A* are very much alike, and that a confusion could easily arise in respect to the first character of the series. *I* and *J*, which are closely related, the one being a vowel and the other the consonantal equivalent, follow each other. The voiceless *S* is followed by the voiced Z (R), which would give the normal order of our alphabet r---s. We have then the four characters *P R S T* in the Latin order. In the second character *U* we have a sound which can easily be confused with the bi-labial lip-consonant, and that could easily have occurred here. With these three changes or transpositions F:A; S:Z(R); U: we now have the following arrangement:

a b c d — g (w) h — i j — p r—s—t—u. This is an order which can be shown to have occurred in the North Italic alphabets. That, as Arnzt points out, cannot be accidental.[87]

It seems clear that a North Italian alphabet formed the basis of the runic, but this does not account for all of the characters of the *futhark.* As the alphabet spread northwards, and as it was used at the beginning mainly for magic purposes, a certain amount of confusion arose on account of the addition of other characters and concepts, which were foreign to the North Italian dialects, and symbols for these sounds had to be changed to fit the new sound system, as happened in the Greek adoption of the alphabet from a Semitic language.

Some of the characters of the runic alphabet are of such a nature that they might occur anywhere as alphabetic or as cult signs, as, for example: 

Some of these do actually occur as cult or magic signs, such as the sign representing the head of an arrow or spear. This can be seen on many of the rock-carvings and paintings of Upper Palaeolithic times. This sign could very well have been used later for the *T* character. And similarly for other symbols of the runic alphabet which have corresponding forms in North Italic letters, the characters for *O, T, H, G, U,* but which also occurred as pre-*futhark* cult-symbols. The *T* symbol points quite naturally to a warlike concept, and it is this symbol which has the name of the war-god Tiu. Of course, the character already existed in the North Italian alphabets, but it was in this way that it acquired its special significance. The Z (*R*) rune in two forms Ψ ᛉ appears to represent the spread fingers of one or in the double form two hands; this is a sign of negation, and this meaning is explicit in the runic character. Similarly the *H* rune with one or more cross strokes had the meaning of destruction (hail); if written on a stone in a grave it meant that destruction was called down upon the desecrator of the grave. From these examples it can be seen that there was by the very nature of things a very close connection between the characters of the *futhark* and the cult, magical or symbolical meaning of some of these signs.[88]

The question as to which Germanic tribe first used the runes and was responsible for their spread to the other Germanic peoples has not yet found a satisfactory answer. To some extent the difficulty lies in the fact that the earliest runes were in all probability inscribed on wood, and have consequently not been preserved. It has therefore not proved possible to set up a distribution map which would indicate the place of origin. If the *futhark* arose in the North as a result of the amber trade with Italy or if some Germanic soldier who had served in the Roman army returned to his northern home with this new creation, it would be necessary to derive the runes directly from the Latin alphabet, and, as we have seen, this is not considered feasible. That the Goths were responsible for the creation of the runes does violence to the chronology. If the earliest runic inscriptions date from about 200, it does not give the Goths sufficient time to get properly settled in the southeast, acquire some knowledge of the culture of the Eastern Roman Empire, create an alphabet and cause it to spread over practically all the areas occupied by the Germanic people by the fourth century. Then too if the runic characters were a Gothic invention, one might wonder why Wulfilas found it undesirable to make use of them for his translation of the Bible instead of creating an entirely new alphabet. After all, even though the characters of the *futhark* were designed for inscribing it would not have been any more difficult for Wulfilas to have designed a cursive script for them than to have created a new alphabet on a Greek basis. If the Goths had invented the runes, one would suppose that the continued use of them would have been a popular act, and as such would offer a decided psychological advantage in the introduction of the teachings of the new religion. All the more so, since the Goths throughout all their history show every sign of being conservative and clinging to the traditional.

It is, of course, quite possible that the Goths were acquainted with the runes before they left their Baltic home for the Black Sea. This knowledge could easily have reached them as the result of a very lively amber trade between the Baltic and Northern Italy. Arntz suggests that the Kowel lance head on which a runic inscription was inscribed was lost on the way from the Baltic to the Black Sea.[89]

There exists some documentary evidence about the use and meaning of the runes and about their earliest appearance. Arntz maintains that the *signa* mentioned by Tacitus were actually inscribed characters or runes, and that the staves (*surculi*) are not essentially different from similar ones of bone and wood with runic characters inscribed upon them which have been found in various areas.[90] Each of the runes on the staves had a specific name, with a cult or magical significance, and the prophecy depended upon the meanings of the three staves chosen at random from a larger number, possibly all of the characters of the *futhark*. Certain combinations of runes would not be more difficult of interpretation than is the case with a pack of fortune-telling cards. If the use of the runes at this time was well known to the *Germani* and to Tacitus he would not have thought it necessary to be more specific about the nature of the *signa*.

It is also possible that the runes were in use in the time of Julius Caesar, which would take us back to the middle of the first century of the former era. Caesar relates that one of his officers, a Valerius Procillus, had been arrested by order of Ariovistus when he came with a message from Caesar. After the battle and during the flight of Ariovistus and his troops the question arose what disposition should be made of the prisoner. Three times the lots were cast, and three times the result was favorable to Procillus. The prisoner eventually rejoined Caesar.[91] Did the one who had cast the lots pick up staves upon which were inscribed runic characters whose symbolic meaning saved the life of Procillus? This is a perfectly reasonable interpretation if it is admitted that the *futhark* was known before the beginning of the present era.

The *Poetic Edda* also bears witness to the same kind of procedure in the casting of lots, when it relates that under the world ash sit the three Norns: *Urd, Verdandi* and *Skuld,* the Past, the Present and the Future who cut staves, cast lots and determined the fate of men. To be sure this was written centuries later, but practices of this kind remain unchanged generation after generation, even outlasting changes in religious belief. It would never occur to anyone to doubt that the staves cut by the Norns had runic characters inscribed upon them, if there had never been any argument about the meaning of the passage in Tacitus.

The number 24 must have had some kind of magical significance, as well as the number 8, since the *futhark* was divided into three groups of eight. Many of the runic inscriptions contain a definite number of characters, the number being as a rule a multiple of 8, and an inscription consisting of the twenty-four characters of the alphabet plus an additional sixteen would have a very powerful magical effect.

Literary references to the nature and use of the runes are of frequent occurrence in early Germanic literature and in the Eddic poems. In the Eddic *Havamal* Wodan is described as hanging nine nights upon the tree. There his only nourishment was the strengthening mead. He learned the secret meaning of the runes and their magic power. And thus he became omniscient.

Hrabanus Maurus in his *History of the Langobards* relates that the Danes are accustomed to inscribe their magic songs, incantations and prophecies, and that they are permeated with heathen practices.[92] In the *Edda* the magic of the runes is used for a great variety of purposes: to ward off sickness, to assure the affection of the loved one, to enquire into the future, to guard oneself against evil incantation, to ensure victory, to calm the waves of a stormy sea, to acquire eloquence and power of thought. Brunhild after being wakened from her long sleep by the youthful Siegfried teaches him the secret power of the runes and how to use them, "Thou must learn the victory runes" she says to him, "thou must carve the victory runes on the sword-hilt on the blade, and twice thou must name the T (Tyr) rune." The N rune (need, distress) was used by the Skaldic poet Egil when Queen Gunhild put poison into his drink. He carved the N rune in the drinking horn, which caused it to break into many pieces. The *th* rune, the rune of the demon, could cause insanity and the servant of Frey threatened Gerd, the daughter of a giant, with this rune if she were not more favorable to his master. Gudrun of the Eddic poem cut runes into the drinking horn when she gave Sigurd the potion of forgetfulness. The magician of the *Havamal* cut runes when he wished to commune with the dead. The Skald Egil used runes to restore an ailing girl to health. Gudrun used runes to send a message of warning to her brothers.

Names such as Sigrun, Gudrun, Albruna, give further evidence of the universality of the use of the runic characters.

Apart from the possibility of the use of the runes for the casting of lots, as described by Caesar and Tacitus, the oldest runic inscriptions have been found in Wolhynia, Upper Silesia, Mark Brandenburg, Gotland, Denmark and Norway. These are all inscriptions on spearheads, swords, shield buckles, clasps, brooches, combs, urns, all belonging to the third century. The Istaby stone from Sweden is an example of the use of the runes for monumental purposes. (Fig. 19).

Some of the inscriptions consist of single runes, such as the lance shafts of Nydam, and these undoubtedly had magic significance, the T rune being the sign of Tiu, the war-god, originally the Sky-God, the R rune, the sign of negation, here the expression of a wish that the spear will not injure its owner, and the runes $A\ U\ L$, actually *alu*, which was a magic formula of good luck, made all the stronger by a transposition of the characters. This particular formula is of very frequent occurrence, and in this particular case can be read as *aul* or backward *lua*, in either case with the same significance. Then too such words as 'linen' and 'leek' are common. Evidently both were regarded as having certain magic properties. In one case a whole series of the A rune followed by other characters and ending with the word *alu* has been found. The A quite clearly stands for *alu*, the whole group contains exactly 24 runes, only one of which is undecipherable:

a a a a a a a a R R R N N ? b m u t t t alu

This must have been a very powerful magic formula.

Sometimes some of the vowels were omitted, as in a clasp from Etelheim (Sweden) about 550 A. D.: *mk mrlawrta*, which means: *mik maerila worta*: (Maerila made me). Sometimes the runes indicate the owner, sometimes the maker of the inscription, sometimes both. In the case of the celebrated horn of Gallehus we have only the name of the inscriber of the runes, and the maker of the horn: *ek HlewagastiR holtijar horna tawido*: (I Louis of Holt made the horn.). This particular horn was later stolen and presumably melted down for the gold that it contained. Fortunately a copy had been made before this happened. Such an inscription as that on the Fonnas clasp from Norway in the sixth century seems to consist of a number of secret formulas, the meaning of which can no longer be deciphered. There is, however, no reason to believe that we have here a meaningless series of symbols:

jIskIR wkshu ijRspjsrbse ihsbidultl

It will be seen that in this magic formula we have twenty-four plus eight characters, which is one of the reasons why it cannot be regarded as a fortuitous association; there are other magic formulas of the same kind.

We can see then that the poet of the *Havamal* was not merely drawing upon his imagination when he wrote:

> Runes shalt thou find, and fateful signs,
> That the king of singers colored,
> And the mighty gods have made;
> Full strong the signs, full mighty the signs
> That the ruler of gods doth write.[93]

The description of the later use of the runes in the Scandinavian North is beyond the frame of our story, but it seems fitting as a conclusion to make mention of the much disputed Kensington Stone found in 1898 near the village of Kensington in the State of Minnesota by a Swedish farmer by the name of Olaf Ohman. The inscription in runic characters was found on a 200-pound stone and has been translated as follows:

> Eight Goths (Swedes) and 22 Norwegians on exploration journey from Vinland westward. We had camp by two skerries on day's journey north from this stone. We were and fish(ed) one day. After we came home (we) found ten (of our men) red with blood and dead. A. V. M. (Ave Virgo Maria) save (us) from evil. (We) have ten men

by the sea to look after our ships fourteen days' journey from this island. Year 1362.[94]

This was regarded with considerable scepticism after it was first reported, and was considered a forgery by the great majority of experts. Prof. Thalbitzer has recently declared that he is not so sure that the inscription is not genuine, since the forger would have had to be "a cunning and sophisticated scholar and something of a genius."[95] If genuine, we have the tragic story of a group of pre-Columbian explorers who appear to have sailed through Hudson's Bay, perhaps to a point near the modern Churchill, to have then penetrated inland south through Manitoba to the State of Minnesota, and there to have met disaster at the hands of hostile Indians, but not before leaving a record of their fate. It is indeed a stirring tale, and by no means beyond the bounds of possibility; many of the Vikings performed just as daring feats. It is to be hoped that the authenticity of the inscription will be definitely and finally established. If genuine, the story of the runes would begin somewhere in Northern Italy before the beginning of the present era and the runes would travel as far as the Middle West of North America before finally yielding priority to their more successful rival in the Latin alphabet.

17. GERMANIC LITERATURE

Tacitus says that the ancient songs of the Germanic peoples are their sole form of history and tradition, and these songs tell of the earth-born god Tuisto, his son Mannus and the three ancestors of the main groups of West Germanic tribes.[96] This meagre information is the only information that we have of a direct nature from the centuries immediately after the beginning of the present era. However, from the words of Tacitus it is possible to conclude that he was acquainted with two varieties of literary expression: songs about or in honor of the gods, and heroic ballads in praise of the reputed tribal ancestors.

It might then be suggested that it is quite useless to discuss a subject about which nothing is known. That nothing is known about ancient Germanic literature is not quite correct, in spite of the absence of early records. The patient searching, analysis, criticism and reconstruction of scholars of the 19th and 20th centuries have borne better results than might have been expected under the circumstances. And just as a great deal has been discovered by comparison and reconstruction about the nature of the Primitive Germanic language, in spite of a total absence of linguistic documents before the fourth century of the present era (with the exception of a few scattered runic inscriptions), and the Bible translation of Wulfilas, so similar methods have succeeded in bringing the few scattered bones of the ancient literature to life again. The skeleton is by no means complete, but its general nature is known, and what is not known can be reasonably conjectured.

Two forms of this ancient Germanic literature can be distinguished: that which was entirely of an oral nature and which was handed down by the singers and tellers of tales from one generation to the next; and the written literature of a somewhat later period which has preserved some of the ancient songs and stories, although undoubtedly in a somewhat altered form. At one point the two varieties coalesce when the oral tradition becomes a part of a literary composition, as quite evidently happened in the case of the *Beowulf* epic. But the popular literature still continues as long as tnere is any interest in the subject; it is changed according to the interest and demands of succeeding generations, and may or may not eventually be incorporated into the more permanent form of written literature.

"Germanic" literature is usually understood to include all the literature, oral and written, which can be regarded as having been common to the Germanic peoples in respect to form and nature of content, although it is not necessary that any early heroic ballad or story which can be reconstructed should have been the common property of all tribes. It is sufficient if the general tenor is such that it bears the stamp of these times, in the same way, for example, as certain literary work may bear the stamp of the Renaissance or of the Age of Rationalism.

The distinction between oral and written literature is quite simple. Oral literature is not in written form; is of a more popular nature, more down to earth, so to speak, than is the written variety. The oral variety tends consequently to be more general, and the written more individual and subjective, or at least more contemplative. It is the difference which is felt between a genuine folksong and a poem of individualistic expression, a difference which is felt but which cannot always be put into words. The distinction is perhaps best realized in the realm of music.

At the same time, however, even a folksong or any product of oral literature owes its origin in the final analysis to some particular individual. Works of art of all kinds and description are individual creations, bearing the stamp, of course, of the cultural and physical environment of their time, as experienced by the individual creator. If the creation belongs to the category of oral literature, it may, and usually does undergo considerable change as the generations pass, except insofar as it expresses some fact of permanent cultural or cult significance. This part usually survives, even after its meaning is no longer thoroughly understood.

Many of the tales and nursery rimes which are told to children and which only within recent times have been reduced to writing contain expressions which are quite obscure without some knowledge of the background. An example is the well-known nursery rime:

"Here we go gathering nuts in May"

May does not seem to be the proper month in which to go gathering nuts, at least not in the northern hemisphere, and that is where the song originated. However, the whole situation becomes clear when it is known that the word 'nuts' is a corruption in this instance of 'knots,' which was used originally to designate a bunch of flowers, and May is the proper month for gathering flowers.

In the same way many of the old ideas and cult formulas have survived in the later literature or in oral tradition which were only in much later times reduced to writing. A reconstruction can often be made of the original concept and in many cases also of the form, for form, if it once becomes traditional, is very persistent.

Very little of the ancient cult-hymns has been preserved in any of the later written works which described the activities of the early missionaries to the Germanic heathen. This is quite natural; the missionaries were anxious to eradicate all remembrance of the ancient cults, and where they could do so with success, they overlaid the heathen product with a Christian varnish. But there were fortunately others who, although Christian, were not working at it quite so eagerly or fanatically. Such were some of the Anglo-Saxon poets, especially the author of the *Beowulf,* and the authors of many of the poems of the *Edda* and some of the Scandinavian Scaldic poets. One might expect that of the *Edda,* for some of these poems were certainly pre-Christian in the North, but the Scaldic poets belong to the Christian era. Fortunately for our knowledge of earlier times, they were not very much concerned with the dogmas of the theologians and had retained a very lively interest in the ideas and cult-symbols of their heathen past. In the same way the author of the *Beowulf* makes use of the ancient stories and the ancient beliefs, and is manifestly full of enthusiasm for the glories of the past, but from time to time feels that he should not be so enthusiastic, and it is then that the Christian references and also the Christian condemnation appear; often it seems, as an afterthought.

In addition to these sources of information there are such works as those of Jordanes, Gregory of Tours, Paulus Diaconus,

Priscus, Saxo Grammaticus, and others. Their works were written in Latin and Greek, but they wrote what they considered to be histories of some of the Germanic peoples and described the earliest times in the popular recollection, in many cases basing their accounts on old heroic ballads which were known to them and to the Germanic peoples of those times. These ballads have not been preserved, or have been preserved only in scattered fragments or as background material in works of later origin. The *Nibelungenlied* is an example; this poem contains references to early Gothic history, although the subject of the epic is not Gothic but Burgundian and Hunnish. The Latin histories have all been carefully combed for information about early Germanic literature, as have also all the later epics and ballads. The final result is that it is possible to give some idea of the nature of the contents and the form of the early Germanic literature.

All the indications point to the use of a definite poetic form in ancient Germanic poetry, both in the structure of the verse and in the rime system which was employed. There is no necessary connection between these two, but they appear to have been part of the traditional equipment of the poet or *scop*, the 'creator' as he is called in Anglo-Saxon poetry.

The structure of the verse depends upon the alternation of stressed and unaccented syllables; syllables with a secondary accent also playing a role. This is quite natural in languages such as the Germanic, which have strong accents as a rule on the root syllable. This causes a tendency to slur unaccented syllables. Where there are many compound words, syllables with secondary accents will be frequent. An example of this in English would be the word 'handbook' (German *Handbuch*) which has both a primary and a secondary accent. With an unaccented syllable an example would be 'eastern time,' written in English as two words but which is to all intents and purposes a compound word. As such it has a main accent, an unstressed syllable and a secondary accent. The German *Eisenbahn* has the same structure. Although the practice of syllable counting and the regular alternation of stressed and unstressed syllables was introduced into the poetry of the various Germanic Languages as the result of contact with the Latin language and Latin literature, the rhythm of Germanic poetry has not changed.

There are many variations of this old Germanic line as it appears in the later ballads, poems and epics, variations which are designed to suit the tempo of the speech, the mood of the passage, the suggestion of the action, description or pathos. Since modern English has lost so many of its unaccented syllables it is difficult to render the old Anglo-Saxon Germanic line in modern verse, but Gummere in his translation of the *Beowulf* has perhaps made the most successful attempt. This basic line appears in all kinds of ancient Germanic poetry, whether cult-hymns, lyric poems, heroic ballads, charms, satiric verse or epic. This inherent metrical and rhythmic structure of Germanic poetry still plays a very important role in our reading of modern English and German verse, regardless of the number of syllables which the line may contain. A good example of this is the natural accentuation in the reading of such a strophe as the first of Heine's *Lorelei*:

Ich weisz nicht was soll es bedeuten,
Dasz ich so traurig bin;
Ein Märchen aus alten Zeiten,
Das kommt mir nicht aus dem Sinn.

It is because of this fundamental structure and of the persistence of the traditional, that it is often possible to find something that is age-old in literary works of much later times, such as, for example, old cult-formulas in the *Poetic Edda*.

The other outstanding characteristic of ancient Germanic poetry was the use of alliteration, that is, the riming of initial syllables instead of the end-rime of modern poetry. This line-scheme is also found in Latin, in Old Irish and in the poetry of many other peoples. The use made of alliteration in Germanic poetry is, however, much more systematic and regulated than in the poetry of any other language. It has become an organized system with much stricter rules than apply elsewhere. In Latin, as in the verses of Virgil, there is no intrinsic connection with the metrical structure of the line as in Germanic; alliteration for the Latin poets was an ornamentation, but for the Germanic poet it was an essential element in every verse, and could not be omitted. The rules regarding the use of alliteration were more strict in Old Irish verse, but still there were basic differences; Old Irish poetry was not structurally bound to any fixed order or position of the alliterating syllables.

It is possible that alliteration owes its origin to a tendency to repetition for purposes of memorization, especially in charms, cult-hymns, invocations and the like, where the exact order of the words is of supreme importance. Certain alliterative phrases have persisted in English such as "bag and baggage," "kith and kin," "man or mouse" and others. These are popular expressions, either of considerable antiquity, or constructed after the same principle as others of the same kind which are no longer in use. Expressions of this kind are of very frequent occurrence in some of the Eddic poems and in the Heroic literature. There is every reason to believe that they are survivals of earlier times and of earlier poetry.

The important basic principles of Germanic alliteration can be seen in certain typical lines from the later poetry:

Beowulf:

Hwaet! we *G*ardena in *g*eardagum...
*i*sig, *u*tfus *ae*thelinges sciff...

Hildebrantslied:

*H*iltibrant *g*imahalta *H*eribrantes sunu....
*g*arutum se iro *g*udhamun *g*urtum sih iro swert ana...
her was eo *f*olches at ente imo was eo *f*ehta to leop...

In the second half of the line there is what is called the main
stave which must be the first of the two stressed syllables of
the half-line, never the second. With the initial sound of
this stressed syllable at least one of the two stressed syllables
of the first half-line must alliterate, and both may. Any vowel
may alliterate with any other vowel, probably because originally
in Germanic there was a strong breath sound before a stressed
vowel, as often occurs in Greek, and as still occurs in the
case of all initial stressed vowels in Modern German.

Similar consonants alliterated with each other, but there was
a restriction in combinations with *s*; in the best Old Germanic
verse *st* alliterated only with *st, sp* with *sp* and *sk* with *sk*.
The *s* and the *k*, for example, were apparently so amalgamated
that the *sk* combination was not regarded as a satisfactory
rime with *st*. The later development of *sk* to the modern *sh*
would seem to support this explanation.

Leaving the last stressed syllable free of the alliterative scheme
made for the avoidance of monotony, although there are cases
where the scheme *A—B A—B* occurs. However, here the
basic principle is maintained, that at least one stressed syllable
of the second half-line alliterates with a stressed syllable of
the first half. The other is just an additional ornament, which
is not of very frequent occurrence.

It does not follow that the alliterative principle of Germanic
poetry is as old as the metrical structure, since there is no
necessary connection, and one could write poetry·in the metrical
structure of the Old Germanic without making use of alliteration. It is difficult to determine the age of the regulated use
of this poetic device in Germanic poetry. It is customary to
regard the inscription on the Horn of Gallehus as being written
in the alliterative form:

ek *h*lewagastir *h*oltijar *h*orna tawido

To be sure, if the name of the maker of the horn began with
h and he came from *H*olt and he was making a *h*orn, he hadn't

very much choice. But he could have written *tawido horna* and in that case it would not have conformed to the structural principle of alliteration. Then too, the line has the same rhythm as a typical line of the later literary period. There are other similar examples from the early runic inscriptions predating any literary manuscript which has survived. It seems probable that these can be accepted as evidence of the existence of the alliterative system at an early time.

It is unfortunate that Tacitus did not give us any samples of the *antiquissima carmina* with which he or his informants were acquainted. De Boor tries to show that the system of the casting of the lots by the use of runes on staves, as described by Tacitus, was based upon the principle of alliterating runes. He interprets the word *ter* to mean that the lot-caster picked up the three runes in a certain order, namely, the first rune and the runic symbol on this stave corresponding to the guiding stave of the second half-line of the Germanic verse. He then determined in order the interpretation of the next two runes.[97] The interpretation of at least one of these two runes would have to conform to the alliterative scheme as determined by the first rune. This would then be evidence of the existence of alliteration as a guiding principle at the time of Tacitus, or about the end of the first century. But there is a difficulty here. Each of the staves had a rune cut on it, if this is the correct interpretation of the *signa* of Tacitus. If the lot-caster had to interpret the last two runes picked up in alliterative terms of the first, he would very frequently have had to do considerable violence to the traditional cult or magical meaning of the other two runes. The explanation must be regarded as doubtful.

That there was originally a connection between the magical significance of the number three and its use in the alliterative structure of the Germanic long-line appears to be more and more probable as further studies are made of the role played in early culture by cult symbols and magic. The number three, as well as the number eight, had a potent magical significance in the arrangement of the runic characters, the 3 x 8 arrangement being essential to achieve the full force of the magic power. The number three is also important in cult ceremonies and Germanic religious belief. There seems to be very good reason for this in cult symbols, since we have here the numerical symbol for the two parents and the divine offspring, as in the case of the Isis-Osiris-Horus of the Egyptians. Under these circumstances this principle of three would impress itself upon the form of address to the deities, and in this way it would pass from a purely cult use to a more secular type of poetry.

We still make frequent use of the principle of the best out of three. It is easy to see how this numeral, which acquired its special meaning in the cult-trinity, could become a mnemonic device in the structure of the poetic line. The effect can still be seen in certain children's ditties such as "Ring around a rosy," or in the German ditty:

Ringel Ringel Reihe
Wir sind der Kinder dreie,
Sitzen unterm Holderbusch,
Machen alle husch husch husch.

Examples of the persistence of this principle of three are quite common in the later poetry of the *Edda,* as, for example, in Brunhild's greeting to the sun after being awakened from the long sleep by Sigurd:

Hail gods! Hail goddesses!
Hail to thee ever fruitful Earth!
Right counsel and rede give us renowned twain
And healing hands.

The principle of three has been preserved in the third line; this sounds like an ancient formula, with the three alliterating staves to aid the memory, and there are many other examples of the same kind. To be sure, this poem dates perhaps from the ninth century, but cult practices and stock expressions live on for many centuries even after the meaning has become obscured.

A similar example of the use of three in address to the deities can be found in an Anglo-Saxon charm:

Erke, Erke, Erke   Earth Mother!

where Erke obviously means 'earth,' and the triune call is important for the attainment of the full magical potency.

There is a surprising number of lines with the three riming staves in the *Beowulf* poem, but by this time it had become merely a principle of rime-structure to avoid the monotony of the normal two-stave riming line. The three-stave line was the original, but this was for very obvious reasons modified to the two-stave line, because after all it is not easy on the spur of the moment to think of the suitable word with the proper initial sound. It is much easier when the poet has only to think of two. Even then in many cases, and this is quite clear when one reads the epic poems, the *scop* had to draw upon his stock of conventional expressions in order to fill out the line with the proper rime-words. He must have had quite a large number of these at his command. Some of this poetry was obviously composed on the spot, as is described in the *Beowulf* when the *scòp* breaks into verse to extol the exploit of Beowulf after his slaying of the mother of Grendel. In order to do this the expert poet would make frequent use of conventional phrases:

From time to time, a thane of the king,
who had made many vaunts, and was mindful of verses,
stored with sagas and songs of old,
bound word to word in well-knit rime,
welded his lay ....

The principle of parallelism or repetition in a slightly different form is well known in Hebrew poetry and it is also characteristic of the poetry of the ancient Germanic peoples, although in Germanic poetry it is altogether likely that this principle of repetition was determined by the use of alliterating stock phrases. An example is the *Skynir* song from the *Edda*:

Angry is Wodan, *a*ngry the All-Father,
Not *f*riendly is Frey.[99]

or such a passage as in *Beowulf*:
So, from Thee,
Thou sovran of the shining-Danes,
Scyldings'-bulwark, a boon I seek, —
and Friend-of-the Folk, refuse it not,
O warrior's-shield, now I've wandered far,[100]

Scores of examples of the repetitive use of stock alliterative phrases can be found in the *Beowulf*. Examples of the similar use of stock phrases with cult significance, either with the three-stave riming scheme or the two, have been collected by de Boor in the section on Religious Poetry.[101] It is a convincing collection, and it is difficult to avoid the conclusion that there was a very intimate connection between the cult practice and the establishment of the alliterative rime scheme as the norm for both cult and secular poetry.

Völuspa is a poem of visionary nature, describing the origin and nature of all created things, man, gods and nature, their inner meaning, their final destruction and the arising of a new heaven and a new earth after the *Götterdämmerung*. The poem is both pessimistic and optimistic, but optimistic only in respect to the "Paradise to be." The poem is essentially pre-Christian, and consequently composed in Iceland before the year 1000 A. D., but how much earlier is largely a matter of speculation. The poet was also to some extent under the influence of Christian dogma, and from this arises the optimistic new Heaven and the new Earth after the fiery destruction of the existing creations, the same line of thought which occurs in the Old High German *Muspilli*. Even though late, however, the poem shows the influence of much earlier structure and phraseology, and the ideas contained in it are so rooted in tradition that they must go back in origin at least to the days of the creation of the "high form" of Germanic religious belief. A few quotations will indicate the nature of this kind of prophetic poetry. Here can be seen the principle of repetition, the occurrence of the ritual triune stave-rime, and the short concise phrases which indicate either a hoary antiquity or an imitation of such antiquity:

> The *s*un knew not the *s*ky above,
> The *m*oon no *m*ore with *m*ight did shine,
> The *s*tars knew not their *s*teadfast course.

> Ax-time, *s*word-time, *s*hields did burst,
> Wind-time, *w*olf-time ere the *w*orld dissolved.

> To the *j*ustice-seat went the *j*udges all,
> Council *h*eld the *h*oly gods.

> *M*uch I tell you, still *m*ore I know
> "Tis truth I *s*peak, *s*eek you still more?

The authors of these poems were evidently gifted with the power of imagination, and with the ability to re-create the past in the minds of the hearers. But they were strongly influenced in their choice of words and phrases by the traditions of the past which were still so real to them, even after the introduction of the new religion. In spite of all the external influences to which the poets of the *Edda*, the authors of the epics, and to a great extent also the Scaldic poets, were subjected, it can with reason be maintained that there is nevertheless a solid foundation of ancient Germanic myth, cult, form and concept.

It is impossible to read the *Mill Song* of the *Edda* and not realize that we have here something that is hundreds of years older than the time of its composition; that it contains traditional phrases and traditional usages of the long-vanished past. The two daughers of giants, Fenja and Menja, represent the Norns, here reduced to two, who weave the fate of men. But instead of weaving, they turn the handmill, which is actually a wishmill, since it grinds out the objects of one's desire. The ancient story has become confused with the story of the downfall of King Frodi. The two daughters of the giants have been captured by him and are required to grind out a never-ending supply of gold to satisfy the unquenchable appetite of Frodi. They grind and grind and eventually grind out the king's downfall as the result of a sudden attack of his enemies:

> We ground out might, we ground out luck,
> We ground out goods on the good-luck mill,
> A seat midst riches, rest on feathers,
> Blissful rest: the best we ground....

One would expect to find old formulas and expressions preserved in charms, since the potency of the charm depends to such a great extent upon the accuracy with which it is repeated and careful performance of the required gestures and mummery. Even in spite of the fact that after the introduction of Christianity many of these charms received a Christian dressing, the disguise is only superficial and one can still see the form of the original heathen charm behind the Christian version. Some of the Anglo-Saxon charms have been subjected in this manner to Christian influence, also some of the Old High German. Charm against a sudden pain in the sides:

> Feverfew and the red nettle which grows through the
> house and plantain, boil in butter —
> Loud were they, lo! when they rode over the hill,
> Resolute were they when they rode over the land.
> Fend thyself now, that thou mayest survive this violence!

Out, little spear, if herein thou be!
I stood under the targe, beneath a light shield,
Where the mighty women made ready their strength
And sent whizzing spears:
I will send them back another
Flying arrow in their faces.
Out, little spear, if herein it be!
The smith sat, forged his little knife,
Sore smitten with iron,
Out, little spear if herein thou be!
Six smiths sat, wrought war-spears.
Out, spear, not in, spear!
If herein be ought of iron,
Work of witch, it shall melt ....

Then follows the final direction: "Take then the knife; plunge it into the liquid."[102] There are certain passages in this charm which must be of considerable antiquity, such as the line: "Out little spear, if herein thou be," and "Six smiths sat, wrought war-spears." The assumption is that the pain is caused by the presence of a foreign body, a piece of a spear thrown by an enemy hand, and hence the plunging of the charmed knife into the prepared liquid.

A wen is an unpleasant disfigurement, and a charm which would act as a cure would naturally be quite popular. Here is one which has survived. There does not seem to be any Christian influence here:

Against Wens
Wen, wen, little wen,
Here thou shalt not build, nor have any abode,
But thou must pass forth to the hill hard by,
Where thou hast a brother in misery.
He shall lay a leaf at the head.
Under the foot of the wolf, under the wing of the eagle,
Under the claw of the eagle, ever mayest thou fade.
Shrivel as coal on the hearth,
Shrink as much in the wall,

And waste away as water in a bucket.
Become as small as a grain of linseed,
And far smaller also than a hand-worm's hip-bone,
And become even so small that thou become nought.[103]

After all that the wen should certainly shrivel away; it must
have been regarded as a powerful charm, and if the wen became
smaller than a worm's hip-bone, it must have been very effective
indeed. Many of these expressions are quite clearly traditional;
are an essential part of the charm, and were used, even
though the meaning was not always clear.

Anyone who is connected with the culture of bees and the
production of honey will recognize how important it is to
have a charm which will prevent the bees from swarming
to the wrong places. Here is such a charm:

> For a Swarm of Bees
>
> Take earth, cast it with thy right hand under thy
> right foot, and say:
> I put it under foot; I have found it.
> Lo, the earth can prevail against all creatures,
> And against injury, and against forgetfulness,
> And against the mighty tongue of man.
> Cast gravel over them when they swarm and say:
> Alright, victorious women, descend to earth!
> Never fly to the wood.
> Be as mindful of my profit
> As every man is of food and fatherland.[104]

The charm is more mindful of the 'profit' of the owner of
the swarm than of the continued good health of the bees.
Perhaps it was necessary to remind them that they were not
working for themselves. As right-handedness for some unknown
reason seems to be normal, it follows that it is more efficacious
to take the earth with the right hand and cast it under the
right foot. The charm has no effect if the directions are not
closely followed.

Most of the older people can remember charms of a similar nature which managed to survive at least until the beginning of the modern atomic age. There was one which would charm away warts; at least it was supposed to do so. If it was not effective one just had not done it correctly.

The following is a charm against the deterioration of the land, doubtless of very great age, and was clearly connected with the worship of the Great Mother, but has been overlaid with a Christian varnish:

> Land-remedy
> Erce, Erce, Erce, mother of earth,
> May the Almighty, the Lord everlasting, grant thee
> Fields growing and flourishing,
> Fruitful and reviving,
> Store of gleaming millet-harvests,
> And broad barley-crops,
> And white wheat-crops,
> And all the crops of the earth...
> Then say thrice, "*Crescite, in nomine patris, sitis benedicti, Amen,* and *Paternoster* thrice."[105]

Just as the Earth Mother is called upon three times, so it is necessary to repeat the blessing, the *Amen* and the *Paternoster* three times in order to achieve the desired effect. This is a very informative version of an ancient Mother Earth charm surviving into Christian times, slightly altered to conform to the requirements of the new belief.

One of the most important of all the Anglo-Saxon charms must have been that against nine infectious diseases; it was purely secular and has not been influenced by Christianity.

> Nine Herbs Charm

> Now these nine herbs avail against nine evil spirits,
> Against nine poisons and against nine infectious diseases,
> Against the red poison, against the running poison,
> Against the white poison, against the blue poison,

Against the yellow poison, against the green poison,
Against the brown poison, against the crimson poison,
Against snake-blister, against water-blister,
Against thorn-blister, against thistle-blister,
Against ice-blister, against poison-blister;
If any poison comes flying from the east or any comes
from the north,
Or any from the west upon the people.

That just about covers all the ailments of man, and the directions of the compass from which these ailments might come, except for some strange reason the south. The direction then continues:

Mugwort, plantain, which is open eastward, lamb's cress, cook's spur grass, mayweed, nettle, crab-apple, thyme and fennel, old soap; crush the herbs to dust, mix with the soap and with the apple's juice. Make a paste of water and ashes; take fennel, boil it in the paste and bathe with egg-mixture, either before or after he puts on the salve. Sing that charm on each of the herbs; thrice before he works them together, and on the apple likewise; and sing that same charm into the man's mouth and into both his ears and into the wound before he puts on the salve.[106]

Students of the ancient pharmacopoeia may be able to determine how effective the prepared salve would be; sometimes the ancients had discovered very efficient practical remedies, even though they may not have known the reason why they were effective. It is, however, quite clear that this particular salve would be useless unless the charm were recited at the proper time and in the proper way.

Two Old High German charms, the *Merseburger Zaubersprüche,* have survived which do not show any indication of Christian influence. In the one, which seems to be a charm to loose the bonds placed by the enemy on the captured, there is an invocation to the *Idisi.* They may represent the three Norns, the weavers of human fate, or they may be simply

the Wise Women. In any case they had power to bind
and to unbind, and are doubtless of considerable antiquity.
In the other charm, Wodan and Balder (Phuol) are riding to
the wood. Balder's horse sprains a fetlock, and Wodan cures
the injury after various others have tried and failed, by the
use of a set formula:

Merseburg Charm 1

Once sat the Idisi, sat here and there.
Some bound the bonds, some harried the foe,
Some mixed up the made-fast fetters:
Escape the binding bonds, escape the foe!

Merseburg Charm 2

To the wood rode Wodan and Balder.
Then sprained was the foot of the filly of Balder.
Then Sinthgund and Sunna her sister sang a charm;
Then sang Freya a charm, and Folla her sister;
Then sang Wodan a charm, as well he could:
Whether bone-sprain or blood-sprain,
Or limb-sprain also:
Bone to bone, blood to blood,
Limb to limb, as if limed together!

There is another very interesting Old High German charm,
also directed against the vagaries of the bees when swarming.
This charm has been influenced by Christian teaching, and
to modern readers sounds rather humorous, but was not
originally intended to be so:

O Christ, the bees are swarming!
Stay here, stay here, bee,
Away you must not, to the woods you must not.
You must not fly away, you must not escape!

Similar charms have been preserved in Icelandic but those
quoted from Anglo-Saxon and Old High German are representative of this kind of Germanic poetry.

There is another variety, the curse formula, which occurs in

some of the runic inscriptions placed in the graves to guard
against any sacrilegious tampering. Such a formula could also
be used against an enemy, as in the case of Sigrun's curse in
the *Helgi* song. Dag has broken an oath of reconciliation with
Helgi, a curse is uttered against the oath-breaker and the
ardent wish expressed that all those things which he may use
will fail him in the hour of need:

> May the *s*hip not *s*ail that *s*wims below thee,
> Though a *s*tiff *s*torm-wind in the *s*ails may blow.
> May the *s*teed not *s*tart that *s*tands below thee,
> Though the *f*oe may *f*ollow *f*ast on your heels.
> May the *s*word not *s*ever that is *s*wung by thee
> Unless it *h*ews from thee the *h*ead from thy trunk.

Very ancient curse-formulas are to be seen in this late rendition.
The poet has made use of the traditional forms with very
little change; parallelism and triple alliteration also reveal
the usages of a still-living past.

In the drinking-horn which the awakened valkyrie Brunhild
gives to the hero Sigurd there is a good-luck formula and a
drink which is:

> Mixed with *s*trength and *s*toutness of heart,
> Full of *w*isdom and *w*insome runes,
> Good magic songs and good-luck staves.

A great many opinions have been expressed about the nature
and the time of origin of the Anglo-Saxon poem *Widsith*,
the Far Traveller. It is possible to interpret the poem as being
the work of a single poet of, say, the eighth century, of a
poet with an excellent command of all the themes of ballad
and epic poetry of the past and also with a fair geographical
knowledge. Such a poet in imagination roams over the history
of the past, and makes brief mention of many themes and
many heroes. That is an explanation which from many points
of view is quite satisfactory. There is another explanation according to which the poem was built up in various stages, three

particularly, and in which each of three poets has added his quota to the whole; the final poet making an attempt to arrange the whole as an artistic unit. The poem is divided into three parts: a catalogue of princes, a catalogue of peoples and a catalogue of heroes. In each of the three catalogues is mentioned a vast amount of material and if there were heroic ballads and epics on such a great variety of subjects as here indicated only the merest fragments of the ancient Germanic poetry has been preserved. It gives some point to the words of the poet of the *Beowulf* when he speaks of the thane of the king,

Who had made many vaunts, and was mindful of verses, stored with sagas and songs of old...

The Far Traveller knows about Caesar, Ermanaric, the king of the East Goths, Attila the king of the Huns; he knows about the Burgundian kings and their heroic end, he knows the names of many peoples who played a part in ancient Germanic history, some a very fleeting part, and the names of many heroes, some of whom are known from other sources, and some of whom would be forgotten if this poem had not been preserved.

Ancient Germanic peoples must have often put into verse, in such form that they could easily be remembered, short expressions of wisdom and moral direction and wise sayings. This gnomic verse, as it is called, is to be found in Icelandic and Anglo-Saxon, and was undoubtedly present also in the Old High German language, but samples of it have unfortunately not been preserved. The following examples from the Icelandic *Havamal* will show the nature of the wisdom-poetry, and even though of later date, must in many cases reflect a much earlier period:

A better burden may no man bear
For wandering wide than wisdom;
It is better than wealth on unknown ways,
And in grief a refuge it gives.

Crooked and far is the road to a foe
Though his house on the highway be;
But wide and straight is the way to a friend
Though far away he fare.

Better a house, though a hut it be,
A man is master at home,
A pair of goats and a patched up roof
Are better far than begging.

To his friend a man a friend shall prove,
To him and the friend of his friend;
But never a man shall friendship make
With one of his foeman's friends.

A little sand has a little sea
And small are the minds of men;
Though all men are not equal in wisdom,
Yet half-wise only are all.

To question and answer must all be ready
Who wish to be known as wise;
Tell one thy thoughts, but beware of two, —
All know what is known to three.

Cattle die and kinsmen die,
And so one dies one's self;
But a noble name will never die,
If good renown one gets.[107]

Another variety of ancient Germanic poetry, the riddles, is
fairly well-represented in Anglo-Saxon manuscripts, and may
have been widespread in much earlier times. Their nature
is such that they are more likely to remain in oral form. Actually
we have in these examples situations which could be represented
as charades. Here are two typical riddles:

    The Swan
My robe is noiseless when I tread the earth,
Or tarry 'neath the banks, or stir the shallows;
But when these shining wings, this depth of air,

Bear me aloft above the bending shores
Where men abode, and far the welkin's strength
Over the multitudes conveys me, then
With rushing whir and clear melodious sound
My raiment sings. And like a wandering spirit
I float unweariedly o'er flood and field.

The Falcon
I'm bosom friend to one of noble blood,
The soldier's comrade, minion of my lord,
And courtier to the king. Sometimes on me
A fair-haired, stately woman lays her hand,
The queenliest daughter of a nobleman.
The bloom of the trees I wear upon my breast![108]

Even when allowance is made for the later date, changes
in customs and beliefs, modifications of form and accumulation
of new experiences, it is clear that the fragments or units
of Germanic poetry which have survived testify to the aptness
of description, the brief and telling metaphor (kenning), the
poetic style, the pungent saying, the romantic and often elegiac
imagination of the makers of the ancient Germanic poetry. The
following examples will make this much clearer than pages
of description could possibly do:

There harps rang out,
Clear song of the singer. He sang who knew
Tales of the early time of man,
how the Almighty made the earth,
Fairest fields enfolded by water,
set, triumphant, sun and moon
For a light to lighten the land-dwellers,
And braided bright the breast of earth
With limbs and leaves, made life for all
Of mortal beings that breathe and move.[109]

If ever the end of ills is fated,
Of cruel contest, if cure shall follow,
And the boiling care-waves cooler grow.[110]

>   He knew there waited
> Fight for the fiend in that festal hall,
> When the sheen of the sun they saw no more,
> And dusk of night sank darkling nigh,
> And shadowy shapes came striding on,
> Wan under welkin...[111]

> How the weary hart away from thence,
> baffled in battle and banned, his steps
> death-marked dragged to the devil's mere.
> Bloody the billows were boiling there,
> Turbid the tide of tumbling waves
> Horribly seething, with sword-blood hot...[112]

And the weary stag would allow itself to be torn to pieces by the threatening hounds rather than leap into the waters of this devil's mere in which the mother of Grendel lived.

By a single phrase the poet can call up in the mind of the hearer a picture of a time of violence and bloodshed:

>   Hengest still
> through the death-dyed winter dwelt with Finn[113]...

The following passage shares the harmonious use of sequent sounds which the translation has in no way exaggerated:

>   Untrod is their home;
> by wolf-cliffs haunt they and windy headlands,
> fenways fearful, where flows the stream
> from mountains gliding to gloom of the rocks,
> underground flood[114]...

And again in describing the same underground haunt of the monster:

> Thence the welter of waters washes up
> wan to welkin when winds bestir
> evil storms, and air grows dusk,
> and the heavens weep[115]...

The poet is describing the melting of Beowulf's sword when it came into contact with the hot blood of the dragon, leaving

the hero helpless and undefended until he sees the ancient heir-
loom-weapon on the wall of the cave, in which the smith
has incorporated all his power of magic:

> 'Twas a wondrous thing
> that all of it melted as ice is wont
> when frosty fetters the Father loosens,
> unwinds the wave-bonds wielding all
> seasons and times[116]....

But the poet can also be elegiac; the warrior's life was not
all grimness and the gore of battle; there was another side to
the picture which the poets at least could use, and this is just
as true of the Icelandic poets as of the Anglo-Saxon, even
though the tellers of the Icelandic stories often attempt to
disguise the realism of their tale by the exhibition of a grim
humor. This elegiac tendency appears to be common to all
Germanic poetry, ancient and modern. It is a product of the
mental and physical environment; it is an element of the
culture. The following passages are typical illustrations:

> The flower of thy might
> lasts now a while: but ere long it shall be
> that sickness or sword thy strength shall minish,
> or fang of fire, or flooding billow,
> or bite of blade, or brandished spear,
> or odious age; or the eye's clear beam
> wax dull or darken: Death even thee
> in haste shall o'erwhelm, thou hero of war![117]

And in the plaint and lament for the death of the great hero:

> No maiden fair
> shall wreathe her neck with noble ring,
> nay, sad in spirit and shorn of her gold,
> now shall pass o'er paths of exile
> now our lord all laughter has laid aside,
> all mirth and revel. Many a spear

morning-cold shall be clasped amain,
lifted aloft; nor shall lilt of harp
those warriors wake; but the wan-hued raven,
fain o'er the fallen, his feast shall praise
and boast to the eagle how bravely he ate
when he and the wolf were wasting the slain.[118]

Similar examples of pathos, elegiac mood and philosophical
reflexion can be found in snatches of lyric poetry which have
survived, as in the *Widsith*:

So, faring aye, are fated to wander
men of song through many lands,
to say their need and to speak their thanks,
or north or south, some one is found,
wise of word and willing of board,
to lift his praise in his liegemen's presence,
to honor his earlship, — till all is fled,
light, and life together, he gets him laud,
holds under heaven a haughty name.[119]

Perhaps the most moving passage in all the ancient Germanic literature is the description of the death of Nyal, his
wife and their little godchild in the burning house where the
aged couple had lived so long, and which they refused to quit
now that the weight of years was upon them and the thought
of leaving all that had been dear to them was more than they
could bear. Even though this was written probably in the
thirteenth century of our era, after the introduction of Christianity
in Iceland, nevertheless there is mirrored here the simplicity,
the genuineness of feeling and the accuracy of description
which from all that can be deduced from the odds and ends,
parts and wholes of ancient Germanic literature, survived
throughout the years and is here once more to be found in
the simple prose of the saga-teller of Iceland. It is a passage
which in its genuine pathos can be compared with the last

speech of Iphigenie to the king in Goethe's play of the same name. The story is relating the death of Nyal:

> Then Flosi went to the door and called to Nyal, and said he wanted to talk with him and Bergthora. Nyal came to the door and Flosi said: "I will give you, Nyal, permission to leave the house, for it is not proper that you should burn inside. "I will not go out," said Nyal, "for I am an old man and I am not able to avenge my sons, but I will not live in dishonor."
>
> Then Flosi said to Bergthora: "You come out, mistress, for I have no desire to burn you inside the house." Bergthora said: "I was given to Nyal when I was young and I promised him that we would share a common lot."
>
> "What shall we do now?" said Bergthora.
>
> "We will go to bed," said Nyal, "and lie down, long ago I would fain have gone to rest."
>
> Then Bergthora said to the boy Thord, Kari's son:
>
> "I will take you out; you shall not burn here."
>
> "You promised me, grandmother," said the boy, "that as long as I wanted to be with you we should never be parted. I would sooner die with you and Nyal than live after you are dead."
>
> Then she carried the boy to the bed, and Nyal spoke to his steward and said: "Notice now where we lay ourselves down, and in what position, for I do not intend to stir at all, no matter how it smokes or burns, and so you will be able to know where to look for our bones."
>
> The steward said he would do as he was told.
>
> An ox had been slaughtered, and the hide was lying there on their bed, and they placed the boy between them. They made the sign of the cross over themselves and the boy, gave their souls into the keeping of God, and that was the last word they were heard to say.[120]

During the centuries of the great phase of the migrations there must have been a very large number of heroic songs extant, but unfortunately very few of them have survived in anything like their original form, and in some cases all we can do is deduce their existence from indications in later writings, both in Latin Chronicles and in such literary epics as the *Beowulf*. The biographer of Charles the Great is authority for the statement that Charles ordered a collection of the old heroic songs to be made. But his son Ludwig or Louis was a man of a different kind. For fear that these heathen heroic songs would take the minds of men away from the contemplation of the Christian virtues, he is said to have had the collection destroyed. If true, and it probably is, this was indeed a tragedy. It is also a tragedy that there was at that time no poet such as the poet of the Anglo-Saxon *Beowulf* who could make use of the old Frankish legends and heroic songs so that they might at least have been preserved in this secondary form.

Just what is meant by the term 'heroic song'? As far as Germanic poetry is concerned the heroic songs belong to the Heroic Age, and the Heroic Age is commonly understood to be that main phase of the Great Migrations which had its prologue in the wars of the *Cimbri* and *Teutones* and the attempt of Ariovistus to found a Germanic kingdom in ancient Gaul. The main action begins with the destruction of the Gothic Empire of Ermanaric in Southern Russia by the Huns and ends with the foundation of the Carolingian supremacy in Western Europe.

During this phase of the Great Migrations the conditions existed which favored the production of heroic poetry, just as Greece also had its Heroic Age and its heroic songs in the poetry of the Heroic cycle. Under conditions of almost constant tribal wars, movements of peoples, long and dangerous migrations, wars against each other and against the forces of the Roman Empire both in the East and the West, there arose strong personalities, leaders of men, chieftains who attracted to themselves others who were desirous of fame and fortune. These were the "Warders of the Hoard," the "battle-famed" of whom the poet of the *Beowulf* speaks; these were the famous leaders about whom the hall-thanes gathered, to whom they swore allegiance even unto death. These were the mighty warriors celebrated in the heroic songs and of whom we hear in those later epics which arose on the foundation of the heroic songs. They lived in common with their followers, the members of the *comitatus* in the great royal halls, about which we hear in the *Beowulf* and the *Nibelungenlied.*

In these halls the great banquets were held; there the *scóps,* those who had stores of songs and sagas of old, those who could create new songs, stirred the imagination of the hall-thanes to the highest pitch by their relation of the deeds of old and by their songs in praise of the still living and especially of the noble chieftain who sat in the seat of honor at the banquet and who led his thanes in the thick of battle.

To be sure, the *scop* counted on a liberal reward, as did all the members of the chieftain's following. They had no other means of subsistence; they were the chieftain's private standing army, his "Knights of the Round Table" of later days. In all the museums showing artifacts of Germanic antiquity in the Iron Age are to be seen spiral arm-rings and similar fabrications of gold which, we are told in the *Beowulf* and in the *Hildebrandslied* as well as in the later Eddic poems, were used as a kind of money with which the followers could be rewarded. Then too there were costly gifts of swords and horses such as Beowulf received from Hrothgar after he had cleansed the kingdom of the devastating monsters. But in addition to the hope of reward there was the desire for fame, the desire to be remembered after death as having been a mighty man of valor, as one who had attained honor and respect among the peoples, as one who had lived nobly and had died a noble death.

Such were the conditions which produced the Heroic Age. Such were the conditions which produced the heroes of the Heroic Age. Such were the heroes who were subjects of the heroic songs. It was an aristocratic society that was described in this poetry, not the society of a peaceful agricultural age. No doubt the vast majority of the people still continued to live in the old-fashioned way when not on the move in search for land, but of the vast majority of the people we hear very little. As far as poetry of the time was concerned they were the submerged mass, the "forgotten men," just as the great mass of the population was in the days of the Knights of the Round Table.

This institution of the *comitatus* meant a breaching of the old tribal traditions of the inviolability of the blood or tribal bonds. The *comitatus* of the chieftain could be formed of men from many tribes, and it quite often happened that a member of a chosen leader's group might have to war against men of his own kith and kin. The oath of fidelity to the leader superseded all other obligations. Thus arose such tragic circumstances as we find described in Matthew Arnold's *Sohrab and Rustum* and in the *Hildebrandslied* when father and son are arrayed on opposing sides. In this way there arose an inner conflict in the minds of those who were forced by circumstances to play such unnatural roles.

There were also other changes in motivation brought about by the unsettled conditions of the Migration Age, as in the case of Kriemhild. This "inner conflict" is claimed by many as an indication of a weakening of the old heroic spirit, as the herald of the beginning of a new age, a period of sentimentality produced to some extent by the humanitarianism of Christianity. But after all there may not have been much of a change in the minds of the actors; the poets required new motivations, they could not always make use of the old traditional forms. Their success often depended upon novelty.

We have no reason to believe that "emotional conflict" is something so entirely new either among the Germanic or other peoples. The heroes of the Greek Homeric epic lamented loudly, exhibited their "ego" in public scenes, wept bitter tears and not always metaphorically "tore their hair." But they were not regarded as any the less heroic for all that, either by their contemporaries or by their modern admirers. Did not even the mighty Roland weep on the battlefield of Ronscevalles? If it is not to be regarded as a weakening of the old heroic spirit in the case of Roland and the Homeric heroes, why should the charge be levelled against some of the characters of Germanic story who do not always act with the grim stoicism of some of the characters in the Icelandic saga or the fanatical fatalism of a Brunhild?

Kriemhild avenging her husband is just as heroic as the earlier Gudrun avenging the death of her brothers. The later Kriemhild and the earlier Brunhild, the Kriemhild of the South and the Brunhild of the North, are in many ways in the same category, and are actuated by the principles of the same heroic code.

There is an inner conflict within every thinking individual and within every people not stultified by the weight of an unchanging tradition. The modern age is inclined to believe that it alone has suffered from inner conflicts, subconscious urges, psychoses and neuroses. The truth is that the earliest ancestor of man underwent all these miseries, otherwise he would have remained an ape! The fashion of exhibiting misery changes from time to time, and one age may be more given to outward manifestation than another, but there is little basic change. There is romanticism and realism, subjectivity and objectivity, impressionism, expressionism and all the other 'isms' in every period of literature and art since the earliest days. The emphasis changes from time to time, in line with changing fashions, and so we call it a Romantic period or a Realistic, and think that by putting a label on it we have given a satisfactory explanation of the cultural environment.

In the report of Priscus on his visits to the court of Attila we are told of poets who sing the praises of the great chieftain while he is still living and in his presence at the banquet table in the great hall. This may have been a custom among

the peoples of Central Asia from where the Huns came, but
it is much more likely that we have here an imitation of a
Gothic custom, for Gothic influence must have played an important role at the court of Attila. Such songs of praise of
a living chieftain are not regarded by some as coming under
the category of heroic songs, which is quite true if these songs
are purely adulatory. We hear, however, similar songs of
praise of Beowulf after his victory over the monsters, and in
this case the *scop* combines his praise of the hero with a
reference to the deeds of Sigmund and his slaying of the
dragon and winning of the hoard. There is no essential difference
between that and a heroic song. It is not necessary to wait
until after the hero's death to compose a heroic song in his
honor.

Cassiodorus-Jordanes must have been acquainted with many
heroic songs and tales about the movements and leaders of the
Goths when they first moved from their Scandinavian home to
settle at the mouth of the Vistula. It is only in this way
that Jordanes, or rather Cassiodorus, from whom he had his
material, could have known that the ancestors of the Goths
came across the Baltic under the leadership of three kings and
in three ships (fleets or expeditions). It is only in this way
that in the sixth century the deeds of Ermanaric who founded
such an extensive Gothic Empire in Eastern Europe could have
been kept alive in the memory of the Gothic people, and it is
only in this way that the story of the deeds of Ermanaric could
have travelled to the Scandinavian North and become a favorite
subject of the poets of the *Edda*. Of course, confusion arose
in respect to many of the historical details. Ermanaric's empire
became in tradition and in song much greater and much more
solidly founded than it could possibly have been in reality.

There are two versions of Ermanaric's death: according to
one, Ermanaric died on his own sword rather than fall into
the hands of the Huns; according to another he died at
the hands of the brothers of Sunhilda, his wife, whom he had

accused of infidelity, and put to death in a most barbarous manner. Which of the two traditions is the true one is impossible to decide at this late date, and it makes little difference. In spite of what has been said for and against, both of them can easily be reconciled with the traditions of the Heroic Age. Many generations later some of the glory associated with Ermanaric must have been transferred to a later Ostrogothic hero, the celebrated Theodoric, who in the *Nibelungenlied* tradition is placed at the court of Attila, something which could not possibly have happened, for Attila was dead and the Hunnish Empire a thing of the past before Theodoric was ever born. But there is a kernel of historical truth in the story and in the songs which celebrated the deeds of Attila, Ermanaric and Theodoric. In the discussion of the historical drama this is sometimes called 'poetic truth.'

The oldest of the heroic songs of the days of the Great Migrations appear to have been of Gothic provenance, and from Southeast Europe they travelled back to the Baltic, and from there to the peoples of the North. Until 400, communications between the Southeast and the Baltic were kept open and many must have passed back and forth, some returning to the homeland, some as traders, some as wandering singers. After the beginning of the fifth century the knowledge of Gothic traditions and Gothic heroic songs was carried to the West by Alaric and his men and by Theodoric and the Ostrogoths. This Gothic heroic material became an intertribal property; it became international, in modern terminology. That is why we hear so much about Gothic heroes in the poetry of the North, and why the Anglo-Saxon poet of the *Widsith* has such an extensive knowledge of the ancient Gothic heroes.

It is very likely that at this time the common Germanic, with some minor changes, was widely understood. It was not until the disruptions of the fifth and following centuries that the various dialects became almost completely mutually unintelligible. A similar situation existed later in the Viking

Age; the Old Norse language was widely understood not only in the countries of the North but also in the Scandinavian settlements of the British Isles. The differentiation began later. But even in those days there were those who spoke more than one language. There were also those who had a command of Greek and Latin as well as of Germanic; Wulfilas was such a one; Cassiodorus and Jordanes were others. It will be recalled that Stilicho was a Vandal, but as a Roman general he must have been able to speak Latin, and as commander of an army in which were many Germanic auxiliaries he must have also been fairly proficient in the various Germanic dialects. And there were many others.

For the most part the direction in which the legends, tales and songs travelled was from south to north. The *Hildebrandslied* was, for example, originally composed in a Bavarian dialect, but in the form in which it has come down to us it is a mixture of the original Bavarian and Saxon forms. Evidently the transcriber was a North German and he used many of the local forms of expression. The same was true of the vast amount of legendary material which accumulated around the name of Theodoric, Dietrich von Bern, in the later epics. This also travelled to the North, is found in the *Poetic Edda* and later a whole saga, *Thidrekssaga,* is devoted to his historical and legendary deeds, mostly legendary. Tales and personalities gathered around the name of Theodoric much in the same way as later around the personality of Charlemagne in the French *Chansons de Geste* and Arthur in the Arthurian romances. This is why the basic material of the *Nibelungen* story plays such an important role in the songs of the *Edda,* although obviously the characters are not Scandinavian in origin. Some of them are Gothic, some from the Hunnish circle, some of them Burgundian and some owe their origin to Merovingian historical characters.

There was a constant interchange of legendary material between the Scandinavian North and the British Isles. The poet of the *Beowulf* deals exclusively with material which was either brought over by his ancestors or which had filtered across the North Sea since the settlements were made. All of his characters are personalities in the history, actual and fictional, of the Danes, the Swedes and the Frisians. And he has a marvellous command of this material; he uses ancient heroic songs, an example of which he gives in the *Finnsburg* story, legends and traditions to give an apparently historical framework to his poem, just in the same way as the writer of a modern historical novel handles his material. He wrote a Germanic epic, not a heroic song. He made use of many heroic songs. He does not represent the Germanic *scop* about whom he speaks; the *scop* belonged to earlier days, but he used the work of many *scòps*.

Somewhere in Southern France, while the Visigoths played such an important role in that area, was preserved the story of the flight of Walther and Hildigund from the court of Attila where they had been held as hostages. It is not likely that the somewhat farcical ending was the original form. This story of the Visigothic Walther was carried to England, and parts of a version in Anglo-Saxon have been preserved; unfortunately only parts, but they seem to give the true ring of the old Germanic heroic song. The full version of the story is in Latin hexameters, written by the poet Ekkehardt of St. Gall. Perhaps Ekkehardt had been stimulated to this poetic work by the literary interests of many of the Irish missionaries in the South, and especially at the monastery of St. Gall. It is unfortunate that it did not occur to him to give us the original with which he must have been acquainted.

There must have been heroic songs written about the out-standing personalities of Frankish-Merovingian history. Their contents have survived only in the Latin chronicles of Gregory and Gregory was not interested in ancient Germanic poetry; he was too much of a propagandist for the good cause. Some of the characters of Merovingian times are mirrored in the

first part of the *Nibelungenlied,* especially such characters as
Fredagonda and Brunhilda. Possibly also the Merovingian Sige-
bert may have added traits to the character of Siegfried, especially in respect to his relationship with the two women
who dominated the times above all others. Perhaps the *Lud-
wigslied* of 881, which celebrates the victory of the Franks
over the Normans at the battle of Saucourt can be taken as
representative of earlier similar songs.

It is a mistake to conclude that nearly all of the ancient
heroic songs were either Gothic or Anglo-Saxon. That is
partly a matter of the accident of survival. Then too the
Gothic material has survived in fair quantity because it was so
widespread.

As far as England was concerned, the transition from the
old heathen beliefs to Christianity took place without any of
the violence which accompanied such change in some continental areas. The result was that there was less bigotry, and the
ancient legends were not considered to be so dangerous to
the immortal souls of the new converts. This can be clearly
seen in the *Beowulf.* Much the same situation prevailed in
Ireland and hence we have the survival of many of the old
pre-Christian poems and tales of the ancient days that have
been of such interest to modern scholars.

Paulus Diaconus in his *Historia Langobardorum* must have
been acquainted with a vast amount of legendary material
and heroic songs of the Langobards. The use that he makes
of some of the ancient themes is proof of this. Then too it was
Paulus who related the story of Alboin and Rosamunda, and
this must have been the subject of many a song.

Saxo Grammaticus likewise in his *Gesta Danorum* has preserved
the contents, if not the form, of many of the early tales and
ballads of the North. It is from Saxo that we know of the
story of Hamlet; it is in Saxo that we get an extensive knowledge of the old warrior Starkad, another such grim character
as Hagen of the *Nibelungenlied.* This same Starkad appears

also in the *Beowulf* in one of the poet's excursions into tribal history. Possibly he is a much grimmer character to the poet of the *Beowulf* than in the thirteenth century account of Saxo, but that is to be expected; Saxo was not nearly so close to the actual time of these stirring events and grim characters as the poet of the *Beowulf*. Saxo has preserved many another similar story, unfortunately again in a Latin version.

Then we have the personality of Irving of Thuringia, who must have made a powerful impression upon the minds of people of his day. His story is preserved in the Latin history of Gregory of Tours, but he also plays a role in the much later mediaeval *Nibelungenlied,* which shows that he survived in song and story through the intervening generations. In a similar way we know of such outstanding subjects of heroic song as Ingeld, Offa and Onela of *Beowulf* fame. These were mighty men of valor in their day, or at least they were made into mighty men of valor by the poets who kept their memory green. We owe a great deal also to the poet of the *Widsith,* the Far Traveller; his catalogue of princes, peoples and heroes is a mine of information, which throws light upon many of the characters in other poems.

Then, as now, rumor played an important part in the appreciation of the characters of the ancient songs and stories. Priscus tells us that after the death of Attila's wife he married a girl by the name of Hildiko, probably a Gothic princess to judge from the form of the name. Attila died, presumably of a hemorrhage, that same night, and very soon after rumor had it that he had been slain by his new wife in revenge for some injury to her people. That was just what the poets needed. This motif was explored and expanded by the poets of the day and carried to the North where it played such a role in those poems of the *Edda* which deal with the character of Attila and his relations with the Burgundians. It was the same kind of popular treatment of historical events which places Theodoric at the court of Attila, which transferred the mighty deeds of Sigmund of Eddic fame to his son Siegfried, and made of Sigmund in the *Nibelungenlied* such an inconspicuous and none-too-daring character. It was the same disregard for historical accuracy that made Theodoric later a hero of romance.

Practically all of the heroes of the ancient Germanic heroic poetry are characters who stand in the shadow of Fate. In this respect they are like the characters of the Greek drama, doomed beyond hope before they ever begin to act. But nevertheless they do act in a supreme defiance of Fate, "goes Wyrd as she must," in a defiance of Fate to express the principle of individual freedom and personality, in a determination to meet the fated end as if it were a matter of free choice, and in any case to die on one's feet. This attitude towards Fate, Freedom and Personality is the outstanding characteristic of the actors in the ancient songs. When that attitude of mind no longer plays a role in the descendants of these ancient heroes then the Germanic people and the Germanic culture will have ceased to be; they will also have passed through their *Götterdämmerung*.

Summary

We are at the end of our story. It began over a hundred thousand years ago according to some calculations and it ends with the dawn of the Viking Age. During the greater part of the Third Interglacial and the early part of the Fourth Glacial, Europe was inhabited by Neanderthal Man, a genus or species of Man quite different in many respects from *Homo sapiens,* to which all living races of Modern Man belong. There is reason for believing that some race mixture between Neanderthal Man and *Homo sapiens* took place in Palestine and possibly at places in North Africa and Eastern Europe in the Third Interglacial. In any case Modern Man was present in Europe during an early stage of the Fourth Glacial, and his appearance is signalized by an Upper Palaeolithic culture associated with his living-sites in caves or in the open in periods of milder climate, as the case may be.

The Upper Palaeolithic cultures are based on the blade technique, cutting instruments and engravers being the common flint implements. Arrowheads and spearheads were also made; the bow, before the end of the period at least, was widely used, as is known from the Central and South Spanish rock-drawings. The three main aspects of the Upper Palaeolithic culture were the Aurignacian, Solutrean and Magdalenian.

During the Magdalenian period which bridges the outgoing Upper Palaeolithic and the Mesolithic very considerable use was made of bone, at first reindeer but later stag horn after the reindeer had begun to move north, following the retreating ice. During the Upper Palaeolithic period we find the first indication of creative art in the fields of engraving, painting, relief work and sculpture. There is a considerable amount of evidence of a widespread animistic belief and of the practice of sympathetic magic. The stage of culture of Upper Palaeolithic Man was that of food-gathering, that is, hunting and the gathering of roots and berries. He was nomadic only when compelled to be so by a changing environment and the necessity of following his food supply. During the colder periods he lived in caves or rock-shelters, and it is there that most of the works of Upper Palaeolithic art have been found.

With the exception of the Negroid Grimaldi type all varieties of Upper Palaeolithic Man belonged to the Primary Caucasian race, or in popular terminology, the White Race, found in the Third Interglacial along the Southern Mediterranean shore. Expansion into Europe took place by way of land-bridges at Gibraltar and Sicily, and into Eastern Europe through the passes of the Caucasus or around the Caspian or over land-bridges in the Aegean when conditions made such movements possible. From these two directions Europe was populated with a new type of man, a type which has remained there ever since. Neanderthal Man became extinct, either being exterminated by *Homo sapiens* or gradually dying out as the result of inability to become adapted to a changing environment.

Although there are several types of man in Upper Palaeolithic times such as Combe Capelle, Brünn, Predmost, Cro Magnon, Chancelade, it is possible to group the important types around two centres: the Combe Capelle and the Cro Magnon. The Combe Capelle is the shorter of the two, more gracile in skeletal and cranial structure, the Cro Magnon type being for the most part tall, at least the men were, with rugged cranial formation and a correspondingly more heavily built body. All types are dolichocranial, but there is a decided tendency in the Cro Magnon type towards mesocrany, which may account for a further development of this factor in later times. There are good reasons for believing that some of the Combe Capelle and Cro Magnon people were either of the blond Nordic variety or were becoming so as the result of adaptation to a glacial climate. The combination of these two types from Upper Palaeolithic times on produced the secondary race of the primary Caucasian which is known in modern terminology as the 'Nordic.' As used here the term 'Nordic' includes both types, such as they appear in Neolithic and later times, now with a greater emphasis on the Combe Capelle, now showing a predominance of the Cro Magnon type.

In parts of Europe, particularly in the West, there was an influx of men of the Mediterranean type with the coming of the microlithic culture from the south at the beginning of the Mesolithic cultural period. This is particularly noticeable in Spain, France and the British Isles, and to some extent also in the North European Plain and in the Danube area. In addition to this there is evidence both in Northern Europe and in Bavaria (Ofnet) for the appearance of the Alpine type of man, whether as a development of already existing factors or as the result of a migration from the southeast, or as the result of both factors combined.

It was during the Mesolithic cultural period, the geological phase which witnessed the melting of the ice in Europe, that Northern Europe was first permanently inhabited. These early inhabitants were hunters and fishers who still lived much the same kind of life as their Upper Palaeolithic ancestors. However, as the climate changed with the changing geological conditions in Northern Europe a more fixed type of settlement can be noticed, especially dependent on the availability of fish, mussels and oysters as well as smaller land game, and therefore quite closely bound to the shores of the lakes and seas. This was the Maglemose culture of the North. This in turn developed into the Ertebölle or Kitchenmidden culture in the *Litorina* geological phase. This culture is a transitional one from the Mesolithic to the Neolithic. It is widespread, being found in many parts of the North European Plain, also in Portugal and on the eastern coast of England, as well as in that area of the North Sea which was then dry land and where the Dogger Banks now lie. It was during the Mesolithic period that the dog was domesticated in the North; during this period also, in the time of the Ertebölle culture, the first pottery makes its appearance in Europe.

This Mesolithic culture is not confined to the Scandinavian North. It is found also in the British Isles, in France, in Poland, in the Danubian area and in the area of Upper Saxony and Thuringia. In this part of Central Germany there developed a special culture which is relatively isolated, and where in Neolithic times is found the culture of the bearers of the Corded Ware Pottery.

The basic type of man throughout the North of Europe and in such a relatively isolated area as Upper Saxony and Thuringia was the Combe Capelle-Cro Magnon complex, or what is here referred to as the Nordic secondary race.

The 'Neolithic Revolution' meant a change from the precarious food-gathering to a food-producing stage of culture, the raising of cereal crops and the keeping of domesticated animals. This caused an increase in population which in turn set in motion a wave of migration from the South into Europe both in the East and in the Southwest. In the east this migration movement brought into Europe the people of the Banded Pottery culture and those of the Painted Pottery; in the west there was a movement along the Atlantic littoral probably both by water and by land, which extended to the British Isles. In Central Germany the two migrations and cultures met, creating many mixed cultures. The Swiss Lake Dwelling cultures are strongly under the influence of the agricultural culture from the east, whose influence extends as far as the Rhine.

In the west of Europe and the British Isles, as also in Northern Europe there is a widespread megalithic culture, the outstanding feature of which was the building of large stone structures to house the dead. This cult. of the dead seems to have come from the Eastern Mediterranean, but not necessarily accompanied by any special migration movement, apart from the wave of Mediterranean people which spread over Western Europe and the British Isles along with the introduction of the agricultural way of life. The North received the new economy and also the cult of the dead, but is not materially affected by the spread of the Mediterranean type. The Mediterranean type is dominant in the Banded Pottery and Painted Pottery cultures. The dominant type in the North still remains the combination of the Combe Capelle-Cro Magnon varieties, with the Cro Magnon being more prevalent in some areas.

Exhaustion of the soil owing to primitive ways of farming and surplus of population caused the *Völkerwanderung* of the Neolithic peoples. The people of the Banded Pottery culture spread into Central Germany and influenced both the Swiss Lake culture and the culture of Upper Saxony and Thuringia. This was, however, mainly a peaceful expansion, since the grave-goods of the Banded Pottery culture give no indication of a warlike equipment. But this was not the case with the Northern culture. First there was a wide expansion of the people of the Northern Megalithic culture, fanning out west, east and south, reaching the Middle Rhine, the Swiss Lake Dwellings and spreading into Eastern Europe even as far as the Caucasus, and further north to the head and middle waters of the Volga. This in turn was closely followed by the expansion of the people of the Corded Ware culture of Upper Saxony and Thuringia, following mostly along the same lines as the migrations of the people of the Northern Megalithic culture, except that this culture expanded also into Northern Europe, especially the Northwest, the Danish continental area and the southern part of Sweden. There was also an Oder and an Eastern German group.

The people of the Corded Ware culture as well as those of the Northern Megalithic were aggressive colonizers, their fighting equipment being mainly maces and very effective battle axes. There can be very little doubt that most of their migrations were of a warlike nature and that they set up military autocracies in the various areas into which they penetrated. These people were all basically of the Nordic type, those of the Corded Ware culture leaning more toward the Combe Capelle variety than the Cro Magnon. It was the people of the Corded Ware, Single Grave culture who were the original Indo-Europeans and who spread the Indo-European languages over the most of Northern, Central and Eastern Europe during the Neolithic period. The assimilation and amalgamation of the Single Grave and Northern Megalithic peoples and cultures during the Bronze Age resulted in the Germanic people and the Germanic language.

In many respects these two cultures are radically different. The graves of the Northern Megalithic were community graves; those of the newcomers were single graves, a survival of the older Mesolithic custom of burial, but influenced to some extent by the Northern culture insofar as a low mound was erected over the grave. But there were other differences; the religious belief of the people of the Northern Megalithic culture was based on the worship of the Earth Mother, an agricultural religion, with a tendency also towards a matriarchal form of society. The religious belief of the newcomers, as that of ·all Indo-Europeans, was based on the worship of the Sky God, was definitely patriarchal and depended more on the raising of flocks and herds than on cereal crops, though cereal agriculture was by no means absent. In the North these two systems merge; the result is the Germanic religious belief of the Bronze Age, which shows such a peculiar mixture of elements from the fertility religions and the worship of the Sky God, and which can be traced right down to the Viking period.

From this cultural mixture arose the Germanic language.

The Single Grave people imposed their Indo-European language upon people speaking a language of an entirely different type, who carried over their native speech habits into the new language, causing certain very definite and radical changes in the language which was introduced.

With the end of the Bronze Age a climatic deterioration set in which brought to a close the period of climatic optimum which had been enjoyed since the time of the Kitchen-midden culture. This climatic deterioration, along with a surplus population, resulted in migration. This phase of the *Völkerwanderung* of the Germanic peoples shows Germanic tribes pushing westward along the North Sea and eastward along the Baltic, where the Illyrian power was not sufficient to halt the movement. In the south, however, the movement was checked for a time by the power of the Celts, who were now, about 500 B. C., at the peak of their strength.

The next phase of the *Völkerwanderung* began with the migration of the *Cimbri* and *Teutones* and Ariovistus in Gaul. This was the beginning of the conflict between the Germanic peoples and the Roman Empire. There was then a pause for some centuries. During this pause the Goths and other Germanic tribes from the Baltic moved into position for an attack on the Roman Empire both in the East and the West, as a result of which the Empire in the East was greatly weakened, but managed to continue a precarious existence. The Empire in the West collapsed and was succeeded by a number of Germanic kingdoms, the only ones able to survive being that of the Franks, and the Anglo-Saxon kingdoms of the British Isles. Out of the complex situation arising from the fall of the Western Roman Empire and the creation of the Holy Roman Empire have developed the modern nations of Europe.

Such in brief is the story of the origin of the Germanic people, their expansion and the development of their culture down to the beginning of the Viking Age. One cannot compare the culture of the Germanic people with that of Egypt or

Greece or Rome. These were essentially urban cultures, and it was quite natural that to both the Greeks and Romans the ancient *Germani* seemed to be "barbarians." They were essentially agricultural peoples, and as such, lacked the industrialization and sophistication of such a metropolis as Rome. They had neither the literature nor the art of a great urban centre. Neither did they have any overruling political unity to direct the various cultural activities along national lines. Only towards the end of the main phase of the Migrations did the urban life of the Roman Empire begin to exercise any marked influence on the Germanic peoples. From that time on they began to acquire a knowledge of foreign cultures, the cultures of the Mediterranean and Christianity. From that time on they ceased to be purely "Germanic" and began the long process which has not yet been completed, of becoming European.

Notes

1. Using the data of variation of the earth's motion, and variation of inclination to the plane of the orbit, changes in the precession of the earth's orbit and in the eccentricity, A. Milankovitch, a Jugoslavian geophysicist and astronomer, calculated the climatic variations for the Northern Hemisphere for the last 600,000 years. According to his calculations the time scale of the glacial and interglacial periods of the Ice Age corresponds very closely to the conclusions of the geologists, based upon entirely different evidence. Milankovitch's results are accepted by Prof. G. Gamow, Professor of Theoretical Physics at George Washington University. Cf. *Biography of the Earth*, Pelican Mentor Book, 1948, New York. There has been a recent revival (C. H. Hapgood: *Earth's Shifting Crust*, Pantheon, 1958) of Alfred Wegener's theory of the shifting of the continents. According to Hapgood's thesis the beginning of the Fourth Glacial would be about 25,000 years ago, as against the much longer time according to Milankovich. However, the basic thesis of this book would not be affected materially if Hapgood's explanation of glaciation proves to be correct.

2. This is the approximate date given by Geophysicist M. Ewing and Meteorologist W. Donn in a report in *Harper's Magazine*, Sept. 1958, on the results of radio-carbon dating of core-samples of sediment in the Caribbean and the Gulf of Mexico. The article also presents a tentative and very novel explanation of the causes of the advance and retreat of the ice.

3. According to the theory of Ewing and Donn, warmer water from the Atlantic penetrates the Arctic and melts the ice. This greatly increases the precipitation over the adjacent land areas in the form of snow which in course of time becomes ice under pressure and begins to flow. The novel element in the theory is that it calls for an open Arctic Ocean during an Ice Age.

4. It is unfortunate that the term "Nordic" has in recent years taken on an unfavorable connotation. The term is scientifically justified, if used correctly, that is, in the strict anthropological sense, without any political connotation.

5. The basic work in this field was done by de Geer and Sernander.

6. Named after a salt water shell-fish.

7. Named after a fresh-water mollusc.

8. The *litorina* is a small shellfish living in salt water.

9. M. Ebert: *Reallexikon der Indogermanischen Altertumskunde*, under *Furfooz* and *Grenelle*.

10. The index is obtained by reckoning the relationship between the breadth and the length. Up to 75 is usually regarded as dolichocranial, from 75 to 80 as mesocranial and from 80 up as brachycranial. The cranial index is the index for the skull of the skeleton, the cephalic index is taken from the measurements of the living and, of course, raises the categories slightly. The index has proved very useful in racial classification, but many other characters must also be taken into consideration. For details of the fossils cf. O. Reche: *Rasse und Heimat der Indogermanen*, pp. 125-126.

11. O. Reche, *Rasse und Heimat*, p. 22.

12. Quoted by Ebert, *Reallexikon, Band,* 12, p. 387.

13. G. Asmus: *Die vorgeschichtlichen und rassischen Verhältnisse in Mecklenburg und Schleswig-Holstein* claims the skull is Neolithic.

14. Quoted by G. Schwantes: *Geschichte Schleswig-Holsteins,* Band I, pp. 132 ff.

15. *Ibid.* p. 135.

16. *Ibid.* p. 135.

17. G. Asmus in a letter from Hannover favors the explanation that the brachycranial skulls developed in isolation out of a local population with a mesocranial tendency.

18. The term "Proto-Nordic" is used here to indicate a stage in the development prior to what may be called the Early Historical Nordic.

For a detailed discussion of the Mesolithic civilization of Northern Europe see Prof. J. D. G. Clark: *Mesolithic Settlements in Northern Europe,* Cambridge, 1936.

NOTES TO CHAPTER II

1. V. G. Childe: *Man Makes Himself,* chapter 5.

2. K. Schuchhardt: *Alteuropa* is an example of such an attempt.

3. K. Kersten: *Zur Älteren Nordischen Bronzezeit.*

4. E. Wahle: *Deutsche Vorzeit,* 1952 revised edition, identifies the people of the Single Grave culture with the Indo-Europeans, p. 62 and p. 111, but derives them from an eastern steppe area *"in einer Osten gelegenen Steppenheimat."*

V. G. Childe: *The Aryans,* pp. 199-200, somewhat reluctantly discards the theory of an origin in south Russia as the result of Tallgren's investigations.

For other discussions of this problem see the works of: S. Müller, Rosenberg, Ebert, Äberg, Schwantes, Sprockhoff, Kossinna, Schulz, von Richthofen, Feist, Hirt.

5. G. Retzius: *Zur Kraniologie der Nordischen Steinzeit,* quoted by W. Scheidt: *Die Rassen der Jüngeren Steinzeit in Europa,* p. 8.

6. C. M. Fürst: *Zur Kraniologie der Schwedischen Steinzeit, Svenska Vetensskaps akademiens Handlingar,* Band 79, 1, 1912.

7. M. H. Nielsen, quoted by W. Scheidt: *Die Rassen der Jüngeren Steinzeit in Europa,* p. 24.

8. H. Hubert: *Les Celtes et l'Expansion Celtique.*

9. G. Kossinna: *Ursprung und Verbreitung der Germanen in vor und frühvorgeschichtlicher Zeit* was for a time a strong advocate of this explanation.

10. O. Schrader: *Prehistoric Antiquities of the Aryan People,* made a list of these words. They are discussed by V. G. Childe: *The Aryans,* pp. 91-92.

11. Some of the important discussions of this problem are: E. Hahn: *Die Haustiere*, p. 186; Ebert: *Reallexikon*, Band X, article by Hilzheimer; G. Menghin: *Weltgeschichte der Steinzeit*, IV, p. 4, *Anmerkung* 19; G. Birnbaum: *Sachsens Vorzeit*, Band II, 1938, pp. 29-33; Hermes: *Anthropos*, XXX, *Hefte* 5, 6; G. Nobis: *Abstammung und Domestikation des Hauspferdes*, not yet published at the time of preparation of this manuscript.

12. H. Hirt: *Etymologie, Konsonantismus, Indogermanische Grammatik*, p. 177.

13. H. Hirt: *Die Indogermanen*, p. 182, places the Indo-Europeans west of the beech-line on the basis of linguistic evidence.

14. W. Sieglin: *Die blonden Haare der Indogermanischen Völker des Altertums*, p. 25.

15. These results are summarized by O. Reche in *Rasse und Heimat der Indogermanen*, pp. 60-61.

16. *Ibid.* p .41; p. 43; pp 51-52.

17. Ebert: *Reallexikon* under *Kurgan;* also O. Reche: *op. cit,* pp. 27-28.

18. O. Reche: *op. cit.,* p. 14.

19. *Ibid.,* p. 39.

20. *Ibid.,* p. 40. Reche quotes F. von Luschan's investigations.

21. C. Kappers and L. Parr: *Anthropology of the Near East,* p. 125.

NOTES TO CHAPTER III

1. E. Sprockhoff: *Zur Entstehung der Germanen*, p. 235, and K. Kerstens: *Zur Älteren Nordischen Bronzezeit, passim.*

2. E. Sprockhoff: *Zur Entstehung der Germanen, Abbildung* 1, *Verbreitung des gemeingermanischen Griffzungenschwertes um etwa* 1200 *v. Chr. Geb.*

3. *Ibid.* p. 261.

4. *Ibid.* p. 265.

5. *Ibid.* p. 266; also K. Kersten: *op. cit.*

6. *Ibid.* p. 262.

7. K. Kersten: *op. cit. passim.*

8. K. H. Jacob-Friesen: *Niedersachsens Urgeschichte, passim.*

9. *Beowulf,* lines 3137-3172, trans. by G. B. Gummere: *The Oldest English Epic.*

10. G. Asmus: *Die vorgeschichtlichen rassischen Verhältnisse in Schleswig-Holstein und Mecklenburg,* p. 523-63.

11. Quoted by G. Asmus, *op. cit.* p. 55.

12. A. Meillet: *Langues de l'Europe Nouvelle,* p. 117.

13. H. Hirt: *Etymologie, Konsonantismus, Indogermanische Grammatik,* Band 1, p. 67.

14. F. Braun: *Die Urbevölkerung Europas und die Herkunft der Germanen, passim.*

Also E. Prokosch: *Sounds and History of the German Language,* pp. 94-95. But in the *Germanic Review,* 1, 1926, he is rather critical of the sub-stratum theory.

15. B. Malmberg: *L'Espagnol dans le Nouveau Monde.*

NOTES TO CHAPTER IV

1. R. L. Carson: *The Sea Around Us,* pp. 177 ff.

2. W. Schulz: *Indogermanen und Germanen,* p. 98.

3. L. Schmidt: *Geschichte der Deutschen Stämme,* I, p. 86.

Also B. von Richthofen: *Zur Vorgeschichte der Germanen,* p. 128.

4. L. Schmidt: *op. cit.,* I, p. 95.

5. B. Nerman: *Die Frühesten Auswanderungen der Germanen,* p. 26.

L. Schmidt: *op. cit.,* I, pp 100 ff.

W. Schulz: *op. cit.,* p. 98.

6. *Encyclopedia Britannica* under *Vandals.*

Migrations of Germanic tribes which began in the preceding era are traced to their conclusion even though that happens in the sequent period.

7. B. Nerman: *op. cit.,* pp 26-33.

L. Schmidt: *op. cit.,* I, pp 565 ff.

Much: *Deutsche Stammeskunde,* p. 115.

8. L. Schmidt: *op. cit.,* I, p. 83.

B. Nerman. *op. cit.,* p. 51.

R. Hoops: *Reallexikon,* V. p. 357.

9. L. Schmidt: *op. cit.,* I, pp. 129 ff.

10. G. Kossinna: *Germanische Kultur im ersten Jahrhundert,* p. 222.

11. L. Schmidt: *op. cit.*, I, pp. 117 ff.

B. Nerman: *op. cit.*, p. 41.

G. Kossinna: *Die Deutsche Vorgeschichte* p. 144.

J. Hoops: *Reallexikon*, IV, p. 4.

12. Julius Caesar: *De Bello Gallico*, I, 53. Trans. by S. A. Handford.

13. Plinius: *Historia Naturalis*, 35, 37 .

14. D. Detlefsen: *Die Entdeckung des Germanischen Nordens im Altertum*, pp 4 ff.

15. Plinius: *op. cit.*, 16, 2.

16. D. Detlefsen: *op. cit.*, pp 28 ff.

17. H. Schneider: *Germanische Altertumskunde*, p. 7. There is no reason to believe that the Celts were hostile to trading voyages overland. Pytheas explored the sea route because transportation by water was cheaper. There was, however, danger from the Carthaginian navy. The Phoenician-Carthaginian merchants wished to maintain a monopoly of the tin trade.

18. H. Schneider: *op. cit.*, p. 7.

19. E. Norden: *Die Antike Kunstprosa, passim.*

20. Julius Caesar: *op. cit.*, VI, 25-28.

21. H. Schneider: *op. cit.*, p. 12.

22. Tacitus: *Germania*, 2.

NOTES TO CHAPTER V

1. B. Nerman: *op. cit.*, p. 58.

2. G. Kossinna: *Germanische Kultur im ersten Jahrhundert*, p. 238.

3. The chief authorities used for the movements of the Goths are:

T. Hodgkins: *Italy and her Invaders* and L. Schmidt: *Geschichte der Deutschen Stämme*, I, pp 195-462.

4. G. Kossinna: *op. cit.*, p. 240.

5. Paulus Diaconus: *Historia Langobardorum*.

6. L. Schmidt: *op. cit.*, I, p. 549.

7. Cassiodorus-Jordanes: *De origine actibusque Getarum*, 117.

8. L. Schmidt: *op. cit.*, I, p. 553.

9. *Ibid.*, I, p. 553.

10. Bede: *Ecclesiastical History of the English People.*

11. L. Schmidt: *op. cit.,* II, pp 123ff.

12. *Ibid.,* II, pp. 152ff.

13. *Ibid.,* II, p. 4.

14. R. Much: *op. cit.,* p. 90.

15. L. Schmidt: *Geschichte der Germanischen Frühzeit,* p. 274.

16. J. Grimm: *Geschichte der Deutschen Sprache,* p. 359.

17. L. Schmidt: *op. cit.,* p. 274.

18. L. Sergeant: *The Franks: The Story of the Nations,* p. 45.

19. Gregory of Tours: *Historia Francorum.*

20. M. Guizot: *Histoire de France,* I, p. 104.

21. V. Duruy: *Histoire de France,* I, p. 84.

22. L. Schmidt: *Geschichte der Deutschen Stämme,* II, p. 443.

23. A. Malet: *Histoire de France,* I, p. 68.

24. *Ibid.* II, p. 25.

25. Gregory of Tours: *op. cit.,* II, 21.

26. G. M. Dalton: *Introduction to Gregory's History of the Franks,* p. 112.

27. E. Lavisse: *Histoire de France,* II, p. 133.

28. F. Funck-Brentano: *The Earliest Times,* p. 278.

   J. Bühler: *Das Erste Reich der Deutschen,* p. 632.

29. E. Lavisse: *op. cit.,* II, p. 260.

30. *Ibid.,* p. 270.

31. *Ibid.,* p. 289.

NOTES TO CHAPTER VI

1. Julius Caesar: *De Bello Gallico,* 21: *pellibus aut parvis rhenorum tegumentis utuntur magna corporis parte nuda.*

2. Tacitus: *Germania,* 17.

3. G. Steinhausen: *Germanische Natur in der Urzeit,* p. 154.

4. H. Schneider: *Germanische Altertumskunde,* p. 83.

5. Tacitus: *Germania,* 17.

6. G. Steinhausen: *op. cit.* p. 154.

7. H. Schneider: *op. cit. Tafel IV.*

8. Tacitus: *Germania,* 14.

9. Julius Caesar: *De Bello Gallico,* 6, 23.

10. Tacitus: *Germania,* 23.

11. T. Edwards: *The Lore of the Honey Bee,* pp. 114-115.

12. Cicero: *de re publica,* 3, 9, 16.

13. Julius Caesar: *De Bello Gallico,* C. A. Handford transl., p. 29. also *De Bello Gallico,* 2, 15 and 4, 2 for similar attitude on the part of the *Suebi.*

Where 'Germans' is used in the translations of Caesar and Tacitus understand *Germani* as used in this book or Germanic people, since at that time there were no 'Germans' in the modern sense.

14. Tacitus: *op. cit.,* 23,   W. H. Fyfe trans.

15. *Ibid.,* 22.   W. H. Fyfe trans.

16. *Beowulf,* lines 494-497, F. B. Gummere trans.

17. *Ibid.,* lines 480-483.

18. *The Poetic Edda,* stanza 24, H. A. Bellows trans.

19. G. Steinhausen: *op. cit.,* p. 171.

Also H. Schneider; *op. cit.,* Monograph by Mohr: *Umwelt und Lebensform,* p. 73.

20. *Beowulf,* lines 612-624, F. B. Gummere trans.

21. Tacitus: *op. cit.,* 12.

22. *Ibid.:* 20.

23. Julius Caesar: *op. cit.,* VI. 21, C. A. Handford trans.

24. *The Seafarer,* R. K. Gordon trans., p. 85.

25. *Ibid.,* p. 84.

26. *Beowulf,* lines 32-33, F. B. Gummere trans.

27. *Ibid.,* line 98.

28. *Ibid.,* lines 217-218.

29. *Ibid.,* line 2890.

30. *Ibid.,* lines 2041-2056.

31. *Ibid.,* lines 138-140.

32. *Ibid.,* lines 2359-2362.

33. *Ibid.,* lines 529-586.

34. Julius Caesar: *op. cit.,* VI. 32, C. A. Handford trans.

35. Tacitus: *op. cit.,* 5, W. H. Fyfe trans.

36. Wilke, G.: *Archäologische Erläuterungen zur Germania des Tacitus,* p. 4.

37. H. Schneider: *op. cit.,* Monograph by Mohr: *Umwelt und Lebensform,* pp. 87 ff.

38. *Ibid.:* p. 91.

39. *Ibid.*: p. 91.

40. *Ibid.*: pp. 91-92.

41. *Ibid.*: p. 92.

42. K. H. Jacob-Friesen: *Niedersachsens Geschichte*, p. 218.

43. *De Bello Gallico*, 6, 23, C. A. Handford Trans.

44. *British Museum Guide to Early Iron Age Antiquities*, p. 35.

45. M. Ebert: *Reallexikon der Indogermanischen Altertumskunde*, under *Bernstein*.

46. *Ibid.*

47. *Ibid.*

48. T. D. Kendrick: *A History of the Vikings*, p. 50.

49. M. Ebert: *op. cit.*, under *La Tènezeit*.

50. W. Boelsche: *Im Bernsteinwald*, p. 7.

51. *Ibid.*: p. 9.

52. *Ibid.*: p. 9.

53. Pliny: *Historia naturalis*, 37, 45.

54. G. Wilke: *op. cit.*, pp. 51-52.

55. Tacitus: *Germania*, 27.

56. *Ibid.*: 2, W. H. Fyfe trans.

57. Tacitus: *Agricola*, 11, W. H. Fyfe trans.

58. Tacitus: *Germania*, 4, W. H. Fyfe trans.

59. Quoted by G. Asmus: die *Vorgeschichtlichen und Rassischen Verhältnisse in Schleswig-Holstein und Mecklenburg*, p. 66.

60. *Ibid.*: p. 72.

61. *Ibid.*: p. 88.

62. H. Schneider: *op. cit.*, p. 222.

63. *Ibid.*: p. 223.

64. *Ibid.*: p. 223.

65. G. Schwantes: *Geschichte Schleswig-Holsteins, Offa*, 1937, Band IV, *Berichte und Mitteilungen des Museums vorgeschichtlicher Altertümer in Kiel*.

66. *Ibid.*: p. 2.

67. *Ibid.*: p. 17.

68. Tacitus: *Germania*, 40.

69. *Ibid.*: 45.

70. Julius Caesar: *De Bello Gallico*, 6, 21.

71. Tacitus: *Germania,* 9, W. H. Fyfe trans.

72. *Ibid.*: 2.

73. H. Schneider: *op. cit.,* p. 240.

74. *Ibid.*: p. 242.

75. *Ibid.*: p. 246.

76. *Ibid.*: p. 431. Monograph *Schrift.*

77. *Ibid.*: pp. 431-432.

78. Mark, 4, 11: *izwis atgiban ist runa thiudangardjos*: Unto you it is given to know the mysteries of the kingdom of heaven.

79. H. Arnzt: *die Runenschrift,* p. 18 f.

80. *Ibid.*: p. 20 f.

81. L. Wimmer: *Runeskriftens oprindelse og udvickling i Norden.* Germ. trans. *die Runenschrift.*

82. O. V. Friesen: *Om runeskriftens härkomst.*

83. C. G. Marstrander: *Om runene og runennavenes oprindelse, Norsk Tideskrift for Sprogvidensskap,* I, 1928.

84. M. Hammarström: *Om runeskriftens härkomst.*

85. *British Museum Guide to Anglo-Saxon Antiquities,* p. 119.

86. H. Arnzt: *op. cit.,* p. 13.

87. *Ibid.*: p. 28.

88. *Ibid.*: pp. 28-29.

89. *Ibid.*: p. 41.

90. *Ibid.*: p. 30.

91. Julius Caesar: *op. cit.,* 1, 53.

92. Quoted by Arnzt: *op. cit.,* p. 33.

93. *The Poetic Edda;* H. A. Bellows trans. stanza 143.

94. *Newsweek,* Oct. 8, 1951.

95. *Ibid.*

96. Tacitus: *Germania,* 2.

97. H. Schneider: *op. cit.,* Monograph *Dichtung,* pp. 315-316.

98. *Beowulf*: F. B. Gummere trans., lines 867-871.

99. *Edda*: *Skynir* song.

100. *Beowulf*: F. B. Gummere trans. lines 3010-3014.

101. H. Schneider: *op. cit.,* Monograph *Dichtung,* p. 317 f.

102. R. K. Gordon: *op. cit.,* pp. 94-95.

103. *Ibid.*: pp. 96-97.

104. *Ibid.*: p. 97.

105. *Ibid.*: p. 99.

106. *Ibid.*: p. 104.

107. *The Poetic Edda*: H. A. Bellows trans. p. 29 f.

108. Cook and Tinker: *Select Translations from Old English Poetry.* Trans. by B. B. Brougham, p. 72 and p. 75.

109. *Beowulf*: F. B. Gummere trans., lines 89-98.

110. *Ibid.*: lines 280-282.

111. *Ibid.*: lines 646-651.

112. *Ibid.*: lines 842-849.

113. *Ibid.*: lines 1127-1128.

114. *Ibid.*: lines 1357-1361.

115. *Ibid.*: lines 1373-1376.

116. *Ibid.*: lines 1607-1611.

117. *Ibid.*: lines 1761-1768.

118. *Ibid.*: lines 3016-3027.

119. *Widsith*: F. B. Gummere trans. in *Oldest English Poetry,* lines 135-143.

120. *The story of Burnt Nyal*: G. W. Dassent trans., *Everyman* Series, pp. 237-238.

Maps and Illustrations

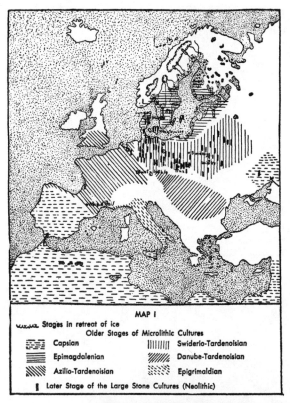

MAP I

Stages in retreat of ice

Older Stages of Microlithic Cultures

Capsian   Swiderio-Tardenoisian

Epimagdalenian   Danube-Tardenoisian

Azilio-Tardenoisian   Epigrimaldian

Later Stage of the Large Stone Cultures (Neolithic)

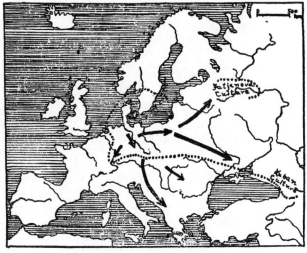

Map II. Expansion of the Northern Megalithic culture (After Schulz).

285

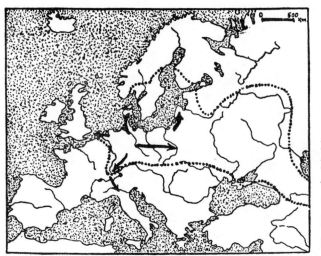

Map III.
Expansion of
the Corded
Ware culture
in Europe
(After Schulz)

//////// Northern Megalithic Culture
\\\\\\ Lake Dwelling Culture ≡≡≡ Danubian Culture
|||||| Painted Pottery Culture ::::::: Corded ware Culture

Map IV. Approximate distribution of Indo-
European languages in prehistoric Europe
before the dispersion in the east and the
approximate areas of Neolithic cultures about
2000 B.C.

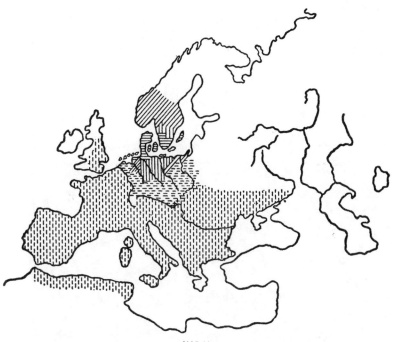

MAP V

Expansion of the Germanic People

≡≡≡ About 1200 B.C.   ═·═·═ About 0

||| About 1000 B.C.   ¦·¦·¦·¦ A.D. 200 - 800

/// About 800 B.C. (towards the end of the Bronze Age)

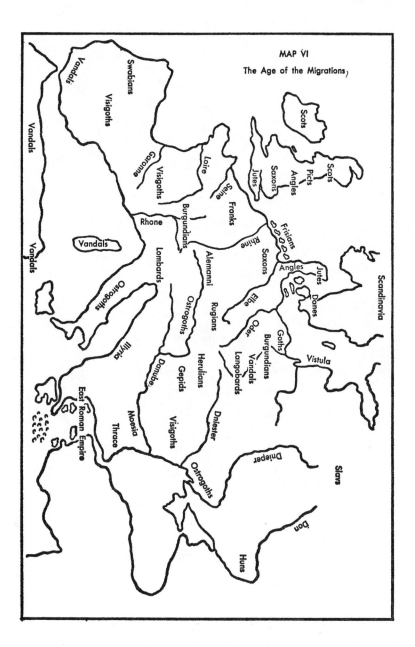

MAP VI

The Age of the Migrations

Fig. 1. Dolmen Grave

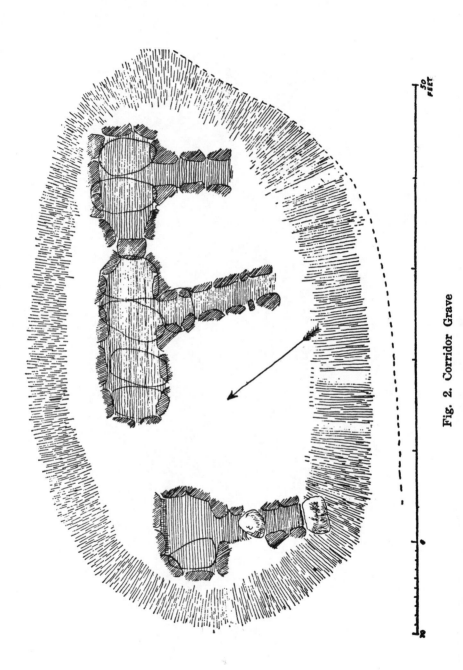

Fig. 2. Corridor Grave

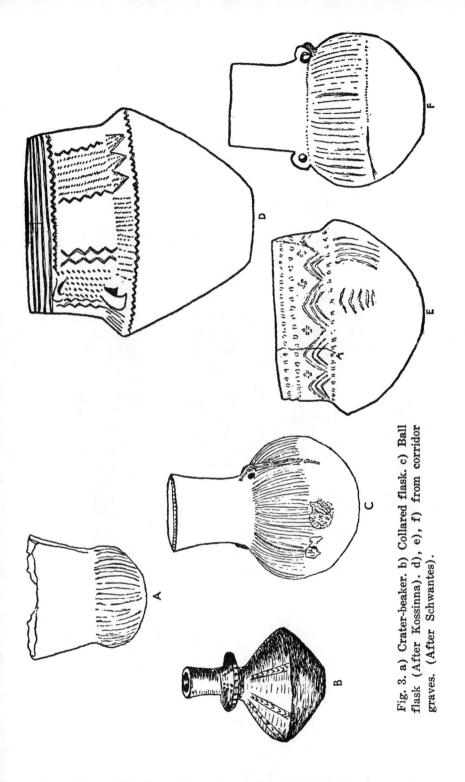

Fig. 3. a) Crater-beaker. b) Collared flask. c) Ball flask. d), e), f) from corridor graves. (After Kossinna). d), e), f) from corridor graves. (After Schwantes).

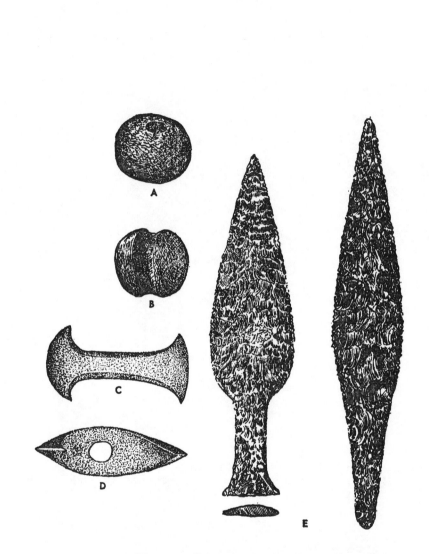

Fig. 4. a), b) Mace-heads. (After Mueller).
c), d) Double-headed axes. (After Schumann).
e) Stone daggers. Courtesy National Museum,
Copenhagen.

Fig. 5. Polished stone work-ax.

Fig. 6. Neolithic house.

Fig. 7. Corded Ware beaker. (After Kossinna).

A

B

Fig. 8. a) Grave-house of the Corded Ware culture. (After Schulz). b) Cross-section of mound with single graves from Jutland. (After Schwantes).

294

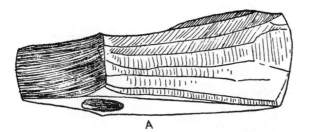

A

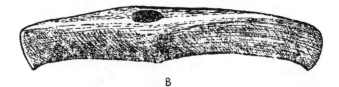

B

Fig. 9. a) Facetted ax. (After Schuchhardt). b) Boat-shaped ax. (After
Mueller).

Fig. 10. Bronze Age people in Denmark (After
drawing by Karl Jensen). Courtesy Provinzial-
Museum, Hannover.

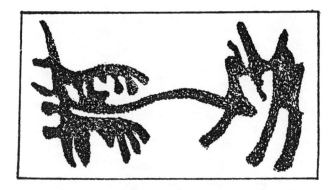

Fig. 11. Rock-drawing of ox-drawn plough
(After Schultz).

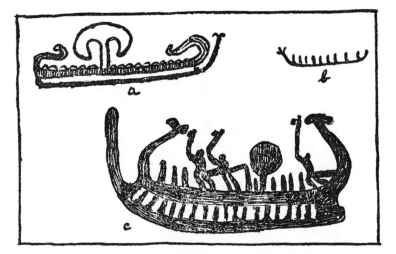

Fig. 12. Boats of the Northern Bronze Age
a) From a knife. b) c) From rock-drawings
(After Hoernes-Behn).

Fig. 13. Swabian Warrior, first century B.C.
(After Behn).

297

Fig. 14. House Interior. (After photograph courtesy of Provinzial-Museum, Hannover).

Fig. 15. Reconstruction of clothing from moor-burials Courtesy Provinzial Museum, Hannover.

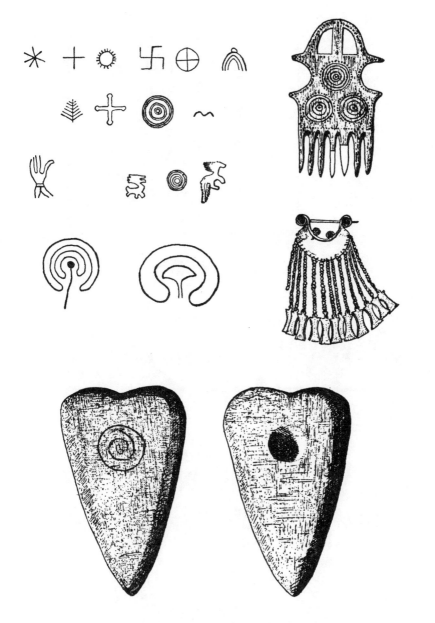

Fig. 16. Cult Symbols.

Fig. 17. Symbols on the Kivik Stone
(After Hilfeling).

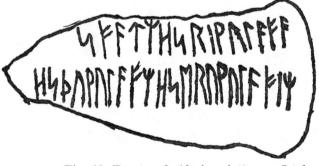

Fig. 18. Front and side inscription on Istaby
Stone. In memory of Herjulf. Half Hjoerulfs-
son inscribed these runes.

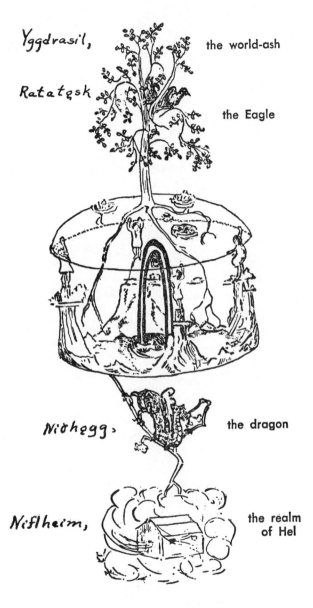

Yggdrasil,   the world-ash

Ratatøsk   the Eagle

Niðhøgg,   the dragon

Niflheim,   the realm of Hel

Fig. 19. The World Tree Iggdrasil
(After Gordon).

301

Bibliography

Arnzt, H.: *Die Runenschrift, ihre Geschichte und ihre Denkmäler.* Halle, 1938.

Asmus, G.: *Die vorgeschichtlichen und rassischen Verhältnisse in Mecklenburg und Schleswig-Holstein,* Neumünster, 1939.

Bede: *Ecclesiastical History of the English People,* London, 1910. Everyman's Library.

Bellows, H. A.: *The Poetic Edda, trans,* New York, 1926. American-Scandinavian Foundation.

Birnbaum, G.: *Sachsens Vorzeit,* Band 2, Leipzig, 1938.

Boelsche, W.: *Im Bernsteinwald,* Stuttgart, 1927.

Braun, F.: *Die Urbevölkwrung Europas und die Herkunft der Germanen,* Berlin 1922.

Brisish Museum: *Guide to Early Iron Age Antiquities,* 1925. *Guide to Anglo-Saxon Antiquities,* 1923.

Bühler, J.: *Das erste Reich der Deutschen,* Leipzig, 1929.

Caesar J.: *De Bello Gallico.*

Carson, R. L.: *The Sea Around Us,* Oxford, 1951.

Cook, A. S. and Tinker, C. B: *Select Translations from Old English Poetry,* Harvard Univ. Press, 1951.

Childe, V. G.: *The Aryans,* London, 1926. *Man makes himself,* London, 1936.

Cicero: *De re publica.*

Dalton, O. M.: *Introduction to and Translation of Gregory's Historia Francorum,* London, 1934.

Dassent, G. W.: *The Story of Burnt Nyal,* trans. from the Icelandic, London, 1931. Everyman's Library.

Detlefsen, D.: *Die Entdeckung des germanischen Nordens im Altertum,* Berlin, 1904.

Diaconus, Paulus,: *Historia Langobardorum.*

Duruy, V.: *Histoire de France,* Paris, 1908

Ebert, M.: *Reallexikon der indogermanischen Altertumskunde,* Berlin, 1924.

303

Edwards, T.: *The Lore of the Honey Bee*, London, 1919.

Von Friesen, O.: *Om runeskriftens härkomst*, Upsala, 1906.

Funck-Bretano, F.: *The Earliest Times*, London, 1927, trans. from the French by E. F. Buckley.

Fürst, C. M.: *Zur Kraniologie der schwedischen Steinzeit, Kungl. svenska Vetenskaps Akademiens Handlingar*, 79, 1, 1912.

Fyfe, W. H.: Tacitus' *Dialogus Agricola and Germania*, trans. Oxford, 1912.

Gordon, R. K.: *Anglo-Saxon Poetry*, London, Everyman's Library.

Gregory of Tours: *Historia Francorum*.

Grimm, J.: *Geschichte der Deutschen Sprache*, 1890.

Guizot, M.: *Histoire de France*, Paris, 1848, trans. by R. Black.

Gummere, F. B.: *The Oldest English Epic*, New York, 1923.

Hahn, E.: *Die Haustiere,* Leipzig, 1896.

Hammerström, M.: *Om runeskriftenshärkomst, Skrifter utgivne av Svenska Literatursälskapet i Finland, Band* 216, 1930.

Handford, S. A.: *The Conquest of Gaul*, trans. of *de Bello Gallico*, Harmondsworth, 1951, Penguin Classics.

Hermes, G.: *Das gezähmte Pferd, Anthropos, Band* 20, *Hefte* 5, 6.

Hirt, H.: *Die Indogermanen, ihre Verbreitung, Urheimat und Kultur*, Strassburg, 1905.
   Etymologie, Konsonantismus, Indogermanische Grammatik, Heidelberg, 1927.

Hodgkin, T.: *Italy and her Invaders*, Oxford, 1892-99.

Hoops, J.: *Reallexikon der germanischen Altertumskunde*, Strassburg, 1911-19.

Hubert, H.: *Les Celtes et l'Expansion celtique*, Paris, 1932.

Jacob-Friesen, K. H.: *Einführung in Niedersachsens Urgeschichte*, Hildesheim and Leipzig, 1939.

Jordanes: *De origine actibusque Getarum*.

Kappers, A. C. and Parr, L.: *An Introduction to the Anthropology of the Near East*, Amsterdam, 1934.

Kendrick, T. D.: *A History of the Vikings*, London, 1930.

Kersten, K.: *Zur älteren nordischen Bronzezeit*, Neumünster, 1935.

Kossinna, G.: *Die Deutsche Vorgeschichte*, Leipzig, 1925.
   Germanische Kultur im ersten Jahrhundert, Leipzig, 1939.

Lavisse, E.: *Histoire de France*, Paris 1900-1908.

Malet, A.: *Histoire de France*, Paris 1918-19.

Malmberg, B.: *L'Espagnol dans le nouveau monde*, Lund 1948.

Marstrander, C. G.: *Om runene og runenavenens oprindelse, Norsk Tideskrift for Sprogvidenskab*, 1, 1928.

Meillet, A.: *Langues de l'Europe nouvelle*, Paris, 1928.

Menghin, O.: *Weltgeschichte der Steinzeit*, Vienna, 1931.

Much, R.: *Deutsche Stammeskunde*, Berlin, 1920.

Nerman, B.: *Die Herkunft und die frühesten Auswanderungen der Germanen,* Stockholm, 1924.

Newsweek, Oct. 8, 1951.

Norden, E.: *Die antike Kunstprosa,* Leipzig and Berlin, 1915-18.

Plinius: *Historia naturalis.*

Prokosch, E.: *Sounds and History of the German Language,* New York, 1916.

Germanic Review, 1.

Ptolemy: *Geographia.*

Reche, O.: *Rasse und Heimat der Indogermanen,* München, 1937.

Retzius, G.: *Zur Kraniologie der nordischen Steinzeit,* Stockholm, 1899.

von Richthofen, Freiherr B.: *Zur Vorgeschichte der Germanen, Sonderdruck aus Vorgeschichte der Menschheit,*

Scheidt, W.: *Die Rassen der jüngeren Steinzeit in Europa,* München, 1924.

Schmidt, L.: *Die Geschichte der germanischen Frühzeit,* Köln, 1934.

Geschichte der deutschen Stämme, Köln, 1920.

Schneider, H.: *Germanische Altertumskunde,* München, 1938.
Monographs by Mohr, de Boor, Reichert and Schneider.

Schuchhardt, K.: *Alteuropa,* Berlin and Leipzig, 1919, 1926.

Schrader, O.: *Reallexikon der indogermanischen Altertumskunde,* Berlin, 1917-29.

Schulz, W.: *Indogermanen und Germanen,* Leipzig, 1936.

Schwantes, G.: *Die Geschichte Schleswig-Holsteins,* Neumünster, 1939.

Offa: Berichte und Mitteilungen des Museums für vorge-schichtliche Altertümer in Kiel, Band, 4, 1939.

Sergeant, L.: *The Franks. The Story of the Nations,* London, 1898.

Sieglin, W.: *Die blonden Haare der indogermanischen Völker des Altertums,* München, 1936.

Sprockhoff, E.: *Zur Entstehung der Germanen,* Berlin, 1936.

Steinhausen, G.: *Germanische Kultur in der Urzeit,* Leipzig and Berlin, 1927.

Tacitus: *Germania.*

Wahle, E.: *Deutsche Vorzeit,* Leipzig, 1932, *Neue Ausgabe,* 1952.

Wilke, G.: *Archäologische Erläuterungen zur Germania des Tacitus,* Leipzig, 1921.

Wimmer, L.: *Runeskriftens oprindelse og udvikling i Norden,* German ed. *Die Runenschrift,* Berlin, 1887.

Index

307